A Practical Guide to

DOCUMENT AUTHENTICATION:

Legalization of Notarized
&
Certified Documents

1998

JOHN P. SINNOTT

OCEANA PUBLICATIONS INC.
DOBBS FERRY, NEW YORK

ISBN: 0-379-21219-6

Manufactured in the United States of America on acid-free paper.

TABLE OF CONTENTS

How to Use This Book i
Introduction to the 1998 Edition iii
Introduction to the First Edition vii

Chapter 1: Consular Legalization 1

Afghanistan 3
Albania 5
Algeria, Democratic and Popular Republic of 6
Angola 8
Anguilla 10
Antigua and Barbuda 11
Argentine Republic 12
Armenia 16
Aruba: See Netherlands Aruba
Australia, Commonwealth of 17
Austria, Republic of.... 21
Azerbaijan 23
Bahamas, Commonwealth of 25
Bahrain, State of 27
Bangladesh 30
Barbados 32
Belarus 34
Belgium, Kingdom of 36
Belize 39
Benin 41
Bermuda 43
Bolivia 44
Bosnia and Herzegovina, Republic of 48
Botswana, Republic of 49
Brazil, Federative Republic of 51
British Antarctic Territory 56
British Virgin Islands 57
Brunei/Darussalam 58
Bulgaria, Republic of 59
Cambodia 61
Cameroon 63
Canada 65
Cape Verde, Republic of 68

Cayman Islands 70
Chad, Republic of 71
Channel Islands 73
Chile, Republic of 74
China, Republic of 78
Colombia, Republic of 83
Comoros, Federal and Islamic Republic of 87
Congo, Democratic Republic of 88
Congo Brazzaville 90
Costa Rica, Republic of 92
Croatia 96
Cuba: See Swiss Confederation, Cuban Interests Section 99
Cyprus, Republic of 100
Czech, Republic, The 104
Denmark, Kingdom of 108
Dominican Republic 112
Ecuador, Republic of 114
Egypt, The Republic of 118
El Salvador, Republic of 123
Eritrea 128
Estonia 129
Ethiopia 131
Falkland Islands 133
Fiji 134
Finland, Republic of 135
France 137
French Guiana 140
French Polynesia 141
Gabon 142
Gambia, Republic of The 144
Georgia 145
Germany, Federal Republic of 147
Ghana, Republic of 151
Gibraltar 153
Great Britain: See United Kingdom
Greece (Hellenic Republic) 154
Guadeloupe 158
Guatemala, Republic of 159
Guinea 162
Guyana 164
Haiti 166

Holy See 168
Honduras, Republic of 169
Hong Kong 171
Hungary, Republic of 172
Iceland 175
India 181
Indonesia 184
Iraq, Republic of 187
Irish Republic 189
Israel, State of 192
Italy 195
Jamaica 199
Japan 202
Jordan 206
Kazakstan 208
Kenya 210
Korea, Democratic People's Republic of (North) 212
Korea, Republic of (South) 213
Kuwait 217
Laos 220
Latvia 222
Lebanon 223
Lesotho 226
Liberia 227
Liechtenstein, The Duchy of 229
Lithuania 230
Luxembourg, Grand Duchy of 232
Madagascar, Democratic Republic of 234
Malawi, Republic of 236
Malaysia 237
Mali 240
Malta 241
Marshall Islands 242
Martinique 243
Mauritania 244
Mauritius 245
Mayotte 246
Mexico 247
Micronesia, Federated States of 248
Moldava 249
Mongolia 251

Montserrat . . . 253
Morocco, Kingdom of . . . 254
Mozambique . . . 256
Myanmar, Union of . . . 257
Nepal, Kingdom of . . . 259
Netherlands, Kingdom of The . . . 261
Netherlands Antilles . . . 269
Netherlands Aruba . . . 270
New Caledonia . . . 271
New Zealand . . . 272
Nicaragua . . . 274
Niger, Republic of . . . 279
Nigeria . . . 280
Norway, Kingdom of . . . 281
Oman, Sultanate of . . . 284
Palau . . . 286
Panama . . . 287
Papua New Guinea . . . 289
Paraguay, Republic of . . . 291
Peru . . . 293
Philippines, The... . . . 296
Poland, Republic of . . . 300
Portuguese Republic . . . 303
Qatar, State of . . . 308
Reunion . . . 310
Romania . . . 311
Russian Federation . . . 314
Rwanda . . . 316
Saudi Arabia, Kingdom of . . . 317
Senegal . . . 319
Seychelles, Republic of . . . 320
Sierra Leone . . . 321
Singapore, Republic of . . . 322
Slovak Republic . . . 324
Slovenia, Republic of . . . 326
South Africa, Republic of . . . 327
Spain . . . 330
Sri Lanka, Democratic Socialist Republic of . . . 333
St. Helena . . . 335
St. Kitts & Nevis . . . 336
St. Lucia . . . 337

St. Pierre and Miquelon 338
Sudan, Democratic Republic of 339
Suriname, Republic of 341
Swaziland, Kingdom of 342
Sweden, Kingdom of 343
Swiss Confederation 345
Swiss Confederation, Cuban Interests Section 345
Syrian Arab Republic 348
Tanzania 350
Thailand, Kingdom of 352
Togo 354
Tonga, Kingdom of 356
Tunisia 357
Turkey, Republic of 359
Turks and Caicos Islands 362
Uganda, Republic of 363
Ukraine 364
United Arab Emirates 367
Great Britain and Northern Ireland, United Kingdom of 369
Uruguay, Oriental Republic of 374
Uzbekistan, Republic of 378
Venezuela, Republic of 379
Vietnam, Socialist Republic of 382
Wallis and Futuna Islands 383
Western Samoa 384
Yemen 385
Yugoslavia 387
Zaire, Republic of: See Congo, Democratic Republic of
Zambia, Republic of 388
Zimbawe, Republic of 390

Chapter 2: Legalization within the United States 393

Alabama 395
Alaska 402
American Samoa 403
Arizona 404
Arkansas 407
California 408
Colorado 409
Connecticut 410

Delaware 411
Florida 412
Georgia 413
Guam 414
Hawaii 415
Idaho 417
Illinois 418
Indiana 419
Iowa 421
Kansas 422
Kentucky 423
Louisiana 424
Maine 425
Maryland 426
Massachusetts 429
Michigan 430
Minnesota 432
Mississippi 433
Missouri 434
Montana 435
Nebraska 437
Nevada 438
New Hampshire 439
New Jersey 440
New Mexico 443
New York 444
North Carolina 449
North Dakota 458
Ohio 459
Oklahoma 467
Oregon...... 476
Pennsylvania 477
Puerto Rico 479
Rhode Island 480
South Carolina 481
South Dakota 482
Tennessee 483
Texas 485
Utah 486
Vermont 488
Virgin Islands 489

Virginia 490
Washington 492
Washington, DC 494
West Virginia 495
Wisconsin 499
Wyoming 501

Appendices 503

Appendix A: Hague Convention 505

Appendix B: Protocol on Uniformity of Powers of Attorney Which Are to be Used Abroad 515

Appendix C: National U.S.-Arab Chamber of Commerce 525

Appendix D: U.S. Department of State 531

HOW TO USE THIS BOOK

To prepare a document, notarized in one state, for submission to a court or government agency in another state, it is usually necessary to have the Notary's power authenticated by the relevant county clerk, to be followed by the Secretary of State for the state in which the county clerk is located. Many states, however, have done away with the need for an intervening county clerk's authentication and have given the power to authenticate notarial status directly to the State Secretary of State.

Chapter 2 of this book lists the individual states and territories, e.g., Guam and American Samoa, alphabetically. Each of these entries describes the local notarial authentication procedure in detail, including addresses, telephone numbers, fees and methods of payment where this information is available. County clerk addresses are also provided for those states in which this intermediate authentication step is necessary.

To prepare a notarized document for use in some judicial or administrative matter outside of the United States, however, there are two possible procedures. Thus, if the foreign nation participates in the Convention Abolishing the Requirement of Legalization for Foreign Public Documents ("The Hague Convention"), it is only necessary when submitting a notarized document to a State Secretary of State to request an "Apostille." State Secretaries of State, among other government officials, are empowered to grant the Apostille. A document bearing an Apostille, is valid in all of the Hague Convention countries without further formalities. The entries in Chapter 2 also provide information about requesting an Apostille from a State Secretary of State or, in the case of United States territories and possessions, the relevant official authorized to grant these certificates. The complete text of the Hague Convention and a current list of Convention member countries is published in Appendix A.

The Protocol on Uniformity of Powers of Attorney Which Are to be Utilized Abroad (see Appendix B) provides for a simplified procedure, similar to that of the Hague Convention, among the United States and some Latin American signatories.

Many foreign jurisdictions have not joined to the Hague Convention. In this circumstance, it is usually necessary to submit the document, after authentication by a State Secretary of State, to the United States Secretary of State and the detailed steps required to achieve this final step in the United States procedure for the document are found in Appendix D.

After authentication by the United States Department of State, the document then must be submitted to the appropriate consular section for the nation in which the document is required. Generally, among those nations that maintain only an embassy or mission in the United States, a consular official will provide the necessary legalization service. Many embassies maintain one or more consular offices in the United States and, quite frequently, these consular offices have exclusive legalization jurisdiction for documents originating in the states for which they are responsible. In every instance, entries for each nation, which are arranged in alphabetical order in Chapter 1, provide detailed guidance with respect to consular legalization requirements and procedures for each of these offices. Illustratively, addresses, telephone and fax numbers, office hours, and legalization fees charged by consular sections in the various embassies and, where appropriate for the consular offices, are described.

As might be expected, a spectrum of special situations arise among the legalization authorities in the United States. The Republic of China, or Taiwan, for example, does not have diplomatic recognition in the United States. As a result, consular legalization activity is carried out through the Taipei Economic and Cultural Representation Offices. On the other end of this spectrum, a few embassies do not provide any Consular legalization services at all.

Every reasonable effort has been made to provide accurate and up-to-date information outlining the specific procedures that must be followed in each of the offices addressed in this book to enable the user to proceed in a step-by-step manner toward the goal of a fully legalized document, produced swiftly and efficiently. A caution with respect to the data, however, should be noted. Consular offices, locations and procedures do change with time. As a result it is possible that changes have occurred since the information in this text was compiled. Because of this possibility, the user is urged to calendarize materials sent to an embassy or consulate. If a response is not received from the embassy or consulate within a few days after the turn around time specified in the entry for the state or country in question, the user would be well advised to make a direct inquiry into the status of the specific legalization request by telephone or in person.

Some embassies and consular offices will permit the legalization procedure to be bypassed if the document is signed in the presence of a consular officer. The texts for those embassies that permit direct signing and specific requirements such as the need for an appointment and specific requirements to establish identity, are stated in the associated texts.

INTRODUCTION TO THE 1998 EDITION

In the course of doing business between states and countries, it is frequently necessary to "legalize" documents. The process of legalizing a document involves notarizing the document, i.e., obtaining the signature of a Notary Public verifying that the document and signature are authentic, and then having this certification authenticated other officials, ending with authentication by the United States Secretary of State in the U.S. or by a consular official from the embassy of the country in which the document is to be used.

Two treaties, the text of which may be found in the appendices, are designed to shorten and simplify the process. The better known is the Convention Abolishing the Requirement of Legalization for Foreign Public Documents, signed at the Hague and popularly known as The Hague Convention." For nations which are parties to the Hague Convention, it is only necessary to obtain a certificate called the Apostille in order to legalize the document(s) in question. Two other steps which serve to shorten the process are sometimes available: they are direct registration of the Notary Public, which involves registering the Notary's signature with an Embassy or Consular Officer making it unnecessary to obtain the intervening signatures, and direct signing of the document in the present of a Consular official.

The steps required for legalization, the materials to be submitted, the fees, the turn around time, and the relevant offices with addresses, telephone numbers and fax numbers when available are listed for nations in Chapter 1: Consular Legalization and for states of the United States in Chapter 2: Legalization within the United States. Following these two chapters are appendices containing the texts of the Hague Convention and the Protocol on Uniformity of Powers of Attorney Which Are to be Utilized Abroad, a listing of the U.S.-Arab Chambers of Commerce which are on occasion involved in the legalization process, and information on the United States Department of State as well as a list of American authorities who can provide the Apostille. To determine how to legalize a document for use in a particular state or nation, look up the state or nation in the table of contents and check the entry. If you have any questions, contact either the embassy or consular section or the state Secretary of State's office.

The following nations have been added to this edition:

- Belarus
- Congo Brazzaville
- The Holy See
- Kazakstan
- Mauritania
- Micronesia
- Moldava
- Pakistan
- The Russian Federation
- Rwanda
- Senegal
- Sierra Leone
- Uzbekistan
- Vietnam
- Yemen

As those who have used earlier editions of this book know, consulates change addresses, telephone numbers and legalization fees. Changes in embassy business hours and legalization jurisdictions also occur frequently. Consequently, speed is important to the preparation of this manuscript in order to reduce the time between data acquisition and publication, thus to reduce the number of possible changes that might occur with respect to the published data in that interval.

Accordingly, the first questionnaires were mailed to the missions that have diplomatic representation in the United States and to the state secretaries of state in June of 1997. October 20, 1997 was chosen as the cut-off date for entries to the text of this 1998 edition. The author and his two assistants, Mrs. Eva Baker and Mrs. Ellen Hunt, decided that the volume of information acquired between those two dates represented the best compromise for a thorough presentation that would also meet the requirement for swift publication.

In this circumstance, a few of the nations canvassed failed to respond to our inquiries before the October 20 final manuscript preparation date. Some of these nations, however, were represented in the sixth edition. Rather than delete these countries from this edition, it was decided to republish in this, the 1998 edition, the data that was presented in the sixth edition. This decision was taken for several reasons. It is, for example, possible that nothing has changed and that the sixth edition information continues to be accurate with respect to consular functions. Even if there have been significant changes, the reader will at least have some useful information, e.g., an address or telephone number, on which to undertake a direct inquiry.

To fully inform the reader about those diplomatic missions with entries in the 1998 edition that did not respond in time to meet the October 20 deadline for this edition, the following is a list of those countries for which the sixth edition data is republished in the 1998 edition without the benefit of any comment from the relevant oficials.

Anguilla
Antigua and Barbuda
Bahrain
Bermuda
British Antarctic Territory
British Virgin Islands
Cayman Islands
Channel Islands
Republic of China (Taiwan)
French Guyana
French Polynesia
Lebanon
Luxembourg
Madagascar
Martinique
Mauritius
Mayotte
Montserrat
New Caledonia
Reunion
St. Helena
St. Kitts & Nevis
St. Pierre et Miquelon
Tonga
Turks and Caicos Islands
Wallis and Futuna Islands
Western Samoa

Because of the diplomatic instabilities that have marked the last few years, some of which are described above, as well as the changes that occur in the normal course of events, it is the author's intent to continue to prepare future revisions to this work annually in order to better present consular legalization requirements to the reader on a timely basis.

At this point it is only fair to extend the personal thanks not only of the author but also of Mrs. Baker and Mrs. Hunt to those diplomatic officers and state secretaries of state who so freely and agreeably provided the information needed to write this 1998 edition. The author also must express his profound thanks to Mrs. Baker and Mrs. Hunt, without whom nothing could have been accomplished. It was Mrs. Baker who prepared the mailings, tallied the returns from the various embassies and state offices and entered the data into the text, which she revised to a certain extent for better presentation. Mrs. Hunt spent hours on the telephone following up among diplomatic missions and state offices that had not responded to letter inquiries and clarifying ambiguities in the written responses.

Further appreciation is due to Mrs. Lucy Curci-Gonzales, the librarian at my law firm, and to Mrs. Jennifer C. Groh, her assistant, who provided much help, not the least of which was an up-to-the-minute list of Hague Convention countries for use in this edition. Ms. Maria Lin, a partner in my firm, is also to be thanked for her helpful comments. Mrs. Anna Hill, my secretary at Morgan & Finnegan, deserves much more than appreciation for her help in preparing this book for publication. Sainthood might be a more appropriate recognition for her tireless effort. Further in this regard I must thank Ms. Lenore Tesch of Andrus, Sceales, Starke & Sawall for her continued assistance in providing important consular information and Mr. Peter J. Bartucca, Manager, Records and Legislative Services, Office of the Connecticut Secretary of State, for his insightful comments about the notarial and legalization process. German Cavalier, Esq. of Cavalier Abogados of Bogota, Colombia, also deserves considerable recognition for making an important Pan American Convention available for republication in this text. Ms. Patricia Klaiber of Bell South International, Inc. also has my profound thanks for making me aware of the need to cross-check data provided by some embassies with other sources to enhance the accuracy of the book.

Mrs. Susan de Maio, my editor at Oceana, also deserves a great deal of credit not only for her professionalism in producing this edition so swiftly but also for her recognition of the need for annual editions and her important encouragement in preparation. Thought should also be given to the late Ed Newman of Oceana, a fellow former officer in the United States Air Force. Ed was a wonderful and understanding legal publishing executive who was the first to recognize the need for this book and to carry it through to its initial publication. Phil Cohen and his son, David, of Oceana also deserve full and favorable recognition for building a legal publishing house of the first rank, with which I am proud to be associated.

Finally, the author wishes to express his appreciation to those other users of the book who have been so kind and thoughtful in sending their comments. This author always welcomes reader comments.

All of the foregoing having been written, it is nevertheless the author's sincere statement that any errors in this, the 1998 edition, are his sole responsibility.

New York, New York
October 20, 1997

John P. Sinnott
Of Counsel
Morgan & Finnegan L.L.P.

INTRODUCTION TO THE FIRST EDITION

The growth of foreign trade, investment and travel, as well as continuing high levels of immigration, to suggest only a few reasons, have introduced into United States legal practice an increasing need for documents that enjoy consular legalization. Typically, this need arises with respect to a document that is to be used outside of the United States, and which nevertheless is signed and notarized within the United States. The requirement for a notarized instrument in many foreign countries, however, cannot be satisfied through a local United States notarization without some additional formalities. Generally, documents of this nature also must bear a consular legalization notice that usually reflects, either directly or indirectly, the good standing of the notary who attested to the signature on the document or to the document's contents.

Powers of attorney for use abroad are, perhaps, among the most prevalent of these documents, and it is the legalization procedures associated with these powers that are the primary focus of this work, Many other attested papers, however, also are required abroad. Birth certificates, transcripts of academic records, certificates of origin, and statements of corporate good standing suggest only a few of the more commonplace needs for documents that bear consular legalization. Consular procedures, and notably the legalization fees that are charged, may be slightly different in a few instances for documents of this nature from those that are applied to powers of attorney. Where these differences are known, they have been specified in the body of the text.

Every nation that has diplomatic representation abroad imposes unique requirements with respect to those documents that will be accepted for consular legalization. From the point of view of the practicing attorney, satisfying these requirements can be a time consuming and occasionally frustrating task that, nevertheless, must be accomplished in order to present a foreign colleague with a legally acceptable instrument. Often, a definite time limit is imposed on the submission of a document in properly legalized form, or significant rights will be lost. In these circumstances, the weeks of delay that are frequently encountered in corresponding with a consulate or an embassy to learn appropriate procedure, only to further learn, after submitting the papers, that legalization will not be forthcoming because of an overlooked or heretofore unknown detail, can be professionally awkward as well as wasteful.

Depending on the nation for which consular legalization is sought, there are a number of possible procedures. For example, consular legalization of a document through direct execution before a consular officer is sometimes possible where this is convenient or economically justified. Direct execution avoids one or more of the usual intervening steps of notarization, county clerk and state secretary of state authentication and United States Secretary of State certification. A few embassies and consulates, moreover, permit direct notarial recognition or registration. Documents acknowledged by these "recognized" notaries are subject to direct legalization by the consular officers with whom these notaries are registered without requiring further intermediate authentications. In other cases, however, the notarized document must be submitted to the county clerk for the county in which notarial powers are effective for authentication before being submitted to a consular officer for legalization. Choosing a specific consulate for this legalization, among the several that a foreign power may maintain in the United States, also can be a somewhat burdensome task because the consulates of a number of countries frequently have responsibility for some states and not for others. Italian consular legalization for a document notarized in Kentucky, for example, must be obtained at the Italian consulate in New Orleans. Italian consulates in other cities are not empowered to act in this circumstance.

When diplomatic representation is limited to an embassy or to a mission, it often becomes necessary to proceed through the entire chain of authentication to include not only that of the relevant county clerk, but also the further authentications of the secretary of state for the state of notarization and the Secretary of State of the United States before the document is in a form acceptable to the embassy in question for final legalization.

These problems are relieved, to a limited extent, by the accession of a number of countries (including the United States) to the "Convention Abolishing the Requirement of Legalization for Foreign Documents," which is republished in this volume. This Convention eliminates the need for consular legalization and substitutes instead an *apostille* that can be executed by the secretary of state of a state or an appropriate deputy.

Although submission of an *apostille* eliminates two steps in the usual legalization process, that is, submission to the Secretary of State of the United States for authentication and final submission to an embassy for consular legalization, there occasionally is an intervening need for a county clerk's certificate as a prerequisite to secretary of state action. Consequently, this volume not only describes detailed procedures for obtaining state or commonwealth secretary of state authentication and *apostille* issuance, but also provides specific information on county clerk certification procedures for those states that require this intermediate step.

Other treaties also might have the potential to reduce the burden that is inherent in the legalization process. Illustratively, Article 4D (2) of the Act of Stockholm under the "International Convention for the Protection of Industrial Property" requires each member nation to accept patent application priority documents that are certified as correct by an appropriate national authority without further authentication. Consequently, if the practitioner must obtain a suitably authenticated document in some specialized legal field that is subject to specific treaty obligations, a careful reading of the pertinent treaty, or treaties, might provide some relief with respect to legalization requirements.

Occasionally, more difficult problems must be confronted. What can be done, for example, if consular legalization is required for a country that does not have direct diplomatic representation in the United States? At this writing (1984), a number of commercially important countries do not have this direct representation. Cuba, the Republic of China (Taiwan), Iran and Libya are illustrative of this group of commercially significant countries that do not have diplomatic officers in the United States.

With respect to Taiwan and some of the Middle Eastern countries, organizations akin to chambers of commerce frequently can provide the necessary legalization service. Sometimes, as in the case of the Czechoslovakian Embassy, the embassy of one nation will provide consular legalization service for another nation that does not have diplomatic representation in the United States.

As a further alternative, a roundabout sequence of consular legalizations might provide the needed formalities. A document, for instance, that is executed in the United States and requires Libyan consular legalization can be prepared in the following manner. After signature and notarization, the correct county clerk's certificate is affixed to the document which is then submitted to the appropriate British Consulate for legalization. This British legalized document is forwarded to London for further authentication at the British Foreign Office. This authenticated document is then submitted to the Libyan Embassy in London for the required Libyan consular legalization.

The practitioner must be alert in circumstances of this character to the possible existence of major legal problems of which these formal difficulties may only hint. Thus, if there is no diplomatic representation for a particular nation in the United States, or even if the responses from the consular staff seem strained, the attorney might well ask himself why this is so. Diplomatic relations may have been severed, as they were with Iran a few years ago, or they may be about to be severed, and the attorney would be well advised to "take the hint" and inquire into the existence of an embargo, or the applicability of one or more of the provisions of the Trading With The Enemies Acts (12 USC 95a et al.), the Export Administration Act (50 USC 2401 et seq.) or any other legislation, Presidential Orders and the like that might prohibit or circumscribe the action that the attorney is trying to take in the country under consideration.

The material in this book reflects, to a large extent, the personal experiences of the author and members of his staff acquired in the course of an active foreign patent and trademark practice. Thus, experience, accumulated through many years, has shown that document legalizations can occupy as much as fifteen percent of the basic clerical workload. Occasionally, consular legalization can become the central problem that must be solved in order to accomplish the client's goal, as in the case of documents required in Libya during a time of ruptured diplomatic relations with the United States. Solving these more difficult problems can occupy a great deal of counsel's time and may even elude satisfactory resolution if an acceptable approach is not chanced upon or come to mind.

Eventually, in every active legal practice - specialized or general - a need for consular legalization will arise and create for the attorney a much greater problem than the situation really justifies, especially if legalization is required for a nation that is not among the commercially more active countries of the world.

Consequently, this work attempts to satisfy the need for current information on precise consular legalization requirements for most of the nations of even occasional interest to the United States legal practitioner. Toward this end, the specific requirements of each embassy or diplomatic mission in the United States that grants consular legalization are enumerated. Each section of the text is specific to an individual nation. These sections, moreover, are arranged in alphabetical order.

Within the sections the procedures for legalization through personal appearance before a consular officer, "direct" registration of the notary with the consulate or embassy, and submission through a chain of certification are described in detail, where appropriate. Because details are paramount in this practice, the information presented in each of the sections is of that character, i.e., a requirement to submit fees only through money order or certified check. Telephone numbers, office hours and requirements for appointments also are noted, where applicable.

Clearly, these details are subject to frequent change, usually without any prior notice. These changes reflect in a small way, perhaps, the general social, diplomatic and economic instabilities that characterize our time. Recognizing that these instabilities are likely to be with us for a long time into the future, this volume has been organized as an annual service in order to make current knowledge of these changes available to the practitioner and to expand the number of countries treated in response to reader interest.

It would not have been possible to assemble and arrange into an orderly form the large mass of data that this work represents without the assistance and experience of my staff. Particularly, credit is due in this respect to Constance J. Nerrie, who developed the general questionnaire format, and with Mrs. Norma E. Betty prepared truly bushels of letters of inquiry for submission to various states, embassies and consulates, and who organized each reply into a coherent whole. The form and content of the book, moreover, reflect their perseverance and professionalism.

My wife, Rose Marie, also assisted in the preparation of this book at a most critical time by extracting information from the completed embassy and consular questionnaires and entering the data into the format for that portion of the work. In many respects, Rose Marie's keen analysis of the project and of the data was the most valuable contribution of all. My son, James, and my daughter-in-law, Stephanie, also deserve a great deal of recognition and appreciation for taking time during their wedding trip to visit a number of embassies and consulates in order to collect valuable information that was not otherwise available. Further in this regard, a good deal of recognition and thanks are owed to my daughter, Jessica, and Ms. Marie Ann Moran of New York City for their general encouragement in my professional writing activity. Naturally, nothing could have been written if the willing and generous cooperation of so many consular and state officials had been lacking. Thus, it is to these persons in their exemplary cooperation in this undertaking that we all are most deeply indebted.

Although this book would not have been possible without the conscientious support and cooperation of many people, any errors in the text are the complete responsibility of the author.

It would not be fair to close this introduction without acknowledging my most profound debt of gratitude to all of those persons and institutions that educated and trained me, tasks that I am sure appeared at many times to be not worth the effort, if not just hopeless! God bless them with their unreasonable optimism and faith in human nature. They represent, indeed, that "unreasonable man upon whom all progress depends."

March 15, 1984

John P. Sinnott
40 West 40th Street
New York, New York 10018

CHAPTER 1

CONSULAR LEGALIZATION

THE ISLAMIC STATE OF AFGHANISTAN

National Holiday: Anniversary of the Saur Revolution, April 27

I. GENERAL INFORMATION

Afghanistan has an Embassy and a Mission to the UN; the Mission does not legalize documents.

II. REQUIREMENTS FOR LEGALIZATION

Prior Authentications Required

1. Notarization
2. Authentication of Notary Signature (In most states this may be done directly by the State Secretary of State; if not, the County Clerk authenticates the signature.)
3. State Secretary of State Certification (In states where the Notary Signature may be authenticated directly by the State Secretary of State, steps 2 and 3 are combined.)
4. U.S. Secretary of State Certification

Materials to be Submitted with Request

1. Original document to be legalized
2. Prepaid, self-addressed return envelope

Direct Registration of Notary Public: Not available

Direct Signing of Document Before Consular Official: Not available

Turn Around Time: If the document is personally delivered, it can be legalized immediately if the work load permits.

Fee: $60.00 per document or signature

Payment Method: Cash, money order, certified check, company check

III. EMBASSY AND MISSION TO THE UN

Address, Phone, Hours	*Jurisdiction*
Embassy of the Islamic State of Afghanistan Chancery 2341 Wyoming Avenue, NW Washington, DC 20008 Tel.: 202-234-3770/1 Fax: 202-328-3516 9:00 AM - 3:00 PM	Entire United States
Afghanistan Mission to the UN 360 Lexington Avenue, 11th Floor New York, NY 10017 Tel.: 212-972-1212 9:00 AM - 4:00 PM	

ALBANIA

I. GENERAL INFORMATION

Albania has an Embassy in the United States, but no consulates.

Documents must be legalized in Albania.

For your convenience, the Embassy is listed below.

II. EMBASSY

Address, Phone, Hours	*Jurisdiction*
Embassy of Albania Suite 1000 1511 K Street, NW Washington, DC 20005 Tel.: 202-393-6255 Fax: 202-628-7342 9:00 AM - 5:00 PM	Entire United States

DEMOCRATIC AND POPULAR REPUBLIC OF ALGERIA

National Holiday: Anniversary of the Revolution, November 1

I. GENERAL INFORMATION

Algeria has an Embassy in the United States, but no consulates. Documents from anywhere in the United States may be sent to the Embassy for legalization.

II. REQUIREMENTS FOR LEGALIZATION

Prior Authentications Required
1. Notarization
2. Authentication of Notary Signature (In most states this may be done directly by the State Secretary of State; if not, the County Clerk authenticates the signature.)
3. State Secretary of State Certification (In states where the Notary Signature may be authenticated directly by the State Secretary of State, steps 2 and 3 are combined.)
4. U.S. Secretary of State Certification

Materials to be Submitted with Request
1. Original document to be legalized
2. Photocopy of the document
3. Prepaid, self-addressed return envelope

Direct Registration of Notary Public: Not available

Direct Signing of Document Before Consular Official: Not available

Turn Around Time: If the document is personally delivered, it must be left for 24 hours for legalization.

Fee: Call 202-265-2800, extension 156 to determine fee.

Payment Method: Money order, certified check

III. EMBASSY

Address, Phone, Hours	*Jurisdiction*
Embassy of Algeria Chancery 2118 Kalorama Road, NW Washington, DC 20008 Tel.: 202-265-2800 9:00 AM - 5:00 PM	Entire United States

ANGOLA

I. GENERAL INFORMATION

Angola legalizes documents originating in the United States and Canada.

II. REQUIREMENTS FOR LEGALIZATION

Prior Authentications Required
1. Notarization
2. Authentication of Notary Signature (In most states this may be done directly by the State Secretary of State; if not, the County Clerk authenticates the signature.)
3. State Secretary of State Certification (In states where the Notary Signature may be authenticated directly by the State Secretary of State, steps 2 and 3 are combined.)
4. U.S. Secretary of State Certification

Materials to be Submitted with Request
1. Original document to be legalized
2. Translations of all documents into Portuguese
3. Prepaid, self-addressed return envelope

Direct Registration of Notary Public: Not available

Direct Signing of Document Before Consular Official: The procedure of certifying the signature of a private person is available. Proper identification should be presented; a driver's license is acceptable identification.

Time Delay: If the document is personally delivered, there will be a delay of from five to seven working days before legalization.

Fee: $15.00 per document or signature

Payment Method: Money order or certified check payable to the Embassy of Angola

II. EMBASSY

Address, Phone, Hours	*Jurisdiction*
Embassy of Angola 1050 Connecticut Avenue, NW Washington, DC 20036 Tel.: 202-452-1042/3 Fax: 202-785-1258 202-822-9049 9:30 AM - 1:00 PM	Entire United States

ANGUILLA

I. GENERAL INFORMATION

Anguilla is a dependency of the United Kingdom, covered by the Hague Convention Abolishing the Requirement for Legalization for Foreign Public Documents.

A document should be sent to the appropriate authority in the state or territory in which the document is notarized in order to obtain the Apostille. For information on obtaining the Apostille for documents originating in the United States, see the procedures specified for each of the individual states under United States jurisdiction in Chapter 2. For the enumeration of Federal authorities competent to provide the Apostille, see Appendix D.

For the text of the Hague Convention, the Apostille, and a list of the parties to the Convention, see Appendix A.

For information on United Kingdom Consulates, see the United Kingdom.

ANTIGUA AND BARBUDA

I. GENERAL INFORMATION

Antigua and Barbuda is a dependency of the United Kingdom, covered by the Hague Convention Abolishing the Requirement for Legalization for Foreign Public Documents.

A document should be sent to the appropriate authority in the state or territory in which the document is notarized in order to obtain the Apostille. For information on obtaining the Apostille for documents originating in the United States, see the procedures specified for each of the individual states under United States jurisdiction in Chapter 2. For the enumeration of Federal authorities competent to provide the Apostille, see Appendix D.

For the text of the Hague Convention, the Apostille, and a list of the parties to the Convention, see Appendix A.

For information on United Kingdom Consulates, see the United Kingdom.

ARGENTINE REPUBLIC

National Holidays: National Day, May 25; Independence Day, July 9

I. GENERAL INFORMATION

The Argentine Republic is a party to the Hague Convention Abolishing the Requirement for Legalization for Foreign Public Documents.

A document should be sent to the appropriate authority in the state or territory in which the document is notarized in order to obtain the Apostille. For information on obtaining the Apostille for documents originating in the United States, see the procedures specified for each of the individual states under United States jurisdiction in Chapter 2. For the enumeration of Federal authorities competent to provide the Apostille, see Appendix D.

For the text of the Hague Convention, the Apostille, and a list of the parties to the Convention, see Appendix A.

For information purposes, the Embassy, Consulates General and Consulate of the Argentine Republic are listed below.

Note: All documents, public or private, not covered by the Hague Convention require prior certification (see steps 1 - 4 below). If the document is certified by a Notary Public and the County Clerk, legalization by the Consulate is required. If the document is certified by the State Secretary of State, the Apostille is not required.

Note that the Embassy does not legalize documents; the Consulates General do, each one legalizing only documents originating in its area of jurisdiction.

II. REQUIREMENTS FOR LEGALIZATION

Prior Authentications Required
1. Notarization
2. Authentication of Notary Signature (In most states this may be done directly by the State Secretary of State; if not, the County Clerk authenticates the signature.)

3. State Secretary of State Certification (In states where the Notary Signature may be authenticated directly by the State Secretary of State, steps 2 and 3 are combined.)
4. U.S. Secretary of State Certification

Materials to be Submitted with Request
1. Original document to be legalized
2. Prepaid, self-addressed return envelope

Direct Registration of Notary Public: The procedure of registering a Notary Public's signature with the Consulate is available, permitting the legalization of the document(s) bearing that Notary's signature and seal without certification by the County Clerk or the Secretary of State. For registration, provide a letter requesting that the signature be accepted and registered by the Consulate and a photocopy of the Notary Public's seal and signature as certified by the County Clerk.

Direct Signing of Document Before Consular Official: Not available

Turn Around Time: If the document is personally delivered, there will be a delay of 24 hours before legalization.

Fee: $30.00 per document or signature

Payment Method: Money order, certified check, cashier's check

III. EMBASSY, CONSULATES GENERAL, AND CONSULATE

Address, Phone, Hours	*Jurisdiction*
Embassy of the Argentine Republic Consular Section 1718 Connecticut Avenue, NW Washington, DC 20009 Tel.: 202-797-8826 Fax: 202-319-1771 9:00 AM - 1:00 PM	Delaware Maryland North Carolina Pennsylvania Virginia Washington, DC West Virginia

Address, Phone, Hours	*Jurisdiction*
Consulate General 245 Peachtree Center Avenue Atlanta, GA 30303 Tel.: 404-880-0805 Fax: 404-880-0806	Alabama Georgia Kentucky Mississippi South Carolina Tennessee
Consulate General 205 North Michigan Avenue Suite 4208 Chicago, IL 60601 Tel.: 312-819-2610 Fax: 312-819-2612	Illinois Indiana Iowa Kansas Michigan Minnesota Missouri Nebraska North Dakota Ohio South Dakota Wisconsin
Consulate 1990 Post Oak Boulevard, Suite 770 Houston, TX 77056 Tel.: 713-871-8935 Fax: 713-871-0639	Arkansas Colorado Louisiana New Mexico Oklahoma Texas
Consulate General 5055 Wilshire Boulevard, Suite 210 Los Angeles, CA 90036 Tel.: 213-954-9155 Fax: 213-934-9076	Alaska Arizona California Hawaii Idaho Montana Nevada Oregon Utah Washington Wyoming Islas del Pacifico e Islas Carolinas

Address, Phone, Hours	*Jurisdiction*
Consulate General 800 Brickell Avenue Miami, FL 33131 Tel.: 305-373-7794 Fax: 305-371-7108	Florida Puerto Rico Bahamas Barbados Dominica Grenada Santa Lucia San Vicente Las Granadinas Virgin Islands
Consulate General 12 West 56th Street New York, NY 10019 Tel.: 212-603-0445 Fax: 212-397-3523 9:00 AM - 1:00 PM	Connecticut Maine Massachusetts New Hampshire New Jersey New York Pennsylvania Rhode Island Vermont

ARMENIA

Armenia is a party to the Hague Convention Abolishing the Requirement for Legalization for Foreign Public Documents.

A document should be sent to the appropriate authority in the state or territory in which the document is notarized in order to obtain the Apostille. For information on obtaining the Apostille for documents originating in the United States, see the procedures specified for each of the individual states under United States jurisdiction in Chapter 2. For the enumeration of Federal authorities competent to provide the Apostille, see Appendix D.

For the text of the Hague Convention, the Apostille, and a list of the parties to the Convention, see Appendix A.

For information purposes, the Embassy is listed below.

II. EMBASSY

Address, Phone, Hours	*Jurisdiction*
Embassy of Armenia 2225 R Street, NW Washington, DC 20008 Tel.: 202-319-1976 Fax: 202-319-2982 10:00 AM - 6:00 PM	

COMMONWEALTH OF AUSTRALIA

National Holiday: Australia Day, January 26

I. GENERAL INFORMATION

Australia is a party to the Hague Convention Abolishing the Requirement for Legalization for Foreign Public Documents.

A document should be sent to the appropriate authority in the state or territory in which the document is notarized in order to obtain the Apostille. For information on obtaining the Apostille for documents originating in the United States, see the procedures specified for each of the individual states under United States jurisdiction in Chapter 2. For the enumeration of Federal authorities competent to provide the Apostille, see Appendix D.

For the text of the Hague Convention, the Apostille, and a list of the parties to the Convention, see Appendix A.

For instances in which legalization by an Australian Consular official is still necessary, the requirements for legalization are given below. The Embassy and Consulates General have legalization functions. Each legalizes documents originating within its jurisdiction. The specific requirements for legalization vary from office to office. The requirements for the Embassy and the Consulates General of Atlanta, Los Angeles, New York, and San Francisco are listed below.

II. REQUIREMENTS FOR LEGALIZATION

Prior Authentications Required
The Embassy and the Consulates General of Atlanta, New York, and San Francisco require steps 1 through 4; the Consulate General of Los Angeles requires steps 1 through 3.

1. Notarization
2. Authentication of Notary Signature (In most states this may be done directly by the State Secretary of State; if not, the County Clerk authenticates the signature.)
3. State Secretary of State Certification (In states where the Notary Signature may be authenticated directly by the State Secretary of State, steps 2 and 3 are combined.)
4. U.S. Secretary of State Certification

Materials to be Submitted with Request

1. Original document to be legalized
2. Photocopy of the document
3. Prepaid, self-addressed return envelope for special mail; an account number for Federal Express

Direct Registration of Notary Public: Not available

Direct Signing of Document Before Consular Official: The procedure of certifying the signature of a private person is available at the Embassy. An appointment is necessary and the signer must present identification (driver's license, credit card, or passport).

Fee: Changes annually, depends on exchange rate and service provided; call Embassy or Consulate General

Payment Method: Cash, money order, certified check, company check, personal check; contact appropriate Consulate

III. EMBASSY AND CONSULATES GENERAL

Address, Phone, Hours	*Jurisdiction*
Embassy of Australia 1601 Massachusetts Avenue, NW Washington, DC 20036 Tel.: 202-797-3139 Fax: 202-797-3132 8:30 AM - 5:00 PM	Delaware Illinois Iowa Kentucky Maryland Minnesota Missouri Texas Virginia Washington, DC West Virginia Wisconsin

Address, Phone, Hours	*Jurisdiction*
Consulate General 1 Peachtree Center, Suite 2920 303 Peachtree Street, NE Atlanta, GA 30308 Tel.: 404-880-1700 8:30 AM - 5:00 PM	Alabama Arkansas Florida Georgia Mississippi North Carolina Oklahoma South Carolina Tennessee
Consulate General 1000 Bishop Street, Suite 507 Honolulu, HI 96813-4299 Tel.: 808-524-5050	Alaska Hawaii American Samoa
Consulate General Century Plaza Tower, 19th Floor 2049 Century Park East Los Angeles, CA 90067 Tel.: 310-229-4800 8:00 AM - 5:00 PM	Arizona California (south) Colorado Kansas New Mexico Utah
Consulate General 630 Fifth Avenue, Suite 420 New York, NY 10111 Tel.: 212-408-8400 9:00 AM - 1:00 PM 2:00 PM - 5:00 PM Appointment necessary	Connecticut Indiana Maine Massachusetts Michigan New Hampshire New Jersey New York Ohio Pennsylvania Puerto Rico Vermont Virgin Islands

Address, Phone, Hours	*Jurisdiction*
Consulate General 1 Bush Street San Francisco, CA 94104 Tel.: 415-362-6160 8:45 AM - 5:06 PM	California (north) Idaho Montana Nebraska Nevada North Dakota Oregon South Dakota Wyoming
Embassy of Australia Federated States of Micronesia H&E Enterprises Building PO Box S Kolonia, Pohnpei Tel.: 011-691-320-5448 Fax: 011-691-320-5449	Guam Mariana Islands

REPUBLIC OF AUSTRIA

National Holiday: October 26

I. GENERAL INFORMATION

Austria is a party to the Hague Convention Abolishing the Requirement for Legalization for Foreign Public Documents.

A document should be sent to the appropriate authority in the state or territory in which the document is notarized in order to obtain the Apostille. For information on obtaining the Apostille for documents originating in the United States, see the procedures specified for each of the individual states under United States jurisdiction in Chapter 2. For the enumeration of Federal authorities competent to provide the Apostille, see Appendix D. For the text of the Hague Convention, the Apostille, and a list of the parties to the Convention, see Appendix A.

For information purposes, the Embassy and Consulates General of Austria are listed below.

II. EMBASSY AND CONSULATES GENERAL

Address, Phone, Hours	*Jurisdiction*
Embassy of Austria 3524 International Court, NW Washington, DC 20008-3022 Tel.: 202-895-6700 Fax: 202-895-6750 9:00 AM - 5:00 PM Consular Section Tel.: 202-895-6767 Fax: 202-905-6773 9:00 AM - 1:00 PM	Alabama Arkansas Delaware Florida Georgia Louisiana Maryland Mississippi North Carolina Oklahoma Puerto Rico South Carolina Tennessee Texas Virginia Washington, DC West Virginia Virgin Islands

Address, Phone, Hours	*Jurisdiction*
Consulate General 400 N. Michigan Avenue, Suite 707 Chicago, IL 60611 Tel.: 312-222-1515 9:00 AM - 12:00 PM	Illinois Indiana Iowa Kansas Kentucky Michigan Minnesota Missouri Nebraska North Dakota Ohio South Dakota Wisconsin
Consulate General 11859 Wilshire Boulevard, Suite 501 Los Angeles, CA 90025 Tel.: 310-444-9310 Fax: 310-477-9897	Alaska Arizona California Colorado Hawaii Idaho Montana Nevada New Mexico Oregon Utah Washington Wyoming U.S. Pacific Trust Territories
Consulate General 31 East 69th Street New York, NY 10021 Tel.: 212-737-6400 Fax: 212-772-8926	Connecticut Maine Massachusetts New Hampshire New Jersey New York Pennsylvania Rhode Island Vermont Bahamas

REPUBLIC OF AZERBAIJAN

National Holidays: American holidays observed

I. GENERAL INFORMATION

Azerbaijan has an Embassy in the United States but no Consulates. Documents from anywhere in the United States may be sent to the Embassy for legalization.

II. REQUIREMENTS FOR LEGALIZATION

Prior Authentications Required

1. Notarization
2. Authentication of Notary Signature (In most states this may be done directly by the State Secretary of State; if not, the County Clerk authenticates the signature.)
3. State Secretary of State Certification (In states where the Notary Signature may be authenticated directly by the State Secretary of State, steps 2 and 3 are combined.)
4. U.S. Secretary of State Certification

Materials to be Submitted with Request

1. Original document to be legalized
2. Photocopy of the document
3. Prepaid, self-addressed return envelope
4. Professional translation of document into Azerbaijani language

Direct Registration of Notary Public: Not available

Direct Signing of Document Before Consular Official: The procedure of certifying the signature of a private person is available at the Embassy. An appointment is necessary. The signer must present a driver's license or Social Security card as identification.

Turn Around Time: If the document is personally delivered, it will be legalized immediately provided that an official is available and that the work load permits.

Fee: $20.00 per document or signature

Payment Method: Money order, certified check, company check payable to The Embassy of the Republic of Azerbaijan

III. EMBASSY

Address, Phone, Hours	*Jurisdiction*
Embassy of the Republic of Azerbaijan 927 Fifteenth Street NW, Suite 700 Washington, DC 20005 Tel.: 202-842-0001 Fax: 202-842-0004 9:00 AM - 5:00 PM	Entire United States

Mailing Address for Certified/Registered Documents
PO Box 27839
Washington, DC 20038-7839

COMMONWEALTH OF THE BAHAMAS

National Holiday: Independence Day, July 10

I. GENERAL INFORMATION

The Bahamas is a party to the Hague Convention Abolishing the Requirement for Legalization for Foreign Public Documents.

A document should be sent to the appropriate authority in the state or territory in which the document is notarized in order to obtain the Apostille. For information on obtaining the Apostille for documents originating in the United States, see the procedures specified for each of the individual states under United States jurisdiction in Chapter 2. For the enumeration of Federal authorities competent to provide the Apostille, see Appendix D.

For the text of the Hague Convention, the Apostille, and a list of the parties to the Convention, see Appendix A.

For information purposes, the Embassy and Consulates General of the Bahamas are listed below.

II. EMBASSY AND CONSULATES GENERAL

Address, Phone, Hours	*Jurisdiction*
Embassy of the Commonwealth of the Bahamas 2220 Massachusetts Avenue NW Washington, DC 20008 Tel.: 202-319-2660/7 Fax: 202-319-2668 9:00 AM - 5:00 PM	Alaska Arizona Arkansas California Colorado Guam Hawaii Idaho Illinois Indiana Iowa Kansas Kentucky Maryland Michigan

Address, Phone, Hours	*Jurisdiction*
	Minnesota Missouri Montana Nebraska Nevada New Mexico North Dakota Ohio Oklahoma Oregon Puerto Rico South Dakota Tennessee Texas Utah Virgin Islands Virginia Washington Washington, DC West Virginia Wisconsin Wyoming
Consulate General Ingraham Building, Suite 818 25 S.E. Second Avenue Miami, FL 33131 Tel.: 305-373-6295 Fax: 305-373-6312 9:00 AM - 5:00 PM	Alabama Florida Georgia Louisiana Mississippi North Carolina South Carolina
Consulate General 231 East 46th Street New York, NY 10017 Tel.: 212-421-6420/3 Fax: 212-759-2135	Connecticut Delaware Massachusetts Maine New Hampshire New Jersey New York Pennsylvania Rhode Island Vermont

STATE OF BAHRAIN

National Holiday: Independence Day, December 16

I. GENERAL INFORMATION

The Embassy and the Consulate in New York have legalization functions. Each will legalize documents originating anywhere in the United States. The information below pertains to the legalization of documents such as Powers of Attorney and Agreements.

Note: The New York Consulate will legalize documents destined for the United Arab Emirates as well as for Bahrain. The requirements for documents destined for those countries are the same as for documents destined for Bahrain.

II. REQUIREMENTS FOR LEGALIZATION

Prior Authentications Required
All shipping documents, commercial invoices, certificates of origin, steamship certificates, and health certificates should be certified before presentation to the Consulate or the Embassy by one of the Arab Chambers of Commerce listed below. See the appropriate section for the requirements of these Arab Chambers of Commerce.

For trademarks, powers of attorney, agreements, assignments and registrations:
1. Notarization
2. Authentication of Notary Signature (In most states this may be done directly by the State Secretary of State; if not, the County Clerk authenticates the signature.)
3. State Secretary of State Certification (In states where the Notary Signature may be authenticated directly by the State Secretary of State, steps 2 and 3 are combined.)
4. U.S. Secretary of State Certification

Materials to be Submitted with Request
1. Original document to be legalized
2. Prepaid, self-addressed return envelope

Direct Registration of Notary Public: Not available

Direct Signing of Document Before Consular Official: Not available

Turn Around Time: 24 hours at the Embassy and New York Consulate

Fees: Embassy: $12.00; New York Consulate: $20.00

Commercial invoices, certificates of origin, steamship certificates, health certificates and additional documents (if required) all are subject to an $8.00 fee.

Legalization fees for U.S. Arab Chamber of Commerce certification, payable by money order or company check made out to the order of the Embassy of Bahrain, are $8.00 for commercial invoices, certificates of origin, steamship certificates, health certificates and additional documents, if required. For information on the National U.S.-Arab Chamber of Commerce, see Appendix C.

Payment Method: Money order payable to the Embassy of Bahrain

III. EMBASSY AND CONSULATE

Address, Phone, Hours	*Jurisdiction*
Embassy of the State of Bahrain 3502 International Drive, NW Washington, DC 20008 Tel.: 202-342-0741/2 9:30 AM - 12:30 PM	United States
Consulate 2 UN Plaza, 25th Floor New York, NY 10017 Tel.: 212-223-6200	United States

IV. CHAMBERS OF COMMERCE

National U. S.-Arab Chamber of Commerce
1100 New York Avenue, NW, Suite 550
Washington, DC 20005
Tel.: 202-289-5920
Fax: 202-289-5938

U.S.-Arab Chamber of Commerce
208 South LaSalle Street, Suite 706
Chicago, IL 60604
Tel.: 312-782-0320
Fax: 312-782-7379

U.S.-Arab Chamber of Commerce
1330 Post Oak Boulevard, Suite 1600
Houston, TX 77056
Tel.: 713-963-4620
Fax: 713-782-7379

U.S.-Arab Chamber of Commerce
8939 S. Sepulveda Boulevard #430
Los Angeles, CA 90045
Tel.: 310-646-1499
Fax: 310-646-2462

U.S.-Arab Chamber of Commerce
420 Lexington Avenue, #2739
New York, NY 10170
Tel.: 212-986-8024
Fax: 212-986-0216

U.S.-Arab Chamber of Commerce
PO Box 422218
San Francisco, CA 94142-2218
Tel.: 415-398-9200
Fax: 415-389-7111

BANGLADESH

National Holiday: March 26

I. REQUIREMENTS FOR LEGALIZATION

Prior Authentications Required
1. Notarization
2. Authentication of Notary Signature (In most states this may be done directly by the State Secretary of State; if not, the County Clerk authenticates the signature.)
3. State Secretary of State Certification (In states where the Notary Signature may be authenticated directly by the State Secretary of State, steps 2 and 3 are combined.)
4. U.S. Secretary of State Certification

Materials to be Submitted with Request
1. Original document to be legalized
2. Photocopy of the document
3. Prepaid, self-addressed return envelope

Direct Registration of Notary Public: The procedure of registering a Notary Public's signature with the Consulate is available, permitting the legalization of the document(s) bearing that Notary's signature and seal without certification by the County Clerk or the Secretary of State.

Direct Signing of Document Before Consular Official: Not available

Turn Around Time: If the document is personally delivered, there will be a delay of 24 hours before legalization.

Fee: $17.00 per document or signture

Payment Method: Money order, certified check, company check payable to the Embassy or Consulate General of Bangladesh

II. EMBASSY AND CONSULATES GENERAL

Address, Phone, Hours	*Jurisdiction*
Embassy of Bangladesh Consular Section 2201 Wisconsin Avenue Washington, DC 20008 Tel.: 202-342-8395 Fax: 202-333-4971 10:30 AM - 12:30 PM 3:00 PM - 4:00 PM	Washington, DC Central states Southern states
Consulate General 211 East 43rd Street, Suite 502 New York, NY 10017 Tel.: 212-599-6767 Fax: 212-682-9211 10:30 AM - 1:00 PM	Connecticut Maine Massachusetts New Hampshire New Jersey New York Pennsylvania Rhode Island Vermont
Consulate General 10850 Wilshire Boulevard, Suite 1250 Los Angeles, CA 90024 Tel.: 310-441-9399 Fax: 310-441-4458 9:00 AM - 5:00 PM	Arizona California Idaho Nevada Oregon Utah Washington Wyoming

BARBADOS

National Holiday: Independence Day, November 30

I. GENERAL INFORMATION

The Embassy and Consulate General in New York have legalization functions. Each will legalize documents originating anywhere in the United States. The specific requirements for the Embassy and the New York Consulate General are given below. Procedures at the Consulate General in Coral Gables may vary.

II. REQUIREMENTS FOR LEGALIZATION

Prior Authentications Required
The Embassy requires steps 1 through 3; the New York Consulate requires steps 1 and 2.

1. Notarization
2. Authentication of Notary Signature (In most states this may be done directly by the State Secretary of State; if not, the County Clerk authenticates the signature.)
3. State Secretary of State Certification (In states where the Notary Signature may be authenticated directly by the State Secretary of State, steps 2 and 3 are combined.)
4. U.S. Secretary of State Certification

Materials to be Submitted with Request
1. Original document to be legalized
2. Prepaid, self-addressed return envelope

Turn Around Time: If the document is personally delivered, there will be a delay of two or more working days before legalization. However, at the Consulate General of New York, if the Notary Public signature is on file, a document which is personally delivered may be legalized immediately.

Direct Registration of Notary Public: Available at the Consulate General of New York

Direct Signing of Document Before Consular Official: Not available

Fee
Embassy: $25.00 per document or signature
New York Consulate: $5.00 per document or signature
Coral Gables Consulate: Contact Consulate

Payment Method: Money order, certified check, company check payable to the Embassy or Consulate General of Barbados

III. EMBASSY AND CONSULATES GENERAL

Address, Phone, Hours	*Jurisdiction*
Embassy of Barbados Chancery 2144 Wyoming Avenue Washington, DC 20008 Tel.: 202-939-9200 Fax: 202-332-7467 9:00 AM - 5:00 PM	Entire United States
Consulate General 800 Second Avenue, 2nd Floor New York, NY 10017 Tel.: 212-867-8435 Fax: 212-986-1030 9:30 AM - 3:00 PM	Connecticut New Jersey New York Pennsylvania
Consulate General 150 Alhambra Circle, Suite 1270 Coral Gables, FL 33134 Tel.: 305-442-1994 Fax: 305-567-2844 9:00 AM - 5:00 PM	Alabama Arkansas Florida Georgia Kentucky Louisiana Mississippi North Carolina South Carolina Tennessee Texas

THE REPUBLIC OF BELARUS

National Holidays: January 1, March 8, May 1, May 9, July 3

I. GENERAL INFORMATION

Belarus is a party to the Hague Convention Abolishing the Requirement for Legalization for Foreign Public Documents.

A document should be sent to the appropriate authority in the state or territory in which the document is notarized in order to obtain the Apostille. For information on obtaining the Apostille for documents originating in the United States, see the procedures specified for each of the individual states under United States jurisdiction in Chapter 2. For the enumeration of Federal authorities competent to provide the Apostille, see Appendix D.

For the text of the Hague Convention, the Apostille, and a list of the parties to the Convention, see Appendix A.

For information purposes, the Embassy of Belarus is listed below.

For instances in which legalization by a Consular official is still necessary, the requirements for legalization by the Embassy are given below.

II. REQUIREMENTS FOR LEGALIZATION

Documents can be legalized at the Embassy only if the applicant appears in person and signs the document in the presence of the Consular officer. Documents may not be mailed to the Embassy for legalization.

Prior Authentications Required
1. Notarization

Materials to be Submitted with Request
1. Original document to be legalized

Direct Registration of Notary Public: Not available

Direct Signing of Document Before Consular Official: The procedure of certifying the signature of a private person is available at the Embassy. An appointment is not necessary. The signer must present a passport or other identification. The Embassy does not accept documents for legalization that are submitted through the mail.

Turn Around Time: Documents must be personally delivered and will be legalized within five working days.

Fee: $200.00 per document or signature

Payment Method: Money order, certified check, company check, personal check payable to the Embassy of Belarus in the USA

III. EMBASSY

Address, Phone, Hours	*Jurisdiction*
Embassy of the Republic of Belarus 1619 New Hampshire Avenue, NW Washington, DC 20009 Tel.: 202-986-1604/6 Fax: 202-986-1805 9:30 AM - 12:30 PM	Entire United States

KINGDOM OF BELGIUM

National Holiday: July 21; King's Day November 15

I. GENERAL INFORMATION

Belgium is a party to the Hague Convention Abolishing the Requirement for Legalization for Foreign Public Documents.

A document should be sent to the appropriate authority in the state or territory in which the document is notarized in order to obtain the Apostille. For information on obtaining the Apostille for documents originating in the United States, see the procedures specified for each of the individual states under United States jurisdiction in Chapter 2. For the enumeration of Federal authorities competent to provide the Apostille, see Appendix D.

For the text of the Hague Convention, the Apostille, and a list of the parties to the Convention, see Appendix A.

For information purposes, the Embassy and Consulates General of Belgium are listed below.

II. EMBASSY AND CONSULATES GENERAL

Address, Phone, Hours	*Jurisdiction*
Embassy of the Kingdom of Belgium 3330 Garfield Street, NW Washington, DC 20008 Tel.: 202-333-6900 Fax: 202-333-3079 9:30 AM - 12:30 PM	Delaware District of Columbia Maryland Puerto Rico Turks and Caicos Islands Virgin Islands Virginia West Virginia

Address, Phone, Hours	*Jurisdiction*
Consulate General Suite 850 235 Peachtree Street, NE Peachtree Center North Tower Atlanta, GA 30303 Tel.: 404-659-2150/1/2/3 9:30 AM - 12:30 PM	Alabama Arkansas Florida Georgia Kentucky Louisiana Mississippi North Carolina South Carolina Tennessee
Consulate General Room 2000 333 No. Michigan Avenue Chicago, IL 60601 Tel.: 312-263-6624/5/6 9:00 AM - 12:00 PM 1:00 PM - 3:00 PM Closed Friday afternoon	Illinois Indiana Iowa Kansas Michigan Minnesota Missouri Nebraska North Dakota Ohio Oklahoma South Dakota Texas Wisconsin
Consulate General 6100 Wilshire Boulevard Suite 1200 Los Angeles, CA 90048 Tel.: 213-857-1244 9:00 AM - 12:00 PM	Alaska American Samoa Arizona California Caroline Islands Colorado Guam Hawaii Idaho Montana Nevada Oregon Utah

Address, Phone, Hours	*Jurisdiction*
	Washington Wyoming
Consulate General ITT Building 1330 Avenue of the Americas, 26th Floor New York, NY 10019-5422 Tel.: 212-586-5110 10:00 AM - 1:00 PM (visas) 2:00 PM - 4:00 PM	Connecticut Maine Massachusetts New Hampshire New Jersey New York Pennsylvania Rhode Island Vermont

BELIZE

National Holiday: September 21

I. GENERAL INFORMATION

Belize is a party to the Hague Convention Abolishing the Requirement for Legalization for Foreign Public Documents.

A document should be sent to the appropriate authority in the state or territory in which the document is notarized in order to obtain the Apostille. For information on obtaining the Apostille for documents originating in the United States, see the procedures specified for each of the individual states under United States jurisdiction in Chapter 2. For the enumeration of Federal authorities competent to provide the Apostille, see Appendix D.

For the text of the Hague Convention, the Apostille, and a list of the parties to the Convention, see Appendix A.

The Embassy, Consulate General and UN Mission will handle legalizations for other countries only if the paperwork comes directly from Belize.

II. REQUIREMENTS FOR LEGALIZATION

Prior Authentications Required

1. Notarization
2. Authentication of Notary Signature (In most states this may be done directly by the State Secretary of State; if not, the County Clerk authenticates the signature.)
3. State Secretary of State Certification (In states where the Notary Signature may be authenticated directly by the State Secretary of State, steps 2 and 3 are combined.)
4. U.S. Secretary of State Certification

Materials to be Submitted with Request

1. Original document to be legalized
2. Prepaid, self-addressed return envelope for specialized mail service

Direct Registration of Notary Public: Not available

Direct Signing of Document Before Consular Official: Not available

Turn Around Time: If the document is personally delivered, there may be a delay of one to two days before legalization.

Fee: $10 per document

Payment Method: Money order

III. EMBASSY, CONSULATE GENERAL, AND UN MISSION

Embassy of Belize 2535 Massachusetts Avenue, NW Washington, DC 20008 Tel.: 202-332-9636 ext. 3008 Fax: 202-332-6888 9:00 AM - 5:00 PM	Entire United States
Consulate General 5825 Sunset Boulevard, Suite 206 Hollywood, CA 90028 Tel.: 213-469-7343	Surrounding states Other states if needed
Permanent Mission to UN 801 Second Avenue New York, NY 10017 Tel.: 212-599-0233	Surrounding states Other states if needed

BENIN

National Holidays: Easter Monday, May 1, August 1, August 15, November 1

I. GENERAL INFORMATION

Benin has an Embassy in the United States and a Consulate in Los Angeles; the Consulate does not legalize documents. Documents from anywhere in the United States may be sent to the Embassy for legalization.

II. REQUIREMENTS FOR LEGALIZATION

Prior Authentications Required

1. Notarization
2. Authentication of Notary Signature (In most states this may be done directly by the State Secretary of State; if not, the County Clerk authenticates the signature.)
3. State Secretary of State Certification (In states where the Notary Signature may be authenticated directly by the State Secretary of State, steps 2 and 3 are combined.)
4. U.S. Secretary of State Certification

Materials to be Submitted with Request

1. Original document to be legalized
2. Photocopy of the document
3. Prepaid, self-addressed return envelope

Direct Registration of Notary Public: Not available

Direct Signing of Document Before Consular Official: The procedure of certifying the signature of a private person is available at the Embassy. An appointment should be made and the signer must present identification such as a driver's license or some form of picture ID.

Turn Around Time: If the document is personally delivered, there will be a delay of three days before legalization.

Fee: $5.00 per document or signature

Payment Method: Cash, money order, certified check, company check

III. EMBASSY AND CONSULATE

Address, Phone, Hours	*Jurisdiction*
Embassy of Benin 2737 Cathedral Avenue NW Washington, DC 20008 Tel.: 202-232-6656 Fax: 202-265-1996 9:00 AM - 1:00 PM	Entire United States
Consulate 91131 South Laciennega Boulevard, Suite 204 Englewood, CA 90301 Tel.: 310-641-3688	

BERMUDA

I. GENERAL INFORMATION

Bermuda is a dependency of the United Kingdom, covered by the Hague Convention Abolishing the Requirement for Legalization for Foreign Public Documents.

A document should be sent to the appropriate authority in the state or territory in which the document is notarized in order to obtain the Apostille. For information on obtaining the Apostille for documents originating in the United States, see the procedures specified for each of the individual states under United States jurisdiction in Chapter 2. For the enumeration of Federal authorities competent to provide the Apostille, see Appendix D.

For the text of the Hague Convention, the Apostille, and a list of the parties to the Convention, see Appendix A.

For information on United Kingdom Consulates, see the United Kingdom.

BOLIVIA

National Holiday: Independence Day, August 6

I. GENERAL INFORMATION

The Consular Section of the Embassy and all of the Consulates General and Honorary Consulates provide legalization functions for Bolivian citizens and foreign nationals for all documents that will be used in Bolivia (powers of attorney, trademarks, certifications, diplomas, etc.)

The requirements for legalization at the Embassy and Consular Offices are listed below. These procedures apply to educational documents issued by universities, colleges and high schools. It is recommended that documents be translated into Spanish.

II. REQUIREMENTS FOR LEGALIZATION

Prior Authentications Required
Original transcripts from elementary and junior high schools may be submitted directly to the Consular Section for certification. Step 4 may be omitted in states not in the jurisdiction of the Consular Section of the Embassy of Bolivia.

1. Notarization
2. Authentication of Notary Signature (In most states this may be done directly by the State Secretary of State; if not, the County Clerk authenticates the signature.)
3. State Secretary of State Certification (In states where the Notary Signature may be authenticated directly by the State Secretary of State, steps 2 and 3 are combined.)
4. U.S. Secretary of State Certification

Materials to be Submitted with Request
1. Original document to be legalized
2. Photocopy of the document
3. Translation of the document into Spanish (recommended)
4. Prepaid, self-addressed return envelope

Direct Registration of Notary Public: Not available

Direct Signing of Document Before Consular Official: The procedure of certifying the signature of a private person is available at the Embassy. An appointment should be made with the Chargé of Consular Affairs and the signer must present identification.

Turn Around Time: If the document is personally delivered, there may be a delay of from one to two days before legalization.

Fee: The fee at the Embassy varies from $10.00 to $100.00.

Payment Method: Cash, money order, certified company check, personal check payable to the Embassy of Bolivia - Consular Section

III. EMBASSY, CONSULATES GENERAL, AND HONORARY CONSULATES

Address, Phone, Hours	*Jurisdiction*
Embassy of Bolivia 3014 Massachusetts Avenue, NW Washington, DC 20008-3603 Tel.: 202-232-4827/8 Fax: 202-328-3712 9:30 AM - 2:00 PM	Delaware Maryland North Carolina Puerto Rico West Virginia Washington, DC Virginia
Consulate General 25 SE Second Avenue, Suite 545 Miami, FL 33131 Tel.: 305-358-3450 Fax: 305-374-8636 9:00 AM - 3:00 PM	Alabama Florida South Carolina
Consulate General 211 East 43rd Street, Suite 702 New York, NY 10017 Tel.: 212-687-0530/1 Fax: 212-687-0532 9:00 AM - 2:00 PM	Connecticut Maine New Hampshire New Jersey New York Pennsylvania Rhode Island Vermont

Address, Phone, Hours	*Jurisdiction*
Consulate General 870 Market Street, Suite 575 San Francisco, CA 94102 Tel.: 415-495-5173 Fax: 415-399-8958 9:00 AM - 2:00 PM	California Hawaii Nevada
Honorary Consulate 1375 Peachtree Street NW, Ste. 180A Atlanta, GA 30309 Tel.: 404-522-0777 Fax: 404-873-3335 By appointment 10:00 AM - 5:00 PM	Georgia Tennessee
Honorary Consulate 85 Devonshire Street, Suite 1000 Boston, MA 02109 Tel.: 617-742-1500 Fax: 617-742-9130 By appointment 9:00 AM - 2:00 PM	Massachusetts
Honorary Consulate 5500 Mapleridge Drive Cincinnati, OH 45227 Tel.: 513-271-5381 Fax: 513-271-8189 By appointment 9:00 AM - 5:00 PM	Kentucky Ohio
Honorary Consulate Ashford Crossing II 1880 Dairy Ashford, Suite 515 Houston, TX 77077 Tel.: 281-497-4068 Fax: 281-589-1358 2:30 PM - 6:00 PM, Tuesday - Friday Saturday by appointment	Arkansas Louisiana Mississippi Oklahoma Texas

Address, Phone, Hours	*Jurisdiction*
Honorary Consulate 1200 West Superior, Suite 101 Melrose Park, IL 60160 Tel.: 708-343-1234 Fax: 708-343-4290 By appointment 11:00 AM - 3:00 PM except Wednesday	Illinois Indiana Iowa Michigan Minnesota Wisconsin
Honorary Consulate David Bell, Esq. McGlinchey, Stafford 643 Magazine Street New Orleans, LA 70130 Tel.: 504-586-1200 Fax: 504-596-2800 By appointment 9:00 AM - 5:00 PM	Louisiana
Honorary Consulate Castillo Co. 2345 East University Drive PO Box 21087 Phoenix, AZ 85036-1087 Tel.: 602-231-9000 Fax: 602-275-8593 By appointment 8:30 AM - 5:30 PM	Arizona New Mexico
Honorary Consulate 5200 Southcenter Boulevard, Suite #5 Seattle, WA 98188 Tel.: 206-244-6696 Fax: 206-243-3795 By appointment 8:30 AM - 5:30 PM	Alaska Idaho Montana Oregon Washington Wyoming
Honorary Consulate 21 Lemond Circle PO Box 6117 Snowmass Village, CO 81615 Tel.: 970-923-2668 Fax: 970-923-6716 By appointment	Colorado Utah

REPUBLIC OF BOSNIA AND HERZEGOVINA

I. GENERAL INFORMATION

The Republic of Bosnia and Herzegovina is a party to the Hague Convention Abolishing the Requirement for Legalization for Foreign Public Documents.

A-document should be sent to the appropriate authority in the state or territory in which the document is notarized in order to obtain the Apostille. For information on obtaining the Apostille for documents originating in the United States, see the procedures specified for each of the individual states under United States jurisdiction in Chapter 2. For the enumeration of Federal authorities competent to provide the Apostille, see Appendix D.

For the text of the Hague Convention, the Apostille, and a list of the parties to the Convention, see Appendix A.

For information purposes, the Embassy and Consulate General of Bosnia and Herzegovina are listed below.

II. EMBASSY AND CONSULATE GENERAL

Embassy of the Republic of Bosnia and Herzegovina
1707 L Street NW
Washington, DC
Tel.: 202-833-3612
Fax: 202-833-2061
9:00 AM - 5:00 PM

Consulate General
866 UN Plaza, Suite 580
New York, NY 10017
Tel.: 212-751-9015

REPUBLIC OF BOTSWANA

National Holidays: Independence Day, September 30; July 21, November 28, December 26

I. REQUIREMENTS FOR LEGALIZATION

Prior Authentications Required
1. Notarization
2. Authentication of Notary Signature (In most states this may be done directly by the State Secretary of State; if not, the County Clerk authenticates the signature.)
3. State Secretary of State Certification (In states where the Notary Signature may be authenticated directly by the State Secretary of State, steps 2 and 3 are combined.)
4. U.S. Secretary of State Certification

Materials to be Submitted with Request
1. Original document to be legalized
2. Photocopy of the document
3. Prepaid, self-addressed return envelope

Direct Registration of Notary Public: Not available

Direct Signing of Document Before Consular Official: The procedure of certifying the signature of a private person is available at the Embassy. An appointment is not necessary. The signer must present identification such as a driver's license or passport.

Turn Around Time: If the document is personally delivered, it will normally be legalized within a day, depending on the type of document. If the document is delivered by mail, it will take two days or longer, depending on the type of document, for legalization.

Fee: None

II. EMBASSY

Address, Phone, Hours	*Jurisdiction*
Embassy of Botswana 3400 International Drive, NW Washington, DC 20008 Tel.: 202-244-4990 Fax: 202-244-4164 9:00 AM - 5:00 PM	Entire United States

FEDERATIVE REPUBLIC OF BRAZIL

National Holiday: Independence Day, September 7

I. GENERAL INFORMATION

The Embassy and Consulates General have legalization functions. Each will legalize documents originating in its jurisdiction.

The specific requirements for legalization may vary from office to office. Those set forth below are for the Embassy and the New York Consulate.

II. REQUIREMENTS FOR LEGALIZATION

Prior Authentications Required
The Embassy requires step 1.
The New York Consulate requires steps 1 and 2.

1. Notarization by Notary within its jurisdiction only. The Notary must be directly registered by the Embassy. Notary cards must be applied for, completed with a Notarial seal affixed, and returned with the documents to be legalized. To obtain cards, request cards by letter to the Embassy and enclose a stamped, self-addressed envelope. Cards may also be picked up in person.
2. Authentication of Notary Signature (In most states this may be done directly by the State Secretary of State; if not, the County Clerk authenticates the signature.)

Materials to be Submitted with Request
1. Original document to be legalized
2. Prepaid, self-addressed return envelope

Direct Registration of Notary Public: Direct registration is available at the Washington DC Embassy and the New York Consulate only in cases of regular legalization requirements by a company. A letter from the company requesting the service is required with a sample of the signature and seal of the Notary Public. Thereafter, documents notarized by the registered Notary can be legalized by the Consulate without intervening authentications.

Direct Signing of Document Before Consular Official: This is available at the Embassy for nationals of Brazil. An appointment is advisable.

Additional Information

1. The signature on the document must be notarized and the signature of the Notary Public must be certified by the County Clerk or the State Secretary of State.
2. The signature of the authority must be handwritten with the name and title stamped or printed underneath.
3. Birth Certificates, Marriage Certificates and Death Certificates must be certified copies.
4. The legalization of the signature of local authorities such as Secretary of State, Judge of the Superior Court, School Official, Public Official of the Department of Health or Agriculture, Police Official, etc. waives requirement No. 1.

Fee: $20.00; Invoice $15.00; School Documents $5.00 - $15.00

Payment Method: Cash (except for requests submitted through the mail), cashier's check, money order, certified check payable to the Consulate General

Turn Around Time: If the document is personally delivered, or delivered by mail for legalization, there may be a delay of 48 hours before legalization, depending on the Consulate General.

III. EMBASSY AND CONSULATES GENERAL

Address, Phone, Hours	*Jurisdiction*
Embassy of the Federative Republic of Brazil Consular Service 3009 Whitehaven Street, NW Washington, DC 20008 Tel.: 202-238-2735 Fax: 202-238-2818 8:00 AM - 1:00 PM	Kentucky Maryland Ohio Virginia Washington, DC West Virginia

Address, Phone, Hours	*Jurisdiction*
Consulate General 229 Peachtree Street NE, Suite 2306 Atlanta, GA 30303 Tel.: 404-521-0061 Fax: 404-521-3449	Alabama Georgia Mississippi North Carolina South Carolina Tennessee
Consulate General The Statler Building 20 Park Plaza Suite 810 Boston, MA 02116 Tel.: 617-542-4000 Fax: 617-542-4318	Maine Massachusetts New Hampshire Rhode Island Vermont
Consulate General 401 N. Michigan Avenue, Suite 3050 Chicago, IL 60611 Tel.: 312-464-0244/5 Fax: 312-464-0299	Illinois Indiana Iowa Michigan Minnesota Missouri Nebraska North Dakota South Dakota Wisconsin
Consulate General 201 Dina House 11 Duddel Street Central, Hong Kong Tel.: 852-2525-7002/3 Fax: 852-2521-8761	Trust Territory of the Pacific: Guam, Caroline Islands, Mariana Islands, Marshall Islands
Consulate General 1700 West Loop South, Suite 1450 Houston, TX 77027 Tel.: 713-961-3063/4/5 Fax: 713-961-3070	Arkansas Colorado Kansas Louisiana New Mexico Oklahoma Texas

Address, Phone, Hours	*Jurisdiction*
Consulate General 8484 Wilshire Boulevard, Suite 730-711 Los Angeles, CA 90211 Tel.: 213-651-2664 Fax: 213-651-1274	Arizona California counties: Imperial, Kern, Los Angeles, Orange, Riverside, San Bernadino, San Diego, San Luis Obispo, Santa Barbara, Ventura Hawaii Idaho Montana Nevada Utah Wyoming
Consulate General 2601 S. Bayshore Drive, Suite 800 Miami, FL 33133 Tel.: 305-285-6200 Fax: 305-285-6229	Florida
Consulate General 630 Fifth Avenue, Room 2720 New York, NY 10111 Tel.: 212-757-3080 Fax: 212-956-3794	Connecticut Delaware New Jersey New York Pennsylvania
Consulado General de Brasil Edificio Antiguo Banco de Ponce Av. Muñoz Rivera 268 8° Piso - Oficina 804 Hato Rey, San Juan Puerto Rico 00919 Tel.: 787-754-7983/65 Fax: 787-754-1494	Puerto Rico Virgin Islands

Address, Phone, Hours	*Jurisdiction*
Consulate General 300 Montgomery Street, Suite 1160 San Francisco, CA 94104 Tel.: 415-981-8170 Fax: 415-981-3628	California counties: Alameda, Alpine, Amador, Butte, Calaveras, Colusa, Contra Costa, Del Norte, El Dorado, Fresno, Glenn, Humboldt, Inyo, Kings, Ladera, Lake, Lassin, Marin Mariposa, Mendocino, Merced, Modoc, Mono, Monterey, Napa, Nevada, Placer, Plumas, Sacramento, San Benedito, San Francisco, San Joaquim, San Mateo, Santa Clara, Santa Cruz, Shasta, Sierra, Siskyou, Solano, Sonoma, Stanislau, Sutter, Tehama, Trinity, Tulare, Tuolumne, Yola, Yuma Alaska Oregon Washington

BRITISH ANTARCTIC TERRITORY

I. GENERAL INFORMATION

The British Antarctic Territory is a dependency of the United Kingdom, covered by the Hague Convention Abolishing the Requirement for Legalization for Foreign Public Documents.

A document should be sent to the appropriate authority in the state or territory in which the document is notarized in order to obtain the Apostille. For information on obtaining the Apostille for documents originating in the United States, see the procedures specified for each of the individual states under United States jurisdiction in Chapter 2. For the enumeration of Federal authorities competent to provide the Apostille, see Appendix D.

The United States, however, does not recognize claims in the Antarctic. Accordingly, the legal status of an Apostille of United States origin, if it can be obtained, is questionable.

For the text of the Hague Convention, the Apostille, and a list of the parties to the Convention, see Appendix A.

For information on United Kingdom Consulates, see the United Kingdom.

BRITISH VIRGIN ISLANDS

I. GENERAL INFORMATION

The British Virgin Islands is a dependency of the United Kingdom, covered by the Hague Convention Abolishing the Requirement for Legalization for Foreign Public Documents.

A document should be sent to the appropriate authority in the state or territory in which the document is notarized in order to obtain the Apostille. For information on obtaining the Apostille for documents originating in the United States, see the procedures specified for each of the individual states under United States jurisdiction in Chapter 2. For the enumeration of Federal authorities competent to provide the Apostille, see Appendix D.

For the text of the Hague Convention, the Apostille, and a list of the parties to the Convention, see Appendix A.

For information on United Kingdom Consulates, see the United Kingdom.

BRUNEI DARUSSALAM

National Holiday: February 23

I. GENERAL INFORMATION

Brunei is a party to the Hague Convention Abolishing the Requirement for Legalization for Foreign Public Documents.

A document should be sent to the appropriate authority in the state or territory in which the document is notarized in order to obtain the Apostille. For information on obtaining the Apostille for documents originating in the United States, see the procedures specified for each of the individual states under United States jurisdiction in Chapter 2. For the enumeration of Federal authorities competent to provide the Apostille, see Appendix D.

For the text of the Hague Convention, the Apostille, and a list of the parties to the Convention, see Appendix A.

The Embassy does not legalize or notarize documents. Contact the Embassy for appropriate procedures.

II. EMBASSY

Embassy of Brunei Darussalam
Watergate, Suite #300
2600 Virginia Avenue, NW
Washington, DC 20037
Tel.: 202-342-0159
Fax: 202-342-0158

REPUBLIC OF BULGARIA

National Holiday: March 3

I. GENERAL INFORMATION

Bulgaria has an Embassy in the United States. Documents from anywhere in the United States may be sent to the Embassy for legalization.

II. REQUIREMENTS FOR LEGALIZATION

Prior Authentications Required
1. Notarization
2. Authentication of Notary Signature (In most states this may be done directly by the State Secretary of State; if not, the County Clerk authenticates the signature.)
3. State Secretary of State Certification (In states where the Notary Signature may be authenticated directly by the State Secretary of State, steps 2 and 3 are combined.)
4. U.S. Secretary of State Certification

Materials to be Submitted with Request
1. Original document to be legalized
2. Prepaid, self-addressed return envelope

Direct Registration of Notary Public: Available. Call the Embassy for requirements for this procedure.

Direct Signing of Document Before Consular Official: The procedure of certifying the signature of a private person is available at the Embassy. An appointment should be made and the signer must present identification, such as a driver's license or a voter registration card.

Turn Around Time: If the document is personally delivered, it can usually be legalized immediately.

Fee: $21.00 per document or signature

Payment Method: Cash, money order or company check payable to the Embassy of Bulgaria

III. EMBASSY

Address, Phone, Hours	*Jurisdiction*
Embassy of Bulgaria 1621 22nd Street NW Washington, DC 20008 Tel.: 202-483-5885 Fax: 202-234-7973 10:30 AM - 12:30 PM	Entire United States

CAMBODIA

National Holiday: October 11, 12, 13

I. GENERAL INFORMATION

Both the Embassy and the Honorary Consulate General have legalization functions.

II. REQUIREMENTS FOR LEGALIZATION

Prior Authentications Required
1. Notarization
2. Authentication of Notary Signature (In most states this may be done directly by the State Secretary of State; if not, the County Clerk authenticates the signature.)
3. State Secretary of State Certification (In states where the Notary Signature may be authenticated directly by the State Secretary of State, steps 2 and 3 are combined.)
4. U.S. Secretary of State Certification

Materials to be Submitted with Request
1. Original document to be legalized
2. Photocopy of the document
3. Prepaid, self-addressed return envelope

Direct Registration of Notary Public: Not available

Direct Signing of Document Before Consular Official: The procedure of certifying the signature of a private person is available at the Embassy and the Honorary Consulate General. An appointment should be made and the signer must present a driver's license or passport as identification.

Turn Around Time: If the document is personally delivered, it will be legalized immediately.

Fee: $50 per document or signature

Payment Method: Money order, certified check, company check payable to the Embassy or Honorary Consulate General of Cambodia

III. EMBASSY AND HONORARY CONSULATE GENERAL

Address, Phone, Hours	*Jurisdiction*
Embassy of Cambodia 4500 16th Street NW Washington, DC 20036 Tel.: 202-726-7742 Fax: 202-726-8381 9:00 AM - 12:00 PM 1:00 PM - 4:00 PM	Entire United States
Honorary Consulate General 306 East Pacific Coast Highway, Suite 205 Long Beach, CA 90806 Tel.: 562-218-2296 Fax: 562-218-2926 9:30 AM - 5:00 PM	Entire United States

CAMEROON

National Holiday: May 20

I. REQUIREMENTS FOR LEGALIZATION

Prior Authentications Required
1. Notarization
2. Authentication of Notary Signature (In most states this may be done directly by the State Secretary of State; if not, the County Clerk authenticates the signature.)
3. State Secretary of State Certification (In states where the Notary Signature may be authenticated directly by the State Secretary of State, steps 2 and 3 are combined.)
4. U.S. Secretary of State Certification

Materials to be Submitted with Request
1. Original document to be legalized
2. Photocopy of the document
3. Prepaid, self-addressed return envelope for specialized mail service

Direct Registration of Notary Public: Not available

Direct Signing of Document Before Consular Official: Not available

Turn Around Time: If the document is personally delivered, it will be legalized within 48 hours if the workload permits.

Fee: Call for current fee schedule

Payment Method: Money order, company check payable to the Embassy of Cameroon

II. EMBASSY

Address, Phone, Hours	*Jurisdiction*
Embassy of Cameroon 2349 Massachusetts Avenue, NW Washington, DC 20008 Tel.: 202-265-8790 Fax: 202-387-3826 9:00 AM - 4:00 PM	Entire United States

CANADA

National Holidays (1997): Good Friday, March 28; Canada Day, July 1; Labor Day, September 1; Thanksgiving, October 13; Remembrance Day, November 11; Boxing Day, December 26

I. REQUIREMENTS FOR LEGALIZATION

Prior Authentications Required

1. State Secretary of State Certification
2. U.S. Secretary of State Certification

Materials to be Submitted with Request

1. Original document to be legalized, containing State Department seal

Direct Registration of Notary Public: Not available

Direct Signing of Document Before Consular Official: The procedure of certifying the signature of a private person is available. An appointment should be made and the signer must present identification such as a passport.

Turn Around Time: If the document is personally delivered, it will be legalized the same day, depending on the workload and type of document. If the document is mailed, it will be legalized the day after it is received.

Fee: $8.00 per document or signature

Payment Method: Cash, money order, certified check payable to the Embassy or Consulate General of Canada

II EMBASSY AND CONSULATES GENERAL

Address, Phone, Hours	*Jurisdiction*
Embassy of Canada 501 Pennsylvania Avenue, NW Washington, DC 20001 Tel.: 202-682-1740 Fax: 202-682-7726	Entire United States For certain State Department matters or third country involvements only the Embassy has jurisdiction.
Consulate General 1175 Peachtree Street NW 1700 - 100 Colony Square Atlanta, GA 30361 Tel.: 404-532-2000 Fax: 404-532-2050	Alabama Florida Georgia Mississippi North Carolina South Carolina Tennessee Puerto Rico Virgin Islands
Consulate General Three Copley Place, Suite 400 Boston, MA 02116 Tel.: 617-262-3760 Fax: 617-262-3415	Maine Massachusetts New Hampshire Rhode Island Vermont Saint-Pierre-et-Miquelon
Consulate General One Marine Midland Center, Suite 3000 Buffalo, NY 14203-2884 Tel.: 716-858-9500 Fax: 716-852-4340	New York (western, central, upstate) Pennsylvania (western) West Virginia
Consulate General Two Prudential Plaza 180 N. Stetson Ave., Suite 2400 Chicago, IL 60601 Tel.: 312-616-1860 Fax: 312-616-1878	Illinois Missouri Wisconsin

Address, Phone, Hours	*Jurisdiction*
Consulate General St. Paul Place, Suite 1700 750 N. St. Paul Street Dallas, TX 75201 Tel.: 214-922-9806 Fax: 214-922-9815	Arkansas Kansas Louisiana New Mexico Oklahoma Texas
Consulate General 600 Renaissance Center, Suite 1100 Detroit, MI 48243-1798 Tel.: 313-567-2340 Fax: 313-567-2164	Indiana Kentucky Michigan Ohio
Consulate General 550 South Hope, 9th Floor Los Angeles, CA 90071-2627 Tel.: 213-346-2700 Fax: 213-346-2767	Arizona California Hawaii Nevada Utah
Consulate General Suite 900, 701 Fourth Avenue South Minneapolis, MN 55415-1899 Tel.: 612-332-7486 Fax: 612-332-4061	Colorado Iowa (except Quad Cities) Minnesota Montana Nebraska North Dakota South Dakota Wyoming
Consulate General 1251 Avenue of the Americas New York, NY 10020-1175 Tel.: 212-596-1600 Fax: 212-596-1793	Connecticut New Jersey New York (southern) Bermuda
Consulate General 412 Plaza 600, Sixth and Stewart Streets Seattle, WA 98101-1286 Tel.: 206-443-1777 Fax: 206-443-9662/9735	Alaska Idaho Oregon Washington

REPUBLIC OF CAPE VERDE

National Holiday: Independence Day, July 5

I. GENERAL INFORMATION

The Embassy and Consulate General have legalization functions. The requirements for the Embassy are given below.

II. REQUIREMENTS FOR LEGALIZATION

Prior Authentications Required
1. Notarization

Materials to be Submitted with Request
1. Original document to be legalized
2. Prepaid, self-addressed return envelope

Direct Registration of Notary Public: Not available

Direct Signing of Document Before Consular Official: The procedure of certifying the signature of a private person is available at the Embassy and General Consulate. An appointment is not necessary. The signer must present identification, i.e., a driver's license or passport.

Turn Around Time: If the document is personally delivered, it can be legalized immediately if the work load permits.

Fee: $9.00 per document or signature

Payment Method: Cash, money order, certified check, company check, personal check payable to the Embassy or Consulate General of Cape Verde

III. EMBASSY AND CONSULATE GENERAL

Address, Phone, Hours	*Jurisdiction*
Embassy of Cape Verde 3415 Massachusetts Avenue, NW Washington, DC 20036 Tel.: 202-965-6820 Fax: 202-965-1207 9:00 AM - 5:00 PM	Entire United States
Consulate General 535 Boylston Street, Second Floor Boston, MA 02116 Tel.: 617-353-0014 9:00 AM - 5:00 PM	Entire United States

CAYMAN ISLANDS

I. GENERAL INFORMATION

The Cayman Islands is a dependency of the United Kingdom, covered by the Hague Convention Abolishing the Requirement for Legalization for Foreign Public Documents.

A document should be sent to the appropriate authority in the state or territory in which the document is notarized in order to obtain the Apostille. For information on obtaining the Apostille for documents originating in the United States, see the procedures specified for each of the individual states under United States jurisdiction in Chapter 2. For the enumeration of Federal authorities competent to provide the Apostille, see Appendix D.

For the text of the Hague Convention, the Apostille, and a list of the parties to the Convention, see Appendix A.

For information on United Kingdom Consulates, see the United Kingdom.

REPUBLIC OF CHAD

National Holiday: Independence Day, August 11

I. GENERAL INFORMATION

Chad has an Embassy but no Consulates. Documents from anywhere in the United States may be submitted to the Embassy for legalization.

II. REQUIREMENTS FOR LEGALIZATION

Prior Authentications Required
1. Notarization
2. Authentication of Notary Signature (In most states this may be done directly by the State Secretary of State; if not, the County Clerk authenticates the signature.)
3. State Secretary of State Certification (In states where the Notary Signature may be authenticated directly by the State Secretary of State, steps 2 and 3 are combined.)
4. U.S. Secretary of State Certification

Materials to be Submitted with Request
1. Original document to be legalized
2. Photocopy of the document
3. Prepaid, self-addressed return certified or registered mail envelope

Direct Registration of Notary Public: Not available

Direct Signing of Document Before Consular Official: Not available

Appointment Required in order to bring document by hand

Fee: $40.00 per document or signature

Payment Method: Money order or check payable to the Embassy of Chad

III. EMBASSY

Embassy of Chad
2002 R Street, NW
Washington, DC 20009
Tel.: 202-462-4009
Fax: 202-265-1937
10:00 AM - 4:00 PM

Entire United States

CHANNEL ISLANDS
(BAILIWICK OF GUERNSEY AND JERSEY)

I. GENERAL INFORMATION

The Channel Islands are Crown Dependencies of the United Kingdom, covered by the Hague Convention Abolishing the Requirement for Legalization for Foreign Public Documents.

A document should be sent to the appropriate authority in the state or territory in which the document is notarized in order to obtain the Apostille. For information on obtaining the Apostille for documents originating in the United States, see the procedures specified for each of the individual states under United States jurisdiction in Chapter 2. For the enumeration of Federal authorities competent to provide the Apostille, see Appendix D.

For the text of the Hague Convention, the Apostille, and a list of the parties to the Convention, see Appendix A.

For information on United Kingdom Consulates, see the United Kingdom.

REPUBLIC OF CHILE

National Holidays: Independence Day, February 12; National Day, September 18

I. GENERAL INFORMATION

The Embassy and Consulates General have legalization functions. The specific requirements for legalization may vary from office to office. The information given below pertains to the Embassy and the Consulates General of Chicago, Houston, and New York.

II. REQUIREMENTS FOR LEGALIZATION

Prior Authentications Required

1. Notarization
2. Authentication of Notary Signature (In most states this may be done directly by the State Secretary of State; if not, the County Clerk authenticates the signature.)
3. State Secretary of State Certification (In states where the Notary Signature may be authenticated directly by the State Secretary of State, steps 2 and 3 are combined.)
4. U.S. Secretary of State Certification

Materials to be Submitted with Request

1. Original document to be legalized
2. Prepaid, self-addressed return envelope

Direct Registration of Notary Public: Not available

Direct Signing of Document Before Consular Official: Not available

Turn Around Time: If the document is personally delivered, there may be a delay of one day before legalization.

Fee: $12.00

Payment Method: Cash, money order, company check

III. EMBASSY AND CONSULATES GENERAL

Address, Phone, Hours	*Jurisdiction*
Embassy of Chile Consulate 1732 Massachusetts Avenue, NW Washington, DC 20036 Tel.: 202-785-1746 Fax: 202-887-5579 9:00 AM - 1:00 PM	Maryland North Carolina Virginia Washington, DC West Virginia
Consulate General 875 North Michigan Avenue, Ste.3352 Chicago, IL 60657 Tel.: 312-654-8780 Fax: 312-654-8948	Illinois Indiana Iowa Kansas Kentucky Michigan Minnesota Missouri Nebraska North Dakota Ohio South Dakota Wisconsin
Consulate General 1360 Post Oak Boulevard, Suite 2330 Houston, TX 77056 Tel.: 713-621-5853 Fax: 713-621-8672 9:00 AM - 5:00 PM	Arkansas Louisiana New Mexico Oklahoma Texas
Consulate General 1900 Avenue of Stars, Ste. 2450 Los Angeles, CA 90067 Tel.: 310-785-0113 Fax: 310-785-0132	Arizona California (southern) Colorado Hawaii Nevada (southern) Utah

Address, Phone, Hours	*Jurisdiction*
Consulate General 800 Brickell Avenue, Ste. 1230 Miami, FL 33131 Tel.: 305-379-8623 Fax: 305-379-6613 9:00 AM - 2:00 PM	Alabama Florida Georgia Mississippi South Carolina Tennessee
Consulate General 866 United Nations Plaza, Ste. 302 New York, NY 10017 Tel.: 212-355-0612 Fax: 212-888-5288 9:00 AM - 1:00 PM	Connecticut Maine Massachusetts New Hampshire New Jersey (north of Trenton) New York Rhode Island Vermont
Consulate General Public Ledger Building, Suite 1030 Chestnut and 6th Street Philadelphia, PA 19106 Tel.: 215-829-9520 Fax: 215-829-0594	Delaware New Jersey (south of Trenton) Pennsylvania
Consulate General 870 Market Street, Suite 1058 San Francisco, CA 94102 Tel.: 415-982-7662 Fax: 415-982-2384	Alaska California (northern) Idaho Montana Nevada (northern) Oregon Washington Wyoming
Consulate General Edificio American Airlines, Suite 800 1509 López Landron, Santurce San Juan, Puerto Rico 00911 Tel.: 787-725-6365 Fax: 787-721-5650 8:00 AM - 1:00 PM	Puerto Rico Caribbean possessions

Address, Phone, Hours	*Jurisdiction*
Consulate General 1732 Massachusetts Avenue, NW Washington, DC 20036 Tel.: 202-785-1746 Fax: 202-887-5579	Maryland North Carolina Virginia Washington, DC West Virginia

REPUBLIC OF CHINA (TAIWAN)

National Holiday: October 10

I. GENERAL INFORMATION

Thirteen Tapei Economic and Cultural Representative Offices (TECRO) located in the United States legalize documents originating in their respective jurisdictions. The requirements may vary from office to office. The information below covers the requirements for the Washington DC, Seattle, Houston, New York and Chicago offices.

II. REQUIREMENTS FOR LEGALIZATION

Prior Authentications Required
The Washington, DC office requires step 1 or step 3 for power of attorney or certificates of nationality (corporation).
The New York and Chicago offices require steps 1 and 2.

1. Notarization
2. Authentication of Notary Signature by the State Secretary of State
3. U.S. Secretary of State Certification

Materials to be Submitted with Request
1. Original document to be legalized
2. Photocopy of the document
3. Application form
4. Prepaid, self-addressed return envelope (must use stamps; meter tape not acceptable)

Direct Registration of Notary Public: Not available

Direct Signing of Document Before Consular Official: Not available

Turn Around Time: If the document is personally delivered, the Chicago office will legalize one document immediately; at the New York office there will be a delay of one to two hours; TECRO in Washington, DC will legalize the document in one day.

Fee: $14.00

Payment Method: Cash or check payable to TECRO

III. ADDITIONAL INFORMATION

To authenticate a letter or contract of employment through the Washington, DC office, the following information must be provided:

1. Employee's full name in both Chinese and English, age (minimum 20), sex, native place and address
2. Nature of work and amount of monthly pay
3. Duration of contract (minimum 12 months)
4. Employer's full name and address

To authenticate letters of invitation for business or training seminars, the following information must be provided in the letter:

1. The trainee's full name, age, sex and address
2. Name of the program, its duration, sponsorship, expenses and allowance provided to the trainee, if any

The New York office requires identity papers (e.g., valid passport, photo-bearing driver's license or a certified copy thereof) if the signatory is an ethnic non-Chinese and the document to be authenticated is an employment certificate, an invitation letter, or a power of attorney for a civil or criminal lawsuit.

IV. TAPEI ECONOMIC AND CULTURAL REPRESENTATION OFFICES

Address, Phone, Hours	*Jurisdiction*
TECRO Service Division 4201 Wisconsin Avenue, NW Washington, DC 20016 Tel.: 202-895-1800 Fax: 202-363-0899 9:00 AM - 5:00 PM Monday through Friday 9:00 AM - 12:00 PM Saturday	Delaware Maryland Virginia Washington, DC West Virginia

Address, Phone, Hours	*Jurisdiction*
TECRO 1349 West Peachtree Street Two Midtown Plaza, Suite 1290 Atlanta, GA 30309 Tel.: 404-872-0123	Alabama Georgia Kentucky North Carolina South Carolina Tennessee Canadian provinces of: New Brunswick Newfoundland Nova Scotia Prince Edward Island Quebec
TECRO 99 Summer Street, Suite 801 Boston, MA 02110 Tel.: 617-737-2050	Maine Massachusetts New Hampshire Rhode Island Vermont Canadian provinces of: Manitoba Northwest Territories Saskatchewan
TECRO Prudential Plaza, 57-58th Floor 180 N. Stetson Avenue Chicago, IL 60601 Tel.: 312-616-0100	Illinois Indiana Iowa Michigan Minnesota Ohio Wisconsin
TECRO Bank of Guam Building, Suite 505 111, Chalan Santo Papa Agana, Guam 96910 Tel.: 671-472-5865	Caroline Islands Guam Mariana Islands Marshall Islands

Address, Phone, Hours	*Jurisdiction*
TECRO 2746 Pali Highway Honolulu, HI 96817 Tel.: 808-595-6347	Hawaii American Samoa
TECRO 11 Greenway Plaza, Suite 2006 Houston, TX 77046 Tel.: 713-626-7445	Arkansas Louisiana Mississippi Oklahoma Texas
TECRO Penntower Office Center, Suite 1001 3100 Broadway Kansas City, MO 64111 Tel.: 816-531-1298	Colorado Kansas Missouri North Dakota South Dakota
TECRO 3731 Wilshire Boulevard, Suite 700 Los Angeles, CA 90010 Tel.: 213-389-1215	Arizona California (south) New Mexico
TECRO 2333 Ponce De Leon Boulevard, Suite 610 Coral Gables, FL 33134 Tel.: 305-443-8917	Florida Puerto Rico Bermuda Virgin Islands
TECRO 885 Second Avenue, 17th Floor New York, NY 10017 Tel.: 212-754-7100 Tel.: 212-486-0088	Connecticut New Jersey New York Pennsylvania
TECRO 555 Montgomery Street, Suite 501 San Francisco, CA 94111 Tel.: 415-362-7680	California (north) Nebraska Nevada Utah

Address, Phone, Hours	*Jurisdiction*
TECRO Westin Building, 24th Floor Sixth Avenue Seattle, WA 98121 Tel.: 206-441-4586	Alaska Idaho Montana Oregon Washington Wyoming

REPUBLIC OF COLOMBIA

National Holidays: Independence Day, July 20; Batalla de Boyaca, August 7

I. GENERAL INFORMATION

The Embassy and Consulates legalize documents originating in their jurisdictions. The specific requirements for legalization may vary from office to office.

The information below pertains to the New York and Washington DC Consulates.

II. REQUIREMENTS FOR LEGALIZATION

Prior Authentications Required
The Embassy requires steps 1 through 4 for international documents. For other documents from its local jurisdiction, steps 1 and 2 are required.

The New York Consulate requires steps 1 and 2. In order to legalize a Power of Attorney, the New York Consulate also requires the submission of a copy, not certified, of the company's certificate of incorporation. In addition, the New York Consulate requires that the signer's signature be legible and that the signer's title be given.

1. Notarization
2. Authentication of Notary Signature (In most states this may be done directly by the State Secretary of State; if not, the County Clerk authenticates the signature.)
3. State Secretary of State Certification (In states where the Notary Signature may be authenticated directly by the State Secretary of State, steps 2 and 3 are combined.)
4. U.S. Secretary of State Certification

Materials to be Submitted with Request
1. Original document to be legalized
2. Prepaid, self-addressed return envelope

Direct Registration of Notary Public: This procedure is available at the Washington, DC Consulate.

Direct Signing of Document Before Consular Official: The procedure of certifying the signature of a private person is available at the Washington, DC Consulate. An appointment must be made and the signer must have proper identification which includes a photograph. The Consulate indicated that this procedure should be available at all other offices as well.

Fees:
$ 21.00 for power of attorney, affidavit, assignment, certification, U.S. trademark, FBI report
$ 36.00 for bank statement or certification
$106.00 for certificate of existence of company
$ 56.00 for other certificates

Payment Method: Money order, certified check, company check

III. EMBASSY AND CONSULATES

Address, Phone, Hours	*Jurisdiction*
Embassy of Colombia 1825 Connecticut Avenue, NW Suite 218 Washington, DC 20009 Tel.: 202-332-7476 Fax: 202-332-7180	Delaware Maryland Virginia Washington, DC West Virginia Bermuda
Consulate 3379 Peachtree Road, Suite 220 Atlanta, GA 30326 Tel.: 404-237-1045 Fax: 404-237-7957	Kentucky Georgia North Carolina South Carolina Tennessee
Consulate 535 Boylston Street, 11th Floor Boston, MA 02116 Tel.: 617-536-6222 Fax: 617-536-9372	Connecticut Maine Massachusetts New Hampshire Vermont

Address, Phone, Hours	*Jurisdiction*
Consulate 500 N. Michigan Avenue, Suite 2040 Chicago, IL 60611-3703 Tel.: 312-923-1196 Fax: 312-923-1197	Illinois Indiana Iowa Kansas Minnesota Missouri Nebraska North Dakota Ohio South Dakota Wisconsin
Consulate 280 Aragon Avenue Coral Gables, FL 33134 Tel.: 305-448-5558 Fax: 305-441-9537	Florida Bahamas Cayman Islands
Consulate Edificacion Mercantil Pl. N. 818, Ave. Ponce de Leon Hato Rey, PR 00918 Tel.: 809-754-1675 Fax: 809-250-1130	La Espanola San Tomas Islas Virgenes Puerto Rico
Consulate 2990 Richmond Avenue, Suite 544 Houston, TX 77098 Tel.: 713-527-8919 Fax: 713-529-3395	Oklahoma Texas
Consulate 3580 Wilshire Boulevard, Ste. 1450 Los Angeles, CA 90010 Tel.: 213-382-1136/7 Fax: 213-383-2785	Arizona California (southern) New Mexico

Address, Phone, Hours	*Jurisdiction*
Consulate 1844 World Trade Center New Orleans, LA 70130 Tel.: 504-525-5580 Fax: 504-525-4903	Alabama Arkansas Louisiana Mississippi
Consulate 10 East 46th Street New York, NY 10017 Tel.: 212-949-9898-01 Fax: 212-972-1725	New Jersey New York Pennsylvania Rhode Island
Consulate 595 Market Street San Francisco, CA 94105 Tel.: 415-495-7195 Fax: 415-717-3731	Alaska California (northern) Colorado Hawaii Idaho Montana Nevada Oregon Utah Washington Wyoming

THE FEDERAL AND ISLAMIC REPUBLIC OF COMOROS

National Holiday: July 6

I. GENERAL INFORMATION

Communicate directly with the Embassy of Comoros for information on legalization procedures.

II. EMBASSY

Embassy of the Federal and Islamic Republic of Comoros
336 East 45th Street, Second Floor
New York, NY 10017
Tel.: 212-972-8010

DEMOCRATIC REPUBLIC OF CONGO
(formerly Zaire)

National Holidays: Colonial Day, December 10; January 4; June 30

I. GENERAL INFORMATION

The Democratic Republic of Congo has an Embassy in the United States but no Consulates. Documents from anywhere in the United States may be sent to the Embassy for legalization.

II. REQUIREMENTS FOR LEGALIZATION

Prior Authentications Required
1. Notarization
2. Authentication of Notary Signature (In most states this may be done directly by the State Secretary of State; if not, the County Clerk authenticates the signature.)
3. State Secretary of State Certification (In states where the Notary Signature may be authenticated directly by the State Secretary of State, steps 2 and 3 are combined.)
4. U.S. Secretary of State Certification

Materials to be Submitted with Request
1. Original document to be legalized
2. Photocopy of the document
3. Prepaid, self-addressed return envelope

Direct Registration of Notary Public: Not available

Direct Signing of Document Before Consular Official: Not available

Turn Around Time: If the document is personally delivered, it will be legalized immediately if the workload permits; otherwise there will be a delay of 48 hours before legalization.

Fee: $15.00 per document or signature

Payment Method: Money order, certified check, company check

III. EMBASSY

Address, Phone, Hours	*Jurisdiction*
Embassy of the Demoratic Republic of Congo 1800 New Hampshire Avenue, NW Washington, DC 20009 Tel.: 202-234-7690 Fax: 202-237-0748 10:00 AM - 3:00 PM	Entire United States

REPUBLIC OF CONGO BRAZZAVILLE

National Holiday: August 15

I. GENERAL INFORMATION

The Republic of Congo Brazzaville has an Embassy in the United States but no Consulates. Documents from anywhere in the United States may be sent to the Embassy for legalization.

II. REQUIREMENTS FOR LEGALIZATION

Prior Authentications Required

1. Notarization
2. Authentication of Notary Signature (In most states this may be done directly by the State Secretary of State; if not, the County Clerk authenticates the signature.)
3. State Secretary of State Certification (In states where the Notary Signature may be authenticated directly by the State Secretary of State, steps 2 and 3 are combined.)
4. U.S. Secretary of State Certification

Materials to be Submitted with Request

1. Original document to be legalized
2. Photocopy of the document
3. Prepaid, self-addressed return envelope

Direct Registration of Notary Public: Not available

Direct Signing of Document Before Consular Official: The procedure of certifying the signature of a private person is available at the Embassy. An appointment should be made and the signer must present identification such as a driver's license or passport.

Turn Around Time: If the document is personally delivered, it will be legalized the same day if the Consular official is in. If the document is mailed, it will take two days for legalization.

Fee: $150.00 per document or signature

Payment Method: Cash, money order, certified check, company check payable to the Embassy of the Republic of Congo Brazzaville

III. EMBASSY

Address, Phone, Hours	*Jurisdiction*
Embassy of the Republic of Congo Brazzaville 4891 Colorado Avenue, NW Washington, DC 20011 Tel.: 202-726-0825 Fax: 202-726-1860 9:00 AM - 5:00 PM	Entire United States

REPUBLIC OF COSTA RICA

National Holiday: Independence Day, September 15

I. GENERAL INFORMATION

The Embassy and Consulates General have legalization functions. The Embassy will legalize documents from anywhere in the United States; the Consulates General will legalize documents originating in their jurisdiction. The specific requirements for legalization may vary from office to office. Requirements of the Embassy and the New York Consulate General are given below.

II. REQUIREMENTS FOR LEGALIZATION

Prior Authentications Required
The Embassy requires steps 1 and 2 for Washington, DC and the surrounding area of Maryland and Virginia; it requires steps 1 through 4 for documents originating elsewhere in the United States.

1. Notarization
2. Authentication of Notary Signature (In most states this may be done directly by the State Secretary of State; if not, the County Clerk authenticates the signature.)
3. State Secretary of State Certification (In states where the Notary Signature may be authenticated directly by the State Secretary of State, steps 2 and 3 are combined.)
4. U.S. Secretary of State Certification

Materials to be Submitted with Request
1. Original document to be legalized
2. Prepaid, self-addressed return envelope

Direct Registration of Notary Public: Not available

Direct Signing of Document Before Consular Official: The procedure of certifying the signature of a private person is available at the New York Consulate. No appointment is necessary. The signer must have proper identification, such as a passport.

Turn Around Time: If the document is personally delivered, there may be a delay of three days before legalization at the Embassy, depending on the content of the document. The New York Consulate may be able to legalize the document immediately; no appointment is necessary.

Fee: $80.00 for regular authorization documents, such as powers of attorney and trademark registration
$40.00 for documents such as certificates of origin
$50.00 for Declarations

Payment Method: Cash, money order, certified check; company checks payable to the Embassy or Consulate General of Costa Rico

III. EMBASSY AND CONSULATES GENERAL

Address, Phone, Hours	*Jurisdiction*
Embassy of Costa Rica Consular Office 2112 S Street, NW Washington, DC 20008 Tel.: 202-328-6628 Fax: 202-797-3916 10:00 AM - 1:00 PM	Entire United States Local: Maryland Virginia Washington, DC
Consulate General 7033 Luella Anne Drive, NE Albuquerque, NM 87109 Tel.: 505-822-1420	New Mexico
Consulate General 8 South Michigan Avenue, Suite 510 Chicago, IL 60603 Tel.: 312-263-2772 10:00 AM - 2:00 PM	Illinois Indiana Iowa Michigan Minnesota Missouri Nebraska North Dakota Ohio South Dakota Wisconsin

Address, Phone, Hours	*Jurisdiction*
Consulate General 11570 Chesswood Houston, TX 77072 Tel.: 713-530-3856	Kansas New Mexico Oklahoma
Consulate General 548 South Spring Street, Suite 101 Los Angeles, CA Tel.: 213-622-6314	California (southern) Nevada Utah
Consulate General 200 SE First Street, Suite 400 Miami, FL 33131 Tel.: 305-377-4242	Florida Georgia North Carolina South Carolina
Consulate General 1901 Paydras Street New Orleans, LA 70112 Tel.: 504-525-6887	Alabama Arkansas Kentucky Louisiana Mississippi Tennessee
Consulate General 80 Wall Street, Suite 1117 New York, NY 10005 Tel.: 212-425-2620 Fax: 212-785-6818 10:00 AM - 3:00 PM	Connecticut Delaware Maine Maryland Massachusetts New Hampshire New Jersey New York Pennsylvania Rhode Island Vermont Virginia West Virginia

Address, Phone, Hours	*Jurisdiction*
Consulate General Avenue Ponce de Leon 431 Hato Rey San Juan Puerto Rico 00917 Tel.: 809-754-0190	Puerto Rico
Consulate General 209 Post Street, Suite 923 San Francisco, CA 94108 Tel.: 415-392-8488	California (northern) Hawaii Idaho Montana Oregon Washington Wyoming

REPUBLIC OF CROATIA

I. GENERAL INFORMATION

Croatia is a party to the Hague Convention Abolishing the Requirement for Legalization for Foreign Public Documents.

A document should be sent to the appropriate authority in the state or territory in which the document is notarized in order to obtain the Apostille. For information on obtaining the Apostille for documents originating in the United States, see the procedures specified for each of the individual states under United States jurisdiction in Chapter 2. For the enumeration of Federal authorities competent to provide the Apostille, see Appendix D.

For the text of the Hague Convention, the Apostille, and a list of the parties to the Convention, see Appendix A.

For information purposes, the Embassy and Consulates General are listed below.

II. EMBASSY AND CONSULATES GENERAL

Address, Phone, Hours	*Jurisdiction*
Embassy of Croatia 2343 Massachusetts Avenue, NW Washington, DC 20008 Tel.: 202-588-5906 Fax: 202-588-8936 10:00 AM - 12:00 PM 2:00 PM - 4:00 PM	Alabama Arkansas Illinois Indiana Iowa Kentucky Louisiana Maryland Michigan Minnesota Mississippi Missouri Pennsylvania Tennessee Virginia West Virginia Wisconsin

Address, Phone, Hours	*Jurisdiction*
Consulate General 34900 Lake Shore Boulevard Eastlake, OH 44095 Tel.: 216-951-4246 Fax: 216-951-4268	Ohio
Consulate General 11766 Wilshire Boulevard, Suite 710 Los Angeles, CA 90025 Tel.: 310-477-1009 Fax: 310-477-1866	Alaska Arizona California Colorado Hawaii Idaho Kansas Montana Nebraska Nevada New Mexico North Dakota Oklahoma Oregon South Dakota Texas Utah Washington Wyoming

Address, Phone, Hours	*Jurisdiction*
Consulate General 369 Lexington Avenue, 11th Floor New York, NY 10017 Tel.: 212-599-3066 Fax: 212-599-3106	Connecticut Delaware Florida Georgia Maine Massachusetts New Hampshire New Jersey New York North Carolina Rhode Island South Carolina Vermont Puerto Rico Virgin Islands

CUBA

I. GENERAL INFORMATION

Cuban diplomatic representation in the United States is maintained through the Cuban Interest Section of the Swiss Embassy. For details about the Cuban Interest Section, please refer to the entry in this chapter for Switzerland.

Cuban consular legalization functions in the United States, however, are provided by Mr. Armando Amieva at the Cuban Interest Section.

II. CUBAN INTEREST SECTION

Cuban Interest Section
2630/2639 16th Street, NW
Washington, DC 20009
Tel.: 202-797-8518/19/20
Fax: 202-797-8521

REPUBLIC OF CYPRUS

National Holiday: Independence Day, October 1

I. GENERAL INFORMATION

Cyprus is a party to the Hague Convention Abolishing the Requirement for Legalization for Foreign Public Documents.

A document should be sent to the appropriate authority in the state or territory in which the document is notarized in order to obtain the Apostille. For information on obtaining the Apostille for documents originating in the United States, see the procedures specified for each of the individual states under United States jurisdiction in Chapter 2. For the enumeration of Federal authorities competent to provide the Apostille, see Appendix D.

For the text of the Hague Convention, the Apostille, and a list of the parties to the Convention, see Appendix A.

For information purposes, the Embassy, Consulate General and major Honorary Consulates of Cyprus are listed below. It should be noted that Honorary Consulates exercise legalization functions.

II. REQUIREMENTS FOR LEGALIZATION

Prior Authentications Required for Submission in Non-Hague Convention Country Circumstances

1. Notarization
2. Authentication of Notary Signature by County Clerk

Fee: $9.90 per document as of May 1997; fee varies according to exchange rate

Payment Method: Money order payable to the Accountant-General of Cyprus

III. EMBASSY, CONSULATE GENERAL, AND HONORARY CONSULATES

Address, Phone, Hours	*Jurisdiction*
Embassy of Cyprus Consul 2211 R Street, NW Washington, DC 20008-4082 Tel.: 202-462-5772 Fax: 202-483-6710	Maryland Virginia Washington, DC
Honorary Consul: Dr. Kyriakos Michaelides 895 Somerset Drive Atlanta, GA 30327 Tel.: 404-941-3764 Fax: 404-941-2109	Georgia
Honorary Consul: Dr. Symeon Symeonides 410 LSU Law Center Baton Rouge, LA 70803-1000 Tel.: 504-388-5088 Fax: 504-388-5935	Louisiana
Honorary Consul: Mr. John Papajohn 70-7 Kirkland Street Cambridge, MA 02138 Tel.: 617-876-0982 Fax: 617-497-0219	Massachusetts
Honorary Consul: Mr. Steve G. Stylianou 15706 Michigan Avenue Dearborn, MI 48126 Tel.: 313-582-1411 Fax: 313-582-6791	Michigan
Honorary Consul: Dr. Charles Kanakis, Jr. Consultants in Cardiology, Ltd. 9301 Golf Road, Suite 303 Des Plaines, IL 60016 Tel.: 708-296-0064 Fax: 708-296-4857	Illinois

Address, Phone, Hours	*Jurisdiction*
Honorary Consul Professor Van Coufoudakis 2402 Oakridge Road Fort Wayne, IN 46805 Tel.: 219-481-6897 Fax: 219-481-6985	Indiana
Honorary Consul: Mr. William Crassas 320 South 66th Street PO Box 9049 Houston, TX 77011 Tel.: 713-928-2264 Fax: 713-928-2093	Texas
Honorary Consul: Mr. Vassos Demetriou 205 Lake Street South, Suite 100 Kirkland, WA 98033 Tel.: 206-827-1700 Fax: 206-889-0308	Washington
Honorary Consul-General Mr. Andreas Kyprianides 4219 Coolidge Avenue Los Angeles, CA 90066 Tel.: 310-397-0771 Fax: 310-398-6775	California (southern)
Consulate General 13 East 40th Street New York, NY 10016 Tel.: 212-686-6016 Fax: 212-685-7316	Entire United States
Honorary Consul-General Dr. Anastassios K Simonides 205 Crocker Avenue Piedmont, CA 94610-1214 Tel.: 510-547-5689 Fax: 510-547-4177	California (northern)

Address, Phone, Hours	*Jurisdiction*
Honorary Consul: Mr. James Oratis 7714 Langdon Street Philadelphia, PA 19111 Tel.: 215-728-6980	Pennsylvania
Honorary Consul: Mr. Stanley J. Dru 1277 East Missouri No. 214 Phoenix, AZ 85014 Tel.: 602-264-9701 Fax: 602-274-8373	Arizona
Honorary Consul: Mr. Alexander Christy Mayer Building, Suite 510 1130 Morrison Street, S.W. Portland, OR 97205 Tel.: 503-248-0500 Tel: 503-227-1411 Fax: 503-227-2086	Oregon
Honorary Consul: Mr. Thomas Kyrus 2973 Shore Drive, Suite 102 Virginia Beach, VA 23451-1248 Tel.: 757-464-5600	Virginia

THE CZECH REPUBLIC

National Holiday: May 8

I. GENERAL INFORMATION

The Embassy, Consulates General, and Honorary Consulates have legalization functions. Requirements for legalization may vary, depending on the document involved.

II. REQUIREMENTS FOR LEGALIZATION

Prior Authentications Required

1. Notarization
2. Authentication of Notary Signature (In most states this may be done directly by the State Secretary of State; if not, the County Clerk authenticates the signature.)
3. State Secretary of State Certification (In states where the Notary Signature may be authenticated directly by the State Secretary of State, steps 2 and 3 are combined.)
4. U.S. Secretary of State Certification

Materials to be Submitted with Request

1. Original document to be legalized
2. Prepaid, self-addressed return envelope for certified mail

Direct Registration of Notary Public: Not available

Direct Signing of Document Before Consular Official: The procedure of certifying the signature of a private person is available at the Embassy, Consulates General, and Honorary Consulates. An appointment should be made and the signer must present identification such as an identification card, passport or driver's license.

Turn Around Time: If the document is personally delivered, there may be a delay of from four to five days before legalization.

Fee: $20.00 per document or signature; legalization fee changes according to the exchange rate; advisable to call in advance to check on current fee

Payment Method: Cash, money order, certified check payable to the Czech Embassy

III. EMBASSY, CONSULATES GENERAL AND HONORARY CONSULATES

Address, Phone, Hours	*Jurisdiction*
Embassy of the Czech Republic 3900 Spring of Freedom Street, NW Washington, DC 20008 Tel.: 202-274-9100 Fax: 202-363-6308 8:30 AM - 11:30 AM	All states except Alaska, Arizona, California, Colorado, Hawaii, Idaho, Montana, New Mexico, Nevada, Oregon, Utah, Washington, Wyoming

Honorary Consul Mr. George A. Novak
2110 Powers Ferry Road, Suite 220
Atlanta, GA 30339
Tel.: 770-859-9402
Fax: 770-951-0751

Honorary Consul Mr. John B. Zavrel
10545 Main Street
Clarence, NY 14031
Tel.: 716-759-6078
Fax: 716-759-7925

Honorary Consul Mr. Jerry G. Bartos
3239 Oradell Lane
Dallas, TX 75220
Tel.: 214-350-6871
Fax: 214-350-9611

Honorary Consul Mr. Alan Becker
c/o Becker & Poliakoff
3111 Sterling Road
Fort Lauderdale, FL 33312
Tel.: 305-985-4127, 954-985-4178
Fax: 305-985-4176

Address, Phone, Hours	*Jurisdiction*
Honorary Consul Mr. Raymond J. Snokhous Stephenson and Snokhous 4544 Post Oak Place Drive, Suite 378 Houston, TX 77027 Tel.: 713-629-6963 Fax: 713-629-9606	
Consulate General 10990 Wilshire Boulevard, Suite 1100 Los Angeles, CA 90024 Tel.: 310-473-0889 Fax: 310-473-9813	Alaska Arizona California Colorado Hawaii Idaho Montana New Mexico Nevada Oregon Utah Washington Wyoming
Consulate General 1109-1111 Madison Avenue New York, NY 100028 Tel.: 212-717-5643 Fax: 212-717-5064	
Honorary Consul Mrs. Marie R. Amicci Lincoln Center Five 10200 SW Greenburg Road, Suite 350 Portland, OR 97223 Tel.: 503-293-9545 Fax: 503-293-9546	
Honorary Consul Mr. Richard Pivnicka 201 Filbert Street, Suite 700 San Francisco, CA 94133-1313 Tel.: 415-391-1313 Fax: 415-391-1895	

Address, Phone, Hours	*Jurisdiction*
Honorary Consul Peter A. Rafaeli 921 Bethlehem Pike, Suite 102 P.O. Box 777 Spring House, PA 19477 Tel.: 215-646-7777 Fax: 215-646-7770	

KINGDOM OF DENMARK

National Holiday: Constitution Day, June 5

I. GENERAL INFORMATION

The Embassy, Consulates General and Consulate have legalization functions. Each will legalize documents originating in its jurisdiction. The specific requirements for the Embassy and the New York Consulate General are given below.

II. REQUIREMENTS FOR LEGALIZATION

Prior Authentications Required
The Embassy requires steps 1 through 4; the New York Consulate requires steps 1, 2 and 3.

1. Notarization
2. Authentication of Notary Signature (In most states this may be done directly by the State Secretary of State; if not, the County Clerk authenticates the signature.)
3. State Secretary of State Certification (In states where the Notary Signature may be authenticated directly by the State Secretary of State, steps 2 and 3 are combined.)
4. U.S. Secretary of State Certification

Materials to be Submitted with Request
1. Original document to be legalized
2. Prepaid, self-addressed return envelope

Direct Registration of Notary Public: Not available

Direct Signing of Document Before Consular Official: The procedure of certifying the signature of a private person is available. An appointment must be made and the signer must present identification issued by a competent authority carrying a photograph, preferably a passport.

Turn Around Time: If the document is personally delivered, it will be legalized immediately if an official is available; it is suggested that one call in advance.

Fee: $19.00, payable in US dollars at the current rate of exchange

III. EMBASSY, CONSULATES GENERAL AND CONSULATE

Address, Phone, Hours	*Jurisdiction*
Royal Danish Embassy 3200 Whitehaven Street, NW Washington, DC 20008-3683 Tel.: 202-234-4300 Fax: 202-328-1470 9:30 AM - 5:00 PM, M - Th 9:30 AM - 4.30 PM, Friday	Entire United States
Consulate General John Hancock Center 875 North Michigan Avenue Chicago, IL 60611-1901 Tel.: 312-787-8780 Fax: 312-787-8744 9:00 AM - 4:00 PM	Arkansas Illinois Indiana Iowa Kansas Kentucky Michigan Minnesota Missouri Nebraska North Dakota Ohio Oklahoma South Dakota Texas Wisconsin

Address, Phone, Hours	*Jurisdiction*
Consulate General 10877 Wilshire Boulevard, Suite 1105 Los Angeles, CA 90024 Tel.: 310-443-2090 Fax: 310-443-2099 8:30 AM - 4:30 PM	Alaska Arizona California (southern) Colorado Hawaii Idaho Montana Nevada New Mexico Oregon Utah Washington Wyoming
Consulate General 1 Dag Hammarskjold Plaza 885 Second Avenue, 18th Floor New York, NY 10017 Tel.: 212-223-4545 Fax: 212-754-1904 10:00 AM - 1:00 PM	Alabama Connecticut Delaware Florida Georgia Louisiana Maine Maryland Massachusetts Mississippi New Hampshire New Jersey New York North Carolina Pennsylvania Puerto Rico Rhode Island South Carolina Tennessee Vermont Virginia West Virginia Virgin Islands

Address, Phone, Hours	*Jurisdiction*
Consulate 601 Montgomery Street, Suite 440 San Francisco, CA 94111 Tel.: 415-391-0100 Fax: 415-391-0181 9:00 AM - 5:00 PM	California (northern)

DOMINICAN REPUBLIC

National Holiday: Independence Day, February 27

I. REQUIREMENTS FOR LEGALIZATION

Prior Authentications Required
1. Notarization
2. Authentication of Notary Signature (In most states this may be done directly by the State Secretary of State; if not, the County Clerk authenticates the signature.)
3. State Secretary of State Certification (In states where the Notary Signature may be authenticated directly by the State Secretary of State, steps 2 and 3 are combined.)
4. U.S. Secretary of State Certification

Materials to be Submitted with Request
1. Original document to be legalized
2. Prepaid, self-addressed return envelope

Direct Registration of Notary Public: Not available

Direct Signing of Document Before Consular Official: Not available

Turn Around Time: If the document is personally delivered, there will be a delay of one day for legalization.

Fee: $25.00 per document or signature

Payment Method: Cash, money order, certified check, company check

II. EMBASSY AND CONSULATES

Embassy of the Dominican Republic
Consular Section
1715 22nd Street, NW 20008
Washington, DC 20009
Tel.: 202-332-6280/2/331-1786
Fax: 202-265-8057
9:00 AM - 4:00 PM

Consulate
3228 W. North Avenue
Chicago, IL 60647
Tel.: 312-772-6363
Fax: 312-772-7626

Consulate
1038 Brickell Avenue
Miami, FL 33131
Tel.: 305-373-4862
Fax: 305-358-2318

Consulate
International Trade Mart Building
World Trade Center, Suite 1647
2 Canal Street 2
New Orleans, LA 70130
Tel.: 504-522-1843
Fax: 504-522-1007

Consulate
One Times Square, 11th Floor
New York, NY 10036
Tel.: 212-768-2480/3
Fax: 212-768-6924

Consulate
870 Marker Street, Suite 915
San Francisco, CA 94102
Tel.: 415-982-5144
Fax: 415-391-6924, 510-887-0615

Consulate
Avianca Building, 7th Floor
Parada 23
Ponce de Leon Avenue 1612
Santurce, Puerto Rico 00903
Tel.: 809-725-9550/4
Fax: 809-721-7820

REPUBLIC OF ECUADOR

National Holiday: Independence Day, August 10

I. GENERAL INFORMATION

The Embassy, Consulates General, and Honorary Consulates have legalization functions. Each will legalize only documents originating in its jurisdiction. Only the Embassy can legalize documents certified by the U.S. Secretary of State. The specific requirements for the Embassy and the New York Consulate General are given below.

II. REQUIREMENTS FOR LEGALIZATION

Prior Authentications Required
1. Notarization
2. Authentication of Notary Signature (In most states this may be done directly by the State Secretary of State; if not, the County Clerk authenticates the signature.)
3. State Secretary of State Certification (In states where the Notary Signature may be authenticated directly by the State Secretary of State, steps 2 and 3 are combined.)
4. U.S. Secretary of State Certification for documents that are to be submitted to the Embassy.

Materials to be Submitted with Request
1. Original document to be legalized
2. Prepaid, self-addressed return envelope

Direct Registration of Notary Public: The procedure of registering a Notary Public's signature with the Embassy's Consulate is available, permitting the legalization of the document(s) bearing that Notary's signature and seal without certification by the County Clerk or the Secretary of State.

Direct Signing of Document Before Consular Official: Not available

Fee: $30.00 per document or signature

Payment Method: Money order, certified check, company check, personal check payable to the Consulate of Ecuador

III. EMBASSY, CONSULATES GENERAL, AND HONORARY CONSULATES

Address, Phone, Hours	*Jurisdiction*
Embassy of the Republic of Ecuador Consulate 2535 15th Street, NW Washington, DC 20009 Tel.: 202-234-7166 Fax: 202-265-9325 9:30 AM - 1:00 PM	Maryland (except Baltimore) Washington DC Virginia West Virginia
Honorary Consulate 2925 North Charles Street Baltimore, MD 21218 Tel.: 301-889-4422/35	Baltimore Delaware
Honorary Consulate 60 State Street, Floor 20 Boston, MA 02109 Tel.: 617-227-7200	Maine Massachusetts
Consulate General 612 North Michigan Avenue, Room 618 Chicago, IL 60611 Tel.: 312-642-8579 10:00 AM - 4:00 PM	Illinois Indiana Iowa Minnesota Missouri Nebraska North Dakota Ohio South Dakota Wisconsin
Honorary Consulate 3500 Paradise Road Las Vegas, NV 89109 Tel.: 702-735-8193	Colorado Nevada

Address, Phone, Hours	*Jurisdiction*
Consulate General 548 South Spring Street Los Angeles, CA 90013 Tel.: 213-628-3014/6	Arizona California (southern) Hawaii Samoa Guam Marshall Islands Caroline Yap Palau Mariana Islands
Consulate General Ingraham Building, Suite 1130 25 SE Second Avenue Miami, FL 33131 Tel.: 305-371-8366	Florida (except for counties of Coral Gables, Dale, and Palm Beach)
Consulate General 1312 World Trade Center 2 Canal Street New Orleans, LA 70130 Tel.: 504-523-3229	Arkansas Alabama Louisiana Mississippi
Consulate General 800 Second Avenue, Suite 501 New York, NY 10017 Tel.: 212-808-0170/1 Fax: 212-808-0188	Connecticut New Hampshire New York Rhode Island Vermont Bermuda
Consulate General 1180 Raymond Boulevard Newark, NJ 07102 Tel.: 201-642-0208 Fax: 201-642-0149 9:00 AM - 2:00 PM	New Jersey Pennsylvania

Address, Phone, Hours	*Jurisdiction*
Honorary Consulate PO Box 430-786 Pontiac, MI 48343 Tel.: 810-332-7356 Fax: 810-332-7881	Michigan
Honorary Consulate Calle Roosevelt 615, Apt. 3A San Juan Puerto Rico 00907 Tel.: 809-781-4408 Fax: 809-723-6572	Puerto Rico
Consulate General The Flood Building, Suite 862 870 Market Street San Francisco, CA 94102 Tel.: 415-391-1148/89 10:00 AM - 2:00 PM	California (northern) Utah
Honorary Consulate 322 Boylston Avenue East Seattle, WA 98102 Tel.: 206-324-4151	Alaska Idaho Montana Oregon Washington Wyoming
Honorary Consulate 2058 Walton Woods Circle Tucker, GA 30084 Tel.: 404-491-6026	Georgia Kentucky North Carolina South Carolina Tennessee

THE REPUBLIC OF EGYPT

National Holiday: Anniversary of the Revolution, July 23

I. GENERAL INFORMATION

The Embassy and Consulates General have legalization functions. Each will legalize documents originating in its jurisdiction.

The specific requirements for legalization vary from office to office. The information in Sections II and III below covers the Embassy and the four Consulates General.

II. REQUIREMENTS FOR LEGALIZATION

The Chicago Consulate requires that all Agency Agreements state the commission in the currency to be given and undertake to inform the Consulate of any future changes.

The New York Consulate requires that alimentary articles being imported into Egypt must be covered by all the necessary certifications, i.e., health certificate, HALAL if applicable, certificate of radiation (certifying that goods are free from radiation), etc. There is a $20.00 fee for certificates of radiation. In the case of imports of tallow, a certificate stating that the tallow is to be used for soap and other detergents and is free from D.D.B. and/or L.A.B.

Prior Authentications Required

1. Notarization
2. Authentication of Notary Signature (In most states this may be done directly by the State Secretary of State; if not, the County Clerk authenticates the signature.)
3. State Secretary of State Certification (In states where the Notary Signature may be authenticated directly by the State Secretary of State, steps 2 and 3 are combined.)
4. U.S. Secretary of State Certification
5. Certification by an American Egyptian Cooperation Foundation branch

The Embassy requires steps 1 through 4 for the legalization of commercial documents such as powers of attorney and steps 1 and 5 for the legalization of documents such as certificates of origin and other shipping documents.

The Chicago Consulate requires steps 1 and 2 plus American Egyptian Cooperation Foundation (AECF) certification from the Chicago branch for the legalization of documents such as powers of attorney and steps 1, 2 and 5 for legalization of shipping documents.

The Houston Consulate requires steps 1 through 3 for the legalization of documents such as powers of attorney and steps 1 and 5 for the legalization of shipping documents.

The New York Consulate requires steps 1 through 2 plus certification from the AECF for the legalization of documents such as powers of attorney and steps 1 and 5 for the legalization of shipping documents.

The San Francisco Consulate requires step 1 for the legalization of shipping documents.

Materials to be Submitted with Request
1. Original document to be legalized
2. Two photocopies of the document: one for the Consulate and one for the AECF
3. Prepaid, self-addressed return envelope

Direct Registration of Notary Public: Not available

Direct Signing of Document Before Consular Official: Not available

Time Delay: If the document is presented by hand for legalization, there will be a delay of two days for legalization. If the document is sent by mail, allow five working days excluding mailing time.

Fees
Embassy: $50.00 per document or signature
Chicago and San Francisco Consulates: $38.00 per document or signature
New York Consulate: $50.00 per document or signature

Payment Method: Cash or money order only for the Embassy; cash, money order, or certified check, payable to Consulate, for Consulates

III. EMBASSY AND CONSULATES

Address, Phone, Hours	*Jurisdiction*
Embassy of the Republic of Egypt 3521 International Court, NW Washington, DC 20008 Tel.: 202-895-5415 Fax: 202-244-4319 9:40 AM - 1:00 PM	Florida Maryland South Carolina Washington, DC
Consulate 500 North Michigan Avenue 19th Floor, Suite 1900 Chicago, IL 60611 Tel.: 312-828-9162	Iowa Kentucky Michigan Minnesota Nebraska North Dakota South Dakota Wisconsin
Consulate 1990 Post Oak Boulevard, Suite 2180 Houston, TX 77056 Tel.: 713-961-4915	Alabama Alaska Colorado Kansas Louisiana Mississippi Missouri New Mexico Oklahoma Tennessee Texas
Consulate 1110 Second Avenue New York, NY 10022 Tel.: 212-759-7120 Fax: 212-697-0465 9:00 AM - 2:00 PM	Connecticut Maine Massachusetts New Hampshire New Jersey New York Ohio

Address, Phone, Hours	*Jurisdiction*
	Pennsylvania Puerto Rico Rhode Island Vermont
Consulate 3001 Pacific Avenue San Francisco, CA 94115 Tel.: 415-346-9700	Arkansas Arizona California Idaho Hawaii Montana Nevada Oregon Washington Wyoming

IV. AMERICAN EGYPTIAN COOPERATION FOUNDATION

The AECF and its branches charge $25.00 to certify each document. This charge is payable by money order or certified check payable to the American Egyptian Cooperation Foundation. The AECF requires the original and two copies of the document submitted for certification.

AECF
625 North Michigan Avenue, Suite 500
Chicago, IL 60611
Tel.: 312-751-5426

AECF
1535 West Loop South, Suite 219A
Houston, TX 77027
Tel.: 713-993-9650

AECF
330 East 39th Street, Suite 32L
New York, NY 10016
Tel.: 212-867-2323
Fax: 212-697-0465
9:00 AM - 5:00 PM

Address, Phone, Hours	*Jurisdiction*
AECF 2277 Van Ness Avenue, Suite 203 San Francisco, CA 94109 Tel.: 415-474-0713	
AECF 733 15th Street, NW, Suite 700 Washington, DC 20005 Tel.: 202-393-3369	

REPUBLIC OF EL SALVADOR

National Holiday: Independence Day, September 15

I. GENERAL INFORMATION

El Salvador is a party to the Hague Convention Abolishing the Requirement for Legalization for Foreign Public Documents.

A document should be sent to the appropriate authority in the state or territory in which the document is notarized in order to obtain the Apostille. For information on obtaining the Apostille for documents originating in the United States, see the procedures specified for each of the individual states under United States jurisdiction in Chapter 2. For the enumeration of Federal authorities competent to provide the Apostille, see Appendix D.

For the text of the Hague Convention, the Apostille, and a list of the parties to the Convention, see Appendix A.

For instances in which legalization by a consular official of El Salvador is still necessary, the requirements for legalization are given below. The Embassy and Consulates General have legalization functions. Documents from anywhere in the United States may be sent to the Embassy for legalization. Each Consulate General will legalize documents originating in its jurisdiction. Requirements for legalization vary.

II. REQUIREMENTS FOR LEGALIZATION

Prior Authentications Required
The Embassy requires steps 1 through 4. All Consulates General require steps 1 and 2. The Consulates General of Dallas, Houston, and San Francisco require step 3 in addition to steps 1 and 2 if there is no Apostille.

1. Notarization
2. Authentication of Notary Signature (In most states this may be done directly by the State Secretary of State; if not, the County Clerk authenticates the signature.)

3. State Secretary of State Certification (In states where the Notary Signature may be authenticated directly by the State Secretary of State, steps 2 and 3 are combined.)
4. U.S. Secretary of State Certification

Materials to be Submitted with Request
1. Original document to be legalized
2. Photocopy of the document (not required at Dallas and Houston Cnsulates General)
3. Prepaid, self-addressed return envelope

Direct Registration of Notary Public: The procedure of registering a Notary Public's signature is available at the Embassy. The Secretary of State should send a letter to the Embassy certifying the signature of the Notary Public. Thereafter, documents notarized by the registered Notary Public can be legalized by the Embassy without intervening authentications.

Direct Signing of Document Before Consular Official: The procedure of certifying the signature of a private person is available at the Embassy and the Consulates General of Dallas, Houston, Miami and New Orleans. The signer must present identification such as a passport or the Cedula de Identidad Personal (identification issued by the government of El Salvador).

Turn Around Time: If the document is personally delivered, the Embassy and a number of the Consulates General will legalize the document immediately or with a brief delay. The Boston Consulate General requires that documents be personally delivered and will legalize them immediately if an appointment has been made. The Chicago Consulate requires an appointment if a document is to be personally delivered.

Fee: $20.00 per document; $30.00 in exact amount, cash only, at Boston Consulate

Payment Method: Cash, money order, and in Dallas, New Orleans and San Francisco, cashier's check payable to the Embassy or Consulate General of El Salvador

III. EMBASSY AND CONSULATES GENERAL

Address, Phone, Hours	*Jurisdiction*
Embassy of the Republic of El Salvador Consulate 1010 16th Street, NW Washington, DC 20036 Tel.: 202-331-4032 Fax: 202-331-4036 9:30 AM - 2:00 PM	Entire United States
Consulate General 222 Third Street, Ste. 1221 Cambridge, MA 02142 Tel.: 617-577-9111 Fax: 617-577-9876 9:30 AM - 3:30 PM	Connecticut (eastern) Maine Massachusetts New Hampshire Rhode Island Vermont
Consulate General 104 South Michigan Avenue, Ste. 423 Chicago, IL 60603 Tel.: 312-332-1393/4 Fax: 312-332-4446 9:00 AM - 3:00 PM	Illinois Indiana Iowa Kentucky Michigan Minnesota Missouri Nebraska North Dakota Ohio South Dakota Wisconsin
Consulate General 1555 W. Mockingbird Lane, Ste. 216 Dallas, TX 75235 Tel.: 214-613-1018/0732 Fax: 214-627-1106 8:00 AM - 2:00 PM	Arkansas Kansas Oklahoma Texas (surrounding areas)

Address, Phone, Hours	*Jurisdiction*
Consulate General 6420 Hillcroft Street, Suite 100 Houston, TX 77081 Tel.: 713-270-6239 Fax: 713-270-9683 8:30 AM - 1:30 PM	Colorado New Mexico Texas (surrounding areas)
Consulate General Central Plaza Building 3450 Wilshire Boulevard, Suite 250 Los Angeles, CA 90010 Tel.: 213-383-8364/5776/6134 Fax: 213-383-8599 8:00 AM - 4:00 PM	California (southern) Hawaii Nevada (some counties)
Consulate General 300 Biscayne Boulevard, Suite 1020 Miami, FL 33131 Tel.: 305-371-8850 Fax: 305-371-7820 9:30 AM - 1:30 PM	Florida Georgia North Carolina South Carolina Virginia West Virginia
Consulate General 2 Canal Street, Suite 1136 New Orleans, LA 70130 Tel.: 504-522-4266/7 Fax: 504-523-5237	Alabama Louisiana Mississippi Missouri
Consulate General 46 Park Avenue New York, NY 10016 Tel.: 212-889-3608 Fax: 212-679-2835	Connecticut (western) Delaware Maryland New Jersey New York Pennsylvania

Address, Phone, Hours	*Jurisdiction*
Consulate General 870 Market Street, Suite 508 San Francisco, CA 94102 Tel.: 415-781-7924 8:00 AM - 4:00 PM	Alaska California (northern) Idaho Minnesota Nevada (some counties) Utah Washington Wyoming
Consulate General 1212 North Broadway, Suite 100 Santa Ana, CA 92701 Tel.: 714-542-3250 Fax: 714-542-3407	Arizona California counties: Orange, Riverside west to border of Utah

ERITREA

National Holiday: May 24

I. REQUIREMENTS FOR LEGALIZATION

Prior Authentications Required
1. Notarization
2. Authentication of Notary Signature (In most states this may be done directly by the State Secretary of State; if not, the County Clerk authenticates the signature.)
3. State Secretary of State Certification (In states where the Notary Signature may be authenticated directly by the State Secretary of State, steps 2 and 3 are combined.)
4. U.S. Secretary of State Certification

Materials to be Submitted with Request
1. Original document to be legalized
2. Prepaid, self-addressed return envelope for specialized mail service

Direct Registration of Notary Public: Not available

Direct Signing of Document Before Consular Official: Not available

Turn Around Time: If the document is personally delivered, there may be a delay of three working days before legalization.

Fee: $50.00 per document or signature

Payment Method: Money order, certified check, company check payable to the Embassy of Eritrea

II. EMBASSY

Address, Phone, Hours	*Jurisdiction*
Embassy of Eritrea 1708 New Hampshire Avenue, NW Washington, DC 20009 Tel.: 202-319-1991 Fax: 202-319-1304 9:00 AM - 1:00 PM	Entire United States South America

REPUBLIC OF ESTONIA

National Holidays: New Year's Day, January 1; Independence Day, February 24; Good Friday; Easter; Spring Holiday, May 1; Whit Sunday; Victory Day (Anniversary of the Battle of Võnnu), June 23; Jaanipäev (St. John's Day), June 24; Christmas, December 25; Boxing Day, December 26

I. GENERAL INFORMATION

The Embassy of the Republic of Estonia and the Consulate General in New York perform legalization functions. Copies and signatures may be certified at the Embassy, the Consulate General, and the Honorary Consulates.

II. REQUIREMENTS FOR LEGALIZATION

Prior Authentications Required

1. Notarization (specific documents such as birth, marriage and death certificates and court files)
2. Authentication of Notary Signature (In most states this may be done directly by the State Secretary of State; if not, the County Clerk authenticates the signature.)
3. State Secretary of State Certification (In states where the Notary Signature may be authenticated directly by the State Secretary of State, steps 2 and 3 are combined.)

Materials to be Submitted with Request

1. Original document to be legalized
2. Prepaid, self-addressed return envelope is required only for specialized mail service

Direct Registration of Notary Public: Not available

Direct Signing of Document Before Consular Official: The procedure of certifying the signature of a private person is available at the Embassy. An appointment should be made and the signer must present identification such as a driver's license.

Turn Around Time: If the document is personally delivered, the document will be legalized in two to seven days.

Fee: $11.00 per document or signature
$ 3.00 per certification of copies and signatures

Payment Method: Certified check, company check, personal check payable to the Embassy of Estonia or the Consulate General of Estonia

III. EMBASSY, CONSUL GENERAL, AND HONORARY CONSULATES

Address, Phone, Hours	*Jurisdiction*
Embassy of the Republic of Estonia 2131 Massachusetts Avenue, NW Washington, DC 20008 Tel.: 202-588-0101 Fax: 202-588-0108 10:00 AM - 12:00 PM 2:00 PM - 4:00 PM	Entire United States
Consulate General 630 Fifth Avenue, Suite 2415 New York, NY 10111 Tel.: 212-247-7634 Fax: 212-262-0893 9:00 AM - 5:00 PM	Entire United States
Honorary Consulate 21515 Vanowen Street, Suite 211 Canoga Park Los Angeles, CA 91303 Tel.: 818-884-5850 Fax: 818-593-2973	California
Honorary Consulate 500 Union Street, Suite 930 Seattle, WA 98101 Tel.: 206-467-1444 Fax: 206-467-8129	Washington

ETHIOPIA

National Holiday: National Revolution Day, September 12

I. GENERAL INFORMATION

The Embassy handles legalization procedures for Great Britain, Canada, Mexico, and Latin America.

II. REQUIREMENTS FOR LEGALIZATION

Prior Authentications Required

1. Notarization
2. Authentication of Notary Signature (In most states this may be done directly by the State Secretary of State; if not, the County Clerk authenticates the signature.)
3. State Secretary of State Certification (In states where the Notary Signature may be authenticated directly by the State Secretary of State, steps 2 and 3 are combined.)
4. U.S. Secretary of State Certification

Materials to be Submitted with Request

1. Original document to be legalized
2. Prepaid, self-addressed return envelope; include extra postage for specialized return

Direct Registration of Notary Public: Not available

Direct Signing of Document Before Consular Official: Not available

Turn Around Time: If the document is personally delivered, there may be a delay of two days before legalization.

Fee: $94.80

Payment Method: Money order, company check payable to the Embassy of Ethiopia

III. EMBASSY

Address, Phone, Hours	*Jurisdiction*
Embassy of Ethiopia 2134 Kalorama Road, NW Washington, DC 20008 Tel.: 202-234-2281 Fax: 202-483-8407 9:00 AM - 2:00 PM	Entire United States Canada Great Britain Latin America Mexico

FALKLAND ISLANDS

I. GENERAL INFORMATION

The Falkland Islands are a dependency of the United Kingdom, covered by the Hague Convention Abolishing the Requirement for Legalization for Foreign Public Documents.

A document should be sent to the appropriate authority in the state or territory in which the document is notarized in order to obtain the Apostille. For information on obtaining the Apostille for documents originating in the United States, see the procedures specified for each of the individual states under United States jurisdiction in Chapter 2. For the enumeration of Federal authorities competent to provide the Apostille, see Appendix D.

For the text of the Hague Convention, the Apostille, and a list of the parties to the Convention, see Appendix A.

For information on United Kingdom Consulates, see the United Kingdom.

The Falkland Islands do not have an Embassy in the United States.

FIJI

National Holiday: Independence Day, October 10

I. GENERAL INFORMATION

Fiji is a party to the Hague Convention Abolishing the Requirement for Legalization for Foreign Public Documents.

A document should be sent to the appropriate authority in the state or territory in which the document is notarized in order to obtain the Apostille. For information on obtaining the Apostille for documents originating in the United States, see the procedures specified for each of the individual states under United States jurisdiction in Chapter 2. For the enumeration of Federal authorities competent to provide the Apostille, see Appendix D.

For the text of the Hague Convention, the Apostille, and a list of the parties to the Convention, see Appendix A.

For information purposes, the Embassy and New York Mission are listed below.

II. EMBASSY AND MISSION TO THE UN

Address, Phone, Hours	*Jurisdiction*
Embassy of Fiji Suite 240 2233 Wisconsin Avenue, NW Washington, DC 20007 Tel.: 202-337-8320 Fax: 202-337-1996	Entire United States and Mexico
Fiji Mission to the UN 630 Third Avenue, 7th Floor New York, NY 10017 Tel.: 212-687-4130	UN and Canada

REPUBLIC OF FINLAND

National Holiday: December 6

I. GENERAL INFORMATION

Finland is a party to the Hague Convention Abolishing the Requirement for Legalization for Foreign Public Documents.

A document should be sent to the appropriate authority in the state or territory in which the document is notarized in order to obtain the Apostille. For information on obtaining the Apostille for documents originating in the United States, see the procedures specified for each of the individual states under United States jurisdiction in Chapter 2. For the enumeration of Federal authorities competent to provide the Apostille, see Appendix D. For the text of the Hague Convention, the Apostille, and a list of the parties to the Convention, see Appendix A.

The Government of Finland considers Diplomatic and Consular Certicates or administrative documents dealing directly with commercial or customs operations to be an exception to the foregoing statements.

For information purposes, the Embassy and Consulates General of Finland are listed below.

II. EMBASSY AND CONSULATES GENERAL

Embassy of the Republic of Finland 3301 Massachusetts Avenue, NW Washington, DC 20008 Tel.: 202-298-5800 8:30 AM - 4:45 PM Appointment necessary	Entire United States
Consulate General 1900 Avenue of the Stars, Suite 1025 Los Angeles, CA 90067 Tel.: 310-203-9903 Fax: 310-203-9186	Western United States including portions of Colorado, Minnesota, New Mexico, and Wyoming

Address, Phone, Hours	*Jurisdiction*
Consulate General 866 United Nations Plaza, Room 250 New York, NY 10017 Tel.: 212-750-4400 Fax: 212-573-6310 8:45 AM - 4:45 PM	Eastern United States through the middle of Colorado, Minnesota, New Mexico, and Wyoming

FRANCE

National Holiday: Taking of the Bastille, July 14

I. GENERAL INFORMATION

France is a party to the Hague Convention Abolishing the Requirement for Legalization for Foreign Public Documents with effect also in French Overseas Departments and Territories.

A document should be sent to the appropriate authority in the state or territory in which the document is notarized in order to obtain the Apostille. For information on obtaining the Apostille for documents originating in the United States, see the procedures specified for each of the individual states under United States jurisdiction in Chapter 2. For the enumeration of Federal authorities competent to provide the Apostille, see Appendix D.

For the text of the Hague Convention, the Apostille, and a list of the parties to the Convention, see Appendix A.

For information purposes, the Consulates General of France are listed below.

II. CONSULATES GENERAL

Consulate General of France 4101 Reservoir Road, NW Washington, DC 20007 Tel.: 202-944-6195 Fax: 202-944-6148 9:00 AM - 1:00 PM 2:00 PM - 5:00 PM by appointment	Delaware Maryland Ohio Pennsylvania Virginia Washington, DC West Virginia
Consulate General 285 Peachtree Center Avenue, Suite 2800 Marquis Two Atlanta, GA 30303 Tel.: 404-522-4226 Fax: 404-880-9408 9:00 AM - 1:30 PM	Alabama Georgia Mississippi North Carolina South Carolina Tennessee

Address, Phone, Hours	*Jurisdiction*
Consulate General Park Square Building, Suite 750 31 Saint James Avenue Boston, MA 02116 Tel.: 617-542-7374 Fax: 617-542-8054 9:00 AM - 12:00 PM 2:00 PM - 5:00 PM by appointment	New Hampshire Maine Massachusetts Rhode Island Vermont
Consulate General 737 North Michigan Avenue, Suite 2020 Chicago, IL 60611 Tel.: 312-787-5358/9/60/61 Fax: 312-664-4196 9:00 AM - 2:00 PM Monday through Friday	Illinois Indiana Iowa Kansas Kentucky Michigan Minnesota Missouri Nebraska North Dakota South Dakota Wisconsin
Consulate General 2777 Allen Parkway, Suite 650 Houston, TX 77019 Tel.: 713-528-2181 Fax: 713-528-1933	Arkansas Oklahoma Texas
Consulate General 10990 Wilshire Boulevard, Suite 300 Los Angeles, CA 90024 Tel.: 310-235-3200 Fax: 310-312-0704	Arizona California counties of: Imperial, Inyo, Kern, Kings, Los Angeles, Mono, Orange, Riverside, San Bernadino, San Diego, San Luis Obispo, Santa Barbara, Ventura Colorado

Address, Phone, Hours	*Jurisdiction*
	Nevada counties of: Clark, Esmeralda et Mineral, Lincoln, Nye New Mexico
Consulate General Biscayne Tower, 17th Floor 2 South Biscayne Boulevard Miami, FL 33131 Tel.: 305-372-9798/9 Fax: 305-372-9549 9:00 AM - 1:00 PM 3:00 PM - 4:00 PM groups	Florida Bahamas Cayman Islands Turks and Caicos Islands Virgin Islands
Consulate General 934 Fifth Avenue New York, NY 10021 Tel.: 212-606-3689 Fax: 212-606-3620 9:00 AM - 1:00 PM	Connecticut New Jersey New York Bermuda
Consulate General Lykes Building 300 Poydras Street, Suite 2105 New Orleans, LA 70130 Tel.: 504-523-5772 Fax: 504-523-5725 9:00 AM - 1:00 PM	Louisiana
Consulate General 540 Bush Street San Francisco, CA 94108 Tel.: 415-397-4330 Fax: 415-433-8357 9:00 AM - 2:00 PM	Alaska California counties not covered by Los Angeles Hawaii Idaho Montana Nevada counties not covered by Los Angeles Oregon Utah Washington Wyoming

FRENCH GUIANA

I. GENERAL INFORMATION

French Guiana is an Overseas Department of France, covered by the Hague Convention Abolishing the Requirement for Legalization for Foreign Public Documents.

A document should be sent to the appropriate authority in the state or territory in which the document is notarized in order to obtain the Apostille. For information on obtaining the Apostille for documents originating in the United States, see the procedures specified for each of the individual states under United States jurisdiction in Chapter 2. For the enumeration of Federal authorities competent to provide the Apostille, see Appendix D.

For the text of the Hague Convention, the Apostille, and a list of the parties to the Convention, see Appendix A.

For information on French Consulates, see France.

FRENCH POLYNESIA

I. GENERAL INFORMATION

French Polynesia is an Overseas Territory of France, covered by the Hague Convention Abolishing the Requirement for Legalization for Foreign Public Documents.

A document should be sent to the appropriate authority in the state or territory in which the document is notarized in order to obtain the Apostille. For information on obtaining the Apostille for documents originating in the United States, see the procedures specified for each of the individual states under United States jurisdiction in Chapter 2. For the enumeration of Federal authorities competent to provide the Apostille, see Appendix D.

For the text of the Hague Convention, the Apostille, and a list of the parties to the Convention, see Appendix A.

For information on French Consulates, see France.

REPUBLIC OF GABON

National Holiday: March 12

I. GENERAL INFORMATION

Both the Embassy in Washington DC and the Consular Section of the Permanent Mission in New York have legalization functions.

II. REQUIREMENTS FOR LEGALIZATION

Prior Authentications Required
1. Notarization
2. State Secretary of State Certification
3. U.S. Secretary of State Certification

Materials to be Submitted with Request
1. Original document to be legalized
2. Photocopy of the document
3. Prepaid, self-addressed return envelope

Direct Registration of Notary Public: Not available

Direct Signing of Document Before Consular Official: Not available

Turn Around Time: If the document is personally delivered, the document will be legalized immediately in most cases.

Fee: $20.00 per document or signature

Payment Method: Cash, certified check, company check

III. EMBASSY AND CONSULATE

Address, Phone, Hours	*Jurisdiction*
Embassy of Gabon 2034 20th Street Washington, DC 20009 Tel.: 202-797-1000 Fax: 202-332-0668 9:00 AM - 5:00 PM	Entire United States

Address, Phone, Hours	*Jurisdiction*
Permanent Mission 18 East 41st Street, 9th Floor New York, NY 10017 Tel.: 212-683-7371 Fax: 212-689-5769 9:00 AM - 5:00 PM	

REPUBLIC OF THE GAMBIA

National Holiday: February 18

I. GENERAL INFORMATION

The Embassy of Gambia does not legalize documents. For information, contact the Attorney General's Chamber, which is listed below.

II. EMBASSY AND ATTORNEY GENERAL'S CHAMBER

Address, Phone, Hours	*Jurisdiction*
Chargé d'Affaires 1155 15th Street, NW Washington, DC 20005 Tel.: 202-785-1399 Fax: 202-785-1430 9:30 AM - 5:00 PM Mon. - Thurs. 9:30 AM - 1:00 PM Friday	Entire United States
Attorney General's Chamber Ministry of Justice Registrar General Marina Parade Banjul, Gambia Tel.: 220-228181 Fax: 220-225352	

REPUBLIC OF GEORGIA

I. GENERAL INFORMATION

Georgia has an Embassy in the United States but no Consulates. The Embassy of Georgia in Washington, DC also handles legalizations for Canada and Mexico.

II. REQUIREMENTS FOR LEGALIZATION

Prior Authentications Required

1. Notarization
2. Authentication of Notary Signature (In most states this may be done directly by the State Secretary of State; if not, the County Clerk authenticates the signature.)
3. State Secretary of State Certification (In states where the Notary Signature may be authenticated directly by the State Secretary of State, steps 2 and 3 are combined.)
4. U.S. Secretary of State Certification

Materials to be Submitted with Request

1. Original document to be legalized
2. Photocopy of the document
3. Prepaid, self-addressed return envelope

Direct Registration of Notary Public: Not available

Direct Signing of Document Before Consular Official: The procedure of certifying the signature of a private person is available at the Embassy. An appointment should be made and the signer must present identification such as a driver's license.

Turn Around Time: If the document is personally delivered, it will be legalized immediately if the workload allows. Otherwise, there may be a delay of two to four days before legalization.

Fee: $100.00 per document for up to and including five documents
$ 50.00 per document for six or more documents

Payment Method: Money order, company check, personal check

III. EMBASSY

Address, Phone, Hours	*Jurisdiction*
Embassy of the Republic of Georgia 1511 K Street NW, Suite 400 Washington, DC 20005 Tel.: 202-393-6060 9:00 AM - 6:00 PM	Entire United States

FEDERAL REPUBLIC OF GERMANY

National Holiday: October 3

I. GENERAL INFORMATION

Germany is a party to the Hague Convention Abolishing the Requirement for Legalization for Foreign Public Documents.

A document should be sent to the appropriate authority in the state or territory in which the document is notarized in order to obtain the Apostille. For information on obtaining the Apostille for documents originating in the United States, see the procedures specified for each of the individual states under United States jurisdiction in Chapter 2. For the enumeration of Federal authorities competent to provide the Apostille, see Appendix D.

For the text of the Hague Convention, the Apostille, and a list of the parties to the Convention, see Appendix A.

For information purposes, the Embassy and Consulates General of Germany are listed below.

II. EMBASSY AND CONSULATES GENERAL

Address, Phone, Hours	*Jurisdiction*
Embassy of the Federal Republic of Germany 4645 Reservoir Road, NW Washington, DC 20007-1998 Tel.: 202-298-4000 Fax: 202-298-4249	Delaware Maryland Virginia Washington, DC West Virginia
Consulate General Marquis Two Tower, Suite 901 285 Peachtree Center Avenue, NE Atlanta, GA 30303-1221 Tel.: 404-659-4760/1/2 Fax: 404-659-1280	Alabama Georgia Mississippi North Carolina South Carolina Tennessee

Address, Phone, Hours	*Jurisdiction*
Consulate General 3 Copley Place, Fifth Floor Boston, MA 02116 Tel.: 617-536-4414 Fax: 617-536-8573	Connecticut (except New York Jurisdiction) Maine Massachusetts New Hampshire Rhode Island Vermont
Consulate General 676 No. Michigan Avenue, Ste. 3200 Chicago, IL 60611 Tel: 312-580-1199 Fax: 312-580-0099 8:30 AM - 12:30 PM	Illinois Iowa Kansas Minnesota Missouri Nebraska North Dakota South Dakota Wisconsin
Consulate General Suite 2100 Edison Plaza 660 Plaza Drive Detroit, MI 48226-1271 Tel.: 313-962-6526 Fax: 313-962-7345	Indiana Kentucky Michigan Ohio
Consulate General 1330 Post Oak Boulevard Suite 1850 Houston, TX 77056-3018 Tel.: 713-627-7770/1/2/3 Fax: 713-627-0506	Arkansas Louisiana New Mexico Oklahoma Texas

Address, Phone, Hours	*Jurisdiction*
Consulate General Suite 500 6222 Wilshire Boulevard Los Angeles, CA 90048 Tel.: 213-930-2703 Fax: 213-930-2805	Arizona California counties of: Imperial, Kern, Los Angeles, Orange, Riverside, San Bernadino San Diego, San Luis Obispo, Santa Barbara, Ventura
Consulate General 100 North Biscayne Boulevard, # 2210 Miami, FL 33132 Tel.: 305-358-0290/1/2 Fax: 305-358-0307	Florida counties: Broward, Charlotte, Dade, Glades, Hendry, Highlands, Indian River, Lee, Martin, Monroe, Okeechobee, Palm Beach, Puerto Rico, Saint Lucie U.S. Virgin Islands
Consulate General 460 Park Avenue New York, NY 10022-1906 Tel.: 212-308-8700 Fax: 212-308-3422	Connecticut county of Fairfield New Jersey New York Pennsylvania
Consulate General 1960 Jackson Street San Francisco, CA 94109 Tel.: 415-775-1061 Fax: 415-775-0187	California (except Los Angeles jurisdiction) Colorado Hawaii Nevada Utah

Address, Phone, Hours	*Jurisdiction*
	Wyoming Midway Islands
Consulate General One Union Square, Suite 2500 600 University Steet Seattle, WA 98101 Tel.: 206-682-4312 Fax: 206-682-3724 Telex: (0230) 312205	Alaska Idaho Montana Oregon Washington

REPUBLIC OF GHANA

National Holiday: Independence Day, March 6

I. GENERAL INFORMATION

Only the Embassy has legalization functions.

II. REQUIREMENTS FOR LEGALIZATION

Prior Authentications Required
1. Notarization
2. Authentication of Notary Signature (In most states this may be done directly by the State Secretary of State; if not, the County Clerk authenticates the signature.)
3. State Secretary of State Certification (In states where the Notary Signature may be authenticated directly by the State Secretary of State, steps 2 and 3 are combined.)
4. U.S. Secretary of State Certification

Materials to be Submitted with Request
1. Original document to be legalized
2. Photocopy of the document
3. Prepaid, self-addressed return envelope

Direct Registration of Notary Public: Not available

Direct Signing of Document Before Consular Official: Not available

Turn Around Time: If the document is personally delivered, legalization of the document will take one to two days.

Fee: $20.00

Payment Method: Cash, money order, certified check payable to the Embassy of Ghana

III. EMBASSY AND CONSULATE GENERAL

Address, Phone, Hours	*Jurisdiction*
Embassy of the Republic of Ghana 3512 International Drive NW Washington, DC 20008 Tel.: 202-686-4520 Fax: 202-686-4527 9:30 AM - 3:00 PM Monday through Thursday	Entire United States

GIBRALTAR

I. GENERAL INFORMATION

Gibraltar is a self-governing dependency of the United Kingdom, covered by the Hague Convention Abolishing the Requirement for Legalization for Foreign Public Documents.

A document should be sent to the appropriate authority in the state or territory in which the document is notarized in order to obtain the Apostille. For information on obtaining the Apostille for documents originating in the United States, see the procedures specified for each of the individual states under United States jurisdiction in Chapter 2. For the enumeration of Federal authorities competent to provide the Apostille, see Appendix D.

For the text of the Hague Convention, the Apostille, and a list of the parties to the Convention, see Appendix A.

For information on United Kingdom Consulates, see the United Kingdom.

Gibraltar has no Embassy in the United States.

HELLENIC REPUBLIC

National Holiday: Independence Day, March 25

I. GENERAL INFORMATION

Greece is a party to the Hague Convention Abolishing the Requirement for Legalization for Foreign Public Documents.

A document should be sent to the appropriate authority in the state or territory in which the document is notarized in order to obtain the Apostille. For information on obtaining the Apostille for documents originating in the United States, see the procedures specified for each of the individual states under United States jurisdiction in Chapter 2. For the enumeration of Federal authorities competent to provide the Apostille, see Appendix D.

For the text of the Hague Convention, the Apostille, and a list of the parties to the Convention, see Appendix A.

For information purposes, the Embassy, Consulates General and Consulates are listed below. For those instances in which legalization by a consular official may still be necessary, the requirements for legalization are given also.

Note that the Washington DC Consular Section and not the Embassy has legalization functions.

II. REQUIREMENTS FOR LEGALIZATION

Prior Authentications Required
1. Notarization
2. Authentication of Notary Signature (In most states this may be done directly by the State Secretary of State; if not, the County Clerk authenticates the signature.)

Materials to be Submitted with Request
1. Original document to be legalized
2. Prepaid, self-addressed return envelope

Direct Registration of Notary Public: Not available

Direct Signing of Document Before Consular Official: The procedure of certifying the signature of a private person is available in Chicago, New York and San Francisco. An appointment is necessary. The signer should have identification bearing a photograph, such as a passport, alien registration card or driver's license.

Turn Around Time: If the document is personally delivered, legalization can generally be handled immediately in New York and Chicago. There will be a delay of three working days in San Francisco.

Fee: Contact Consulate for information on fees.

Payment Method
Cash, certified check, company check, money order

III. EMBASSY, CONSULATES GENERAL AND CONSULATES

Address, Phone, Hours	*Jurisdiction*
Embassy of the Hellenic Republic 1701 New Hampshire Avenue, NW Washington, DC 20009 Tel.: 202-265-2561 Fax: 202-265-2468	Delaware Maryland North Carolina Washington, DC West Virginia Virginia
Consulate Tower Place, Suite 1670 3340 Peachtree Road, NE Atlanta, GA 30326 Tel.: 404-261-3313 Fax: 404-262-2798	Florida Georgia South Carolina
Consulate General Statler Office Building, Suite 526 20 Park Plaza Boston, MA 02116 Tel.: 617-542-3240	Maine Massachusetts New Hampshire Rhode Island Vermont

Address, Phone, Hours	*Jurisdiction*
Consulate General 168 N. Michigan Avenue Chicago, IL 60601 Tel.: 312-372-5356 9:30 AM - 2:00 PM	Illinois Iowa Indiana Kansas Kentucky Michigan Minnesota Missouri Nebraska North Dakota Ohio South Dakota Tennessee Wisconsin
Consulate International Trade Mart Building 2 Canal Street New Orleans, LA 70130 Tel.: 504-523-1167 Fax: 504-524-3610	Alabama Arkansas Louisiana Mississippi Puerto Rico Virgin Islands
Consulate General 69 East 79th Street New York, NY 10021 Tel.: 212-988-5500 Fax: 212-734-8492 9:00 AM - 2:30 PM	Connecticut New Jersey New York Pennsylvania
Consulate General 2441 Gough Street San Francisco, CA 94123 Tel.: 415-775-2102 Fax: 415-776-6815	Alaska California (except counties in Los Angeles jurisdiction) Idaho Montana Nevada Oregon Utah Washington

Address, Phone, Hours	*Jurisdiction*
	American Pacific Territories American Samoa Guam
Consulate General 3255 Wilshire Building Building G, Suite 1103 Los Angeles, CA 90010 Tel.: 213-385-1447 213-385-1660 213-385-1822	Arizona California counties of: Imperial, Los Angeles, San Bernadino, San Diego, Ventura Colorado Hawaii New Mexico Wyoming

GUADELOUPE

I. GENERAL INFORMATION

Guadeloupe is an Overseas Department of France, covered by the Hague Convention Abolishing the Requirement for Legalization for Foreign Public Documents.

A document should be sent to the appropriate authority in the state or territory in which the document is notarized in order to obtain the Apostille. For information on obtaining the Apostille for documents originating in the United States, see the procedures specified for each of the individual states under United States jurisdiction in Chapter 2. For the enumeration of Federal authorities competent to provide the Apostille, see Appendix D.

For the text of the Hague Convention, the Apostille, and a list of the parties to the Convention, see Appendix A.

For information on French Consulates, see France.

Guadeloupe has no Embassy in the United States.

REPUBLIC OF GUATEMALA

National Holiday: Independence Day, September 15

I. GENERAL INFORMATION

The Embassy and Consulates General have legalization functions. Each will legalize documents originating in its jurisdiction. The specific requirements for legalization may vary from office to office; to confirm requirements, contact the Consulate General for your jurisdiction. The requirements for the Embassy are set forth below.

II. REQUIREMENTS FOR LEGALIZATION

Prior Authentications Required

1. Notarization
2. Authentication of Notary Signature (In most states this may be done directly by the State Secretary of State; if not, the County Clerk authenticates the signature.)
3. State Secretary of State Certification (In states where the Notary Signature may be authenticated directly by the State Secretary of State, steps 2 and 3 are combined.)
4. U.S. Secretary of State Certification

Materials to be Submitted with Request

1. Original document to be legalized
2. Photocopy of the document, except for patents
3. Prepaid, self-addressed return envelope

Note: Contact the Embassy for materials required for DHL or UPS delivery service.

Direct Registration of Notary Public: Not available

Direct Signing of Document Before Consular Official: Not available

Turn Around Time: If the document is personally delivered, there will be a delay of 24 to 48 hours for legalization. If the document is mailed, the average turn around time, including mailing time, is two days.

Fee: $10.00 per document or signature for patents; $15 per document or signature for invoices, bills of lading, and other commercial documents

Payment Method: Cash, money order, certified check, company check payable to the Embassy of Guatemala

III. EMBASSY AND CONSULATES GENERAL

Address, Phone, Hours	*Jurisdiction*
Embassy of the Republic of Guatamala Consular Section 2220 R Street, NW Washington, DC 20008 Tel.: 202-745-4952, ext. 107 Fax: 202-745-1908 9:00 AM - 12:30 PM	Delaware Kentucky Maryland Ohio Puerto Rico Tennessee Virginia Washington, DC West Virginia
Consulate General 230 North Michigan Avenue, Suite 1000 Chicago, IL 60601 Tel.: 312-332-3170 Fax: 312-332-4256	Illinois Indiana Iowa Michigan Minnesota Missouri North Dakota South Dakota Wisconsin
Consulate General 300 Sevilla Avenue, Suite 210 Coral Gables, FL 33134 Tel.: 305-443-4828/9 Fax: 305-443-4830	Alabama Florida Georgia North Carolina South Carolina
Consulate General 3600 South Gessner Road, Suite 200 Houston, TX 77063 Tel.: 713-953-9531 Fax: 713-353-1127	Arkansas Kansas Louisiana Mississippi Nebraska Oklahoma Texas

Address, Phone, Hours	*Jurisdiction*
Consulate General 2975 Wilshire Boulevard, Suite 101 Los Angeles, CA 90010 Tel.: 213-365-9251/2 Fax: 213-365-9245	Arizona California (southern) Colorado Hawaii New Mexico Utah
Consulate General 57 Park Avenue New York, NY 10016 Tel.: 212-686-3837	Connecticut Maine Massachusetts New Hampshire New Jersey New York Pennsylvania Rhode Island Vermont
Consulate General 870 Market Street, Suite 667 San Francisco, CA 94102 Tel.: 415-788-5651 Fax: 415-788-5653	Alaska California (northern) Idaho Montana Nevada Oregon Washington Wyoming

GUINEA

National Holiday: October 2

I. GENERAL INFORMATION

Only the Embassy legalizes documents.

II. REQUIREMENTS FOR LEGALIZATION

Prior Authentications Required

1. Notarization
2. Authentication of Notary Signature (In most states this may be done directly by the State Secretary of State; if not, the County Clerk authenticates the signature.)
3. State Secretary of State Certification (In states where the Notary Signature may be authenticated directly by the State Secretary of State, steps 2 and 3 are combined.)
4. U.S. Secretary of State Certification

Materials to be Submitted with Request

1. Original document to be legalized
2. Photocopy of the document
3. Prepaid, self-addressed return envelope

Direct Registration of Notary Public: Not available

Direct Signing of Document Before Consular Official: Not available

Turn Around Time: If the document is personally delivered, it will be legalized immediately if the work load is not too great.

Fee: Varies depending upon the type of document

Payment Method: Cash, money order, certified check, company check

III. EMBASSY

Address, Phone, Hours	*Jurisdiction*
Embassy of Guinea 2112 Leroy Place, NW Washington DC Tel.: 202-483-9420 Fax: 202-483-8688 9:30 AM - 5:00 PM	Entire United States

GUYANA

I. GENERAL INFORMATION

Only the Embassy has legalization functions.

II. REQUIREMENTS FOR LEGALIZATION

Prior Authentications Required

1. Notarization
2. Authentication of Notary Signature (In most states this may be done directly by the State Secretary of State; if not, the County Clerk authenticates the signature.)
3. State Secretary of State Certification (In states where the Notary Signature may be authenticated directly by the State Secretary of State, steps 2 and 3 are combined.)

Materials to be Submitted with Request

1. Original document to be legalized
2. Prepaid, self-addressed return envelope

Direct Registration of Notary Public: Not available

Direct Signing of Document Before Consular Official: The procedure of certifying the signature of a private person is available at the Embassy. The signer must present identification in the form of a driver's license or passport. Documents should be brought in on Monday or Wednesday; they will be signed on Tuesday or Thursday and should be picked up the following day, i.e., Wednesday or Friday.

Fee: $5.20 per document or signature

Payment Method: Cash, money order, certified check payable to the Embassy of Guyana

II. EMBASSY

Address, Phone, Hours	*Jurisdiction*
Embassy 2490 Tracy Place, NW Washington DC Tel.: 202-265-6900 Fax: 202-232-1297 9:00 AM - 5:00 PM	Entire United States

HAITI

National Holiday: January 1

I. GENERAL INFORMATION

The Embassy and Consulates General legalize documents. The procedures outlined below pertain to the Embassy and may not apply to all Consulates.

II. REQUIREMENTS FOR LEGALIZATION

Prior Authentications Required

1. Notarization
2. Authentication of Notary Signature (In most states this may be done directly by the State Secretary of State; if not, the County Clerk authenticates the signature.)
3. State Secretary of State Certification (In states where the Notary Signature may be authenticated directly by the State Secretary of State, steps 2 and 3 are combined.)
4. U.S. Secretary of State Certification

Materials to be Submitted with Request

1. Original document to be legalized
2. Prepaid, self-addressed return envelope

Direct Registration of Notary Public: Not available

Direct Signing of Document Before Consular Official: Not available

Turn Around Time: If the document is personally delivered, it may be legalized immediately if an official is available; otherwise there will be a delay of one day.

Fee: $10.50 per document or signature

Payment Method: Money order, certified check, company check

III. EMBASSY AND CONSULATES GENERAL

Address, Phone, Hours	*Jurisdiction*
Embassy of Haiti 2311 Massachusetts Avenue, NW Washington DC 20008 Tel.: 202-332-4090 9:00 AM - 2:00 PM	Entire US
Consulate General 545 Boylston Street, Suite 201 Boston, MA 02116 Tel.: 617-266-3660 Fax: 617-266-4060	New England
Consulate General 220 South State Street, Suite 2110 Chicago, IL 60604 Tel.: 312-922-4004 Fax: 312-922-7122	Midwest
Consulate General 259 South West 13th Street Miami, FL 33130 Tel.: 305-859-2003 Fax: 305-854-7441	Florida Georgia
Consulate General 271 Madison Avenue, 17th Floor New York, NY 10016 Tel.: 212-697-9767	Connecticut New Jersey New York
Consulate General IBM Building, Suite 833 654 Munoz Rivera Avenue Hato Rey, Puerto Rico 00918 Tel.: 787-764-1392 Fax: 787-764-3109	US Virgin Islands

HOLY SEE

National Holiday: October 16

I. GENERAL INFORMATION

The Holy See legalizes ecclesiastic documents. Documents to be legalized must be authenticated by the Holy See Offices, the Archibishop's See, the Bishop's See, and the Embassy to the Holy See.

II. REQUIREMENTS FOR LEGALIZATION

Materials to be Submitted with Request
1. Original document to be legalized

Direct Registration of Notary Public: Not available

Direct Signing of Document Before Consular Official: Not available

Turn Around Time: If the document is personally delivered, it will be legalized the same day.

Payment Method: Cash

III. EMBASSY

Secretariate of State
Vatican City State
Tel.: 6982

REPUBLIC OF HONDURAS

National Holiday: Independence Day, September 15

I. GENERAL INFORMATION

The Embassy and Consulates General have legalization functions; the Embassy can cover the entire United States if needed.

II. REQUIREMENTS FOR LEGALIZATION

Prior Authentications Required

1. Notarization
2. State Secretary of State Certification (In states where the Notary Signature may be authenticated directly by the State Secretary of State, steps 2 and 3 are combined.)
3. U.S. Secretary of State Certification

Materials to be Submitted with Request

1. Original document to be legalized
2. Prepaid, self-addressed return envelope

Direct Registration of Notary Public: Not available

Direct Signing of Document Before Consular Official: The procedure of certifying the signature of a private person is available at the Embassy, General Consulates, and Consulate. No appointment is necessary and no identification is required.

Turn Around Time: If the document is personally delivered, there will be a delay of one day before legalization.

Fee: $50.00 per document or signature; fee may vary

Payment Method: Cash, money order, certified check, company check

III. EMBASSY AND CONSULATE GENERAL

Address, Phone, Hours	*Jurisdiction*
Embassy of Honduras 1612 K Street NW Washington, DC 20006 Tel.: 202-223-0185 9:30 AM - 2:00 PM	Delaware Maryland Virginia Washington, DC Entire United States if necessary
Consulate General 80 Wallace Street, 4th Floor New York, NY 10005 Tel.: 212-269-3612 Fax: 212-509-8391 9:00 AM - 2:00 PM	Connecticut Maine Massachusetts New Hampshire New Jersey New York Pennsylvania Rhode Island Vermont

HONG KONG

I. GENERAL INFORMATION

Hong Kong, a dependency of the United Kingdom until July of 1997, is an autonomous territory covered by the Hague Convention Abolishing the Requirement for Legalization for Foreign Public Documents.

A document should be sent to the appropriate authority in the state or territory in which the document is notarized in order to obtain the Apostille. For information on obtaining the Apostille for documents originating in the United States, see the procedures specified for each of the individual states under United States jurisdiction in Chapter 2. For the enumeration of Federal authorities competent to provide the Apostille, see Appendix D.

For the text of the Hague Convention, the Apostille, and a list of the parties to the Convention, see Appendix A.

For information purposes, the economic trade office of Hong Kong is listed below.

II. ECONOMIC TRADE OFFICE

Address, Phone, Hours	*Jurisdiction*
Hong Kong Economic and Trade Office 1150 18th Street NW Washington, DC 20036 Tel.: 202-331-8947	
Hong Kong Economic and Trade Office 680 Fifth Avenue, 22nd Floor New York, NY Tel.: 212-265-8888 9:30 AM - 4:30 PM	

REPUBLIC OF HUNGARY

National Holiday: August 20

I. GENERAL INFORMATION

Hungary is a party to the Hague Convention Abolishing the Requirement for Legalization for Foreign Public Documents.

A document should be sent to the appropriate authority in the state or territory in which the document is notarized in order to obtain the Apostille. For information on obtaining the Apostille for documents originating in the United States, see the procedures specified for each of the individual states under United States jurisdiction in Chapter 2. For the enumeration of Federal authorities competent to provide the Apostille, see Appendix D. For the text of the Hague Convention, the Apostille, and a list of the parties to the Convention, see Appendix A.

For those instances in which legalization by a Hungarian consulate official may still be necessary, the requirements for legalization are given below. The Embassy and Consulates General have legalization functions. Each will legalize documents originating in its jurisdiction. The requirements are the same for all offices.

II. REQUIREMENTS FOR NON-HAGUE CONVENTION LEGALIZATION

Prior Authentications Required
1. Notarization
2. Authentication of Notary Signature (In most states this may be done directly by the State Secretary of State; if not, the County Clerk authenticates the signature.)
3. State Secretary of State Certification (In states where the Notary Signature may be authenticated directly by the State Secretary of State, steps 2 and 3 are combined.)

Materials to be Submitted with Request
1. Original document to be legalized
2. Prepaid, self-addressed return envelope
3. Fee ($20.00/document)

Direct Registration of Notary Public: The procedure of registering a Notary Public's signature with the Consulate is available, permitting the legalization of the document(s) bearing that Notary's signature and seal without certification by the County Clerk or the Secretary of State. For registration, the Consulate requires the Notary's stamp and signature, as well as the attestation of his state's Secretary of State.

Direct Signing of Document Before Consular Official: The procedure of certifying the signature of a private person is available at the Embassy and Consulates General. An appointment should be made and the signer must present an official document with the signer's name and picture on it, such as a passport, driver's license, or green card, as identification as well as the $30.00 certification fee.

Turn Around Time: If the document is personally delivered, an appointment should be made with the consul in order to insure prompt handling.

Fee: $20.00 per document for legalization
$30.00 per document for certification

Payment Method: Cash, money order, certified check, company check, personal check payable to the Embassy of Hungary

III. EMBASSY AND CONSULATES GENERAL

Address, Phone, Hours	*Jurisdiction*
Embassy of the Republic of Hungary Consular Section 3910 Shoemaker Street, NW Washington, DC 20008 Tel.: 202-364-8218 Fax: 202-686-6412 9:00 AM - 2:00 PM	Alabama Arkansas Florida Georgia Kentucky Louisiana Maryland Mississippi North Carolina Ohio Pennsylvania South Carolina Tennessee Virginia

Address, Phone, Hours	*Jurisdiction*
	Washington DC West Virginia Puerto Rico
Consulate General 223 East 52nd Street New York, NY 10022 Tel.: 212-752-0661 9:30 AM - 12:30 PM	Connecticut Delaware Illinois Indiana Iowa Maine Massachusetts Michigan Minnesota Missouri New Hampshire New Jersey New York Rhode Island Vermont Wisconsin
Consulate General 11766 Wilshire Boulevard, Suite 410 Los Angeles, CA 90025 Tel.: 310-473-9344	Alaska Arizona California Colorado Hawaii Idaho Kansas Montana Nebraska Nevada New Mexico North Dakota Oklahoma Oregon South Dakota Texas Utah Washington Wyoming

ICELAND

National Holiday: June 17

I. GENERAL INFORMATION

The Embassy and Honorary Consuls have legalization functions. Each office serves the entire United States.

II. REQUIREMENTS FOR LEGALIZATION

Prior Authentications Required

1. Notarization
2. Authentication of Notary Signature (In most states this may be done directly by the State Secretary of State; if not, the County Clerk authenticates the signature.)
3. State Secretary of State Certification (In states where the Notary Signature may be authenticated directly by the State Secretary of State, steps 2 and 3 are combined.)
4. U.S. Secretary of State Certification

Materials to be Submitted with Request

1. Original document to be legalized
2. Photocopy of the document
3. Prepaid, self-addressed return envelope is not required but is appreciated

Direct Registration of Notary Public: Not available

Direct Signing of Document Before Consular Official: The procedure of certifying the signature of a private person is available at the Embassy and Honorary Consulates. An appointment should be made and the signer must present identification in the form of a driver's license or passport.

Turn Around Time: If the document is personally delivered, there will be a delay of two days before legalization.

Fee: $15.00 per document or signature

Payment Method: Cash, money order, certified check payable to the Embassy of Iceland

III. EMBASSY, CONSULS GENERAL, CONSULS AND VICE CONSULS

Address, Phone, Hours	*Jurisdiction*
Embassy of Iceland 1156 15th Street NW, Suite 1200 Washington, DC 20005-1704 Tel.: 202-265-6653 Fax: 202-265-6656 9:00 AM - 12:00 PM 1:00 PM - 5:00 PM	North and South America
Consul Philip W. Benediktsson 3915 Locarno Drive Anchorage, AK 99508 Tel.: 907-561-1492 Fax: 907-562-4263	Entire United States
Consul General Maurice K. Horowitz Suite 118 1677 Tullie Circle, NE Atlanta, GA 30329 Tel.: 404-321-0777 Fax: 404-634-9640	Entire United States
Consul Antonio Ruiz Ochoa Islandia Street # 2 Flamboyant Gardens Bayamon, PR 00959 Tel.: 787-786-7171 Fax: 787-740-2888	Entire United States
Consul Elisha Flagg Lee Winslow Evans & Crocker 33 Broad Street Boston, MA 02210 Tel.: 617-227-4300 Fax: 617-227-5505	Entire United States

Address, Phone, Hours	*Jurisdiction*
Consul Örn Arnar 6428 Nordic Circle Edina, MN 55439 Tel.: 612-863-3838 Fax: 612-863-3764	Entire United States
Consul Vigdis Aðalsteinsdóttir Taylor 7100 East 131 Street Grandview, MO 64030-3317 Tel.: 816-763-2046	Entire United States
Consul Edward K. Christian Saga Communications, Inc. 73 Kercheval Avenue Grosse Pointe Farms, MI 48236 Tel.: 313-836-2596 Fax: 313-886-7150	Entire United States
Consul Thorir Gröndal 5220 North Ocean Drive Hollywood, FL 33019 Tel.: 954-920-7977 Fax: 954-920-6977	Entire United States
Consul Hubert J. Georges 2015 D, South Point Drive Hummelstown, PA 17036 Tel.: 717-566-7791 Fax: 717-566-7792	Entire United States
Consul Pamela Kay Bauer 3205 Seaside Irving, TX 75062 Tel.: 214-699-5417 Fax: 214-255-3916	Entire United States

Address, Phone, Hours	*Jurisdiction*
Vice Consul Örn Eggert Guðmundsson Consul Jón Sigurður Guðmundsson 2600 Highway 146 East La Grange, KY 40031 Tel.: 502-222-1441 Fax: 502-222-1445	Entire United States
Consul General Halla Linker 1551 Westwood Boulevard, Suite 108 Los Angeles, CA 90024 Tel.: 310-474-8485 Fax: 310-474-8728	Entire United States
Consul Greg Beuerman 228 St. Charles Avenue, Suite 1333 New Orleans, LA 70130 Tel.: 504-524-3342 Fax: 504-524-3344	Entire United States
Consul General 800 Third Avenue, 36th Floor New York, NY 10022 Tel.: 212-593-2700 Fax: 212-593-6269	Entire United States
Vice Consul James F. Gerrity III Gerrity Company 90 Oak Street Newton Upper Falls, MA 02164-9111 Tel.: 617-928-3330 Fax: 617-928-3336	Entire United States
Consul Gerald L. Parks Capes Shipping Agencies Inc. 1128 West Olney Road Norfolk, VA 23507 Tel.: 757-625-3658 Fax: 757-625-6942	Entire United States

Address, Phone, Hours	*Jurisdiction*
Vice Consul Aristotle Halikias Consul General Edward Derwinski Inter-Continental Real Estate & Development 15750 South Harlem Avenue Orland Park, IL 60611 Tel.: 708-429-1126 Fax: 708-429-9972	Entire United States
Consul Omer K. Reed Napili/Pentegra 2999 North 44th Street, Suite 650 Phoenix, AZ 85018	Entire United States
Consul Clark T. Thorstenson 2797 Apache Lane Provo, UT 84604 Tel.: 801-378-3337 Fax: 801-378-7860	Entire United States
Vice Consul Robert E. Cartwright, Jr. The Cartwright & Alexander Law Firm 222 Front Street, Fifth Floor San Francisco, CA 94111 Tel.: 415-433-0444 Fax: 415-433-0449	Entire United States
Consul General Jón Marvin Jónsson 5610 20th Avenue NW Seattle, WA 98107 Tel.: 206-783-4100 Fax: 206-784-8916	Entire United States
Vice Consul J. Brent Haymond 164 West 200 South Springville, UT 84663 Tel.: 801-498-6221 Fax: 801-489-0436	Entire United States

Address, Phone, Hours	*Jurisdiction*
Consul General Hilmar Skagfield 270 Crossway Road PO Box 753 Tallahassee, FL 32302 Tel.: 904-878-1144 Fax: 904-878-6093	Entire United States
Consul Ólafur A. Ásgeirsson 2348 West Settler's Way The Woodlands, TX 77380 Tel.: 713-367-2777 Fax: 281-362-4388	Entire United States

INDIA

National Holidays: Anniversary of the Proclamation of the Republic, January 26; July 18; August 15; October 2; October 11; October 30; November 14

I. GENERAL INFORMATION

The Embassy and Consulates General have legalization functions. Each will legalize documents originating in its jurisdiction. Specific requirements for legalization may vary from office to office. The requirements below are for the Embassy and the New York and Houston Consulates General.

II. REQUIREMENTS FOR LEGALIZATION

Prior Authentications Required
The Embassy and New York Consulate General require steps 1 through 4; the Houston Consulate General requires step 1.

1. Notarization
2. Authentication of Notary Signature (In most states this may be done directly by the State Secretary of State; if not, the County Clerk authenticates the signature.)
3. State Secretary of State Certification (In states where the Notary Signature may be authenticated directly by the State Secretary of State, steps 2 and 3 are combined.)
4. U.S. Secretary of State Certification

Materials to be Submitted with Request
1. Original document to be legalized
2. Photocopy of the document
3. Prepaid, self-addressed return envelope

Direct Registration of Notary Public: Not available

Direct Signing of Document Before Consular Official: The procedure of certifying the signature of a private person is available for Indian citizens only.

Turn Around Time: If the document is personally delivered to the Embassy or Houston Consulate General by noon, it can be picked up between 4:00 and 5:00 PM. If the document is personally delivered to the New York Consulate General by 11:00 AM, it can be picked up between 4:30 and 5:15 PM. Allow two weeks for documents mailed to the Embassy, five business days for documents mailed to Houston, and 48 hours for documents mailed to New York.

Fee: $51.00 per document or signature at the Embassy, between $11.00 and $52.00 per document or signature at the Houston Consulate General, and $21 per document or signature at the New York Consulate General

Payment Method: Cash, money order, company check payable to the Embassy or Consulate General.

III. EMBASSY AND CONSULATES GENERAL

Address, Phone, Hours	*Jurisdiction*
Embassy of India 2107 Massachusetts Avenue, NW Washington, DC 20008 Tel.: 202-939-7000 Fax: 202-797-4693 9:30 AM - 12:30 PM 4:00 PM - 5:00 PM	Delaware Kentucky Maryland North Carolina South Carolina Tennessee Virginia Washington, DC West Virginia
Consulate General 455 North City Plaza Drive, Ste. 850 Chicago, IL 60611 Tel.: 312-595-0405 Fax: 312-595-0418 9:00 AM - 12:00 PM	Illinois Indiana Iowa Michigan Minnesota Missouri North Dakota South Dakota Wisconsin

Address, Phone, Hours	*Jurisdiction*
Consulate General 1990 Post Oak Boulevard, Ste. 600 Houston, TX 77056 Tel.: 713-626-3252 Fax: 713-626-2450	Alabama Arkansas Florida Georgia Kansas Louisiana Mississippi Oklahoma Texas
Consulate General Consular Wing 3 East 64th Street New York, NY 10021-7097 Tel.: 212-774-0600, ext. 667 Fax: 212-570-9581 9:15 AM - 1:00 PM 2:00 PM - 5:15 PM	Connecticut Maine Massachusetts New Hampshire New Jersey New York Ohio Pennsylvania Puerto Rico Rhode Island Vermont
Consulate General Consular Wing 540 Arguello Boulevard San Francisco, CA 94118 Tel.: 415-668-0662	Alaska Arizona California Colorado Hawaii Idaho Montana Nebraska New Mexico Nevada Oregon Utah Washington Wyoming

INDONESIA

National Holiday: August 17

I. GENERAL INFORMATION

The Embassy, Consulate General, and Consulates have legalization functions. Each will legalize documents originating in its jurisdiction. Requirements for the various Consulates may differ.

II. REQUIREMENTS FOR LEGALIZATION

Prior Authentications Required
1. Notarization
2. Authentication of Notary Signature (In most states this may be done directly by the State Secretary of State; if not, the County Clerk authenticates the signature.)
3. State Secretary of State Certification (In states where the Notary Signature may be authenticated directly by the State Secretary of State, steps 2 and 3 are combined.)
4. U.S. Secretary of State Certification

Materials to be Submitted with Request
1. Original document to be legalized
2. Photocopy of the document
3. Prepaid, self-addressed return envelope

Direct Registration of Notary Public: Not available

Direct Signing of Document Before Consular Official: Not available

Turn Around Time: If the document is personally delivered, there will be a delay of three working days before legalization.

Fee: $10.00 per document or signature

Payment Method: Cash, money order, certified check, company check payable to the Embassy, Consulate General or Consulate of Indonesia

III. EMBASSY, CONSULATE GENERAL, AND CONSULATES

Address, Phone, Hours	*Jurisdiction*
Embassy of Indonesia 2020 Massachusetts Avenue, NW Washington, DC 20036 Tel.: 202-775-5314 Fax: 202-775-5365 1:30 PM - 3:00 PM Monday - Thursday 10:00 AM - 12:30 PM Friday	Washington, DC
Consulate 2 Illinois Center 233 North Michigan Avenue Chicago, IL 60601 Tel.: 312-938-0101 Fax: 312-938-3148 9:00 AM - 5:00 PM	Illinois Indiana Iowa Kansas Kentucky Michigan Minnesota Missouri Nebraska Ohio North Dakota South Dakota Wisconsin
Consulate 10900 Richmond Avenue Houston, TX 77042 Tel.: 713-780-9644 Fax: 713-780-9644	Alabama Arkansas Florida Georgia Mississippi New Mexico Puerto Rico Tennessee Texas Virgin Islands Washington

Address, Phone, Hours	*Jurisdiction*
Consulate 3457 Wilshire Boulevard Los Angeles, CA 90010 Tel.: 213-383-5126 Fax: 213-487-3971 9:00 AM - 12:00 PM Mon. - Fri. 1:00 PM - 5:00 PM Mon. - Thurs. 2:00 PM - 5:00 PM Friday	Arizona California (southern) Colorado Hawaii Montana Nevada (southern) Utah Wyoming United States Islands of the Pacific
Consulate General 5 East 68th Street New York, NY 10021 Tel.: 212-879-0600 Fax: 212-487-3971 10:00 AM - 1:00 PM	Connecticut Delaware Maine Maryland Massachusetts New Hampshire New Jersey New York North Carolina Pennsylvania Rhode Island South Carolina Vermont Virginia West Virginia
Consulate 1111 Columbus Avenue San Francisco, CA 94133 Tel.: 415-474-9571 Fax: 415-441-4320 9:00 AM - 1:00 PM	Alaska California (northern) Idaho Nevada (northern) Oregon Washington

REPUBLIC OF IRAQ

I. GENERAL INFORMATION

The Iraq Interests Section of the Algerian Embassy will legalize documents originating anywhere in the United States.

II. REQUIREMENTS FOR LEGALIZATION

Prior Authentications Required
1. Notarization
2. Authentication of Notary Signature (In most states this may be done directly by the State Secretary of State; if not, the County Clerk authenticates the signature.)
3. State Secretary of State Certification (In states where the Notary Signature may be authenticated directly by the State Secretary of State, steps 2 and 3 are combined.)
4. U.S. Secretary of State Certification

Materials to be Submitted with Request
1. Original document to be legalized
2. Photocopy of the document
3. Prepaid, self-addressed return envelope

Direct Registration of Notary Public: Not available

Direct Signing of Document Before Consular Official: Not available

Turn Around Time: If the document is personally delivered, there may be a delay of from one to two days before legalization.

Fee: Contact Embassy; fees vary.

Payment Method: Certified check made payable to Iraq Interests Section

III. EMBASSY

Address, Phone, Hours	*Jurisdiction*
Iraq Interests Section Embassy of the Republic of Algeria 1801 P Street, NW Washington, DC 20036 Tel.: 202-483-7500 Fax: 202-462-5066 10:00 AM - 3:00 PM Monday through Friday	Entire United States

IRISH REPUBLIC

National Holiday: St. Patrick's Day, March 17

I. GENERAL INFORMATION

The Embassy and Consulates General have legalization functions. Each will legalize documents originating in its jurisdiction. The specific requirements for the Embassy and the New York Consulate General are given below.

The Embassy can legalize a document originating anywhere in the United States if the document is certified by the U.S. Department of State. It is preferred, however, that documents be presented for legalization at the appropriate local Consulate.

II. REQUIREMENTS FOR LEGALIZATION

Prior Authentications Required
The Embassy requires steps 1 through 4.
The New York Consulate requires steps 1, 2, and 3.

1. Notarization
2. Authentication of Notary Signature (In most states this may be done directly by the State Secretary of State; if not, the County Clerk authenticates the signature.)
3. State Secretary of State Certification (In states where the Notary Signature may be authenticated directly by the State Secretary of State, steps 2 and 3 are combined.)
4. U.S. Secretary of State Certification

Materials to be Submitted with Request
1. Original document to be legalized
2. Photocopy of the document required at the Embassy; photocopy not required at the Consulate
3. Prepaid, self-addressed return envelope for return service other than first class, which is advised

Direct Registration of Notary Public: Not available

Direct Signing of Document Before Consular Official: The procedure of certifying the signature of a private person is not available at the Embassy. The procedure of certifying the signature of a private person, however, is available at the New York Consulate. The signer must have proper identification with a photograph and signature, such as a passport and a driver's license. The New York Consulate requires two pieces of identification.

Turn Around Time: If the document is personally delivered, there will be a delay of two or three business days at the Embassy; the time at the New York Consulate depends on the volume of business.

Fee: $17.00 per document or signature

Payment Method: Cash, money order, certified check payable to the Embassy of the Irish Republic or Irish Consulate

III. EMBASSY AND CONSULATES GENERAL

Address, Phone, Hours	*Jurisdiction*
Embassy of the Irish Republic 2234 Massachusetts Avenue, NW Washington, DC 20008 Tel.: 202-462-3939 Fax: 202-232-5993 9:00 AM - 1:00 PM 2:00 PM - 4:00 PM	Maryland Virginia Washington, DC
Consulate General 535 Boylston Street Boston, MA 02116 Tel.: 617-267-9330	Maine Massachusetts New Hampshire Rhode Island Vermont
Consulate General 400 N. Michigan Avenue Chicago, IL 60611 Tel.: 312-337-1868 10:00 AM - 12:00 PM 2:00 PM - 4:00 PM	Alabama Arkansas Illinois Indiana Iowa Kansas Kentucky

Address, Phone, Hours	*Jurisdiction*
	Louisiana Michigan Minnesota Mississippi Missouri Nebraska North Dakota Ohio Oklahoma South Dakota Tennessee Texas Wisconsin
Consulate General 345 Park Avenue, 17th Floor New York, NY 10154 Tel.: 212-319-2555 10:00 AM - 3:00 PM	Connecticut Delaware Florida Georgia New Jersey New York North Carolina Pennsylvania South Carolina West Virginia
Consulate General 655 Montgomery Street, Suite 930 San Francisco, CA 94111 Tel.: 415-392-4214	Alaska Arizona California Colorado Hawaii Idaho Montana Nevada New Mexico Oregon Utah Washington Wyoming

STATE OF ISRAEL

National Holiday: Independence Day (Gregorian calendar date varies)

I. GENERAL INFORMATION

Israel is a party to the Hague Convention Abolishing the Requirement for Legalization for Foreign Public Documents.

A document should be sent to the appropriate authority in the state or territory in which the document is notarized in order to obtain the Apostille. For information on obtaining the Apostille for documents originating in the United States, see the procedures specified for each of the individual states under United States jurisdiction in Chapter 2. For the enumeration of Federal authorities competent to provide the Apostille, see Appendix D.

For the text of the Hague Convention, the Apostille, and a list of the parties to the Convention, see Appendix A.

For other services and fee information, please call the Embassy or one of the Consulates. Fees may be paid by cash or money order. For information purposes, the Embassy and Consulates General of Israel are listed below.

II. EMBASSY AND CONSULATES GENERAL

Address, Phone, Hours	*Jurisdiction*
Embassy of the State of Israel 3514 International Drive, NW Washington, DC 20008 Tel.: 202-364-5500 Fax: 202-364-5423	Maryland Virginia Washington, DC
Consulate General 1100 Spring Street, Suite 440 Atlanta, GA 30309-2823 Tel.: 404-875-7851/2 Fax: 404-874-5364	Alabama Georgia Mississippi North Carolina South Carolina Tennessee

Address, Phone, Hours	*Jurisdiction*
Consulate General 1020 Statler Office Building 20 Park Plaza Boston, MA 02116 Tel.: 617-542-0041/2/5 Fax: 617-338-4995	Maine Massachusetts New Hampshire Rhode Island Vermont
Consulate General 111 East Wacker Drive, Suite 1308 Chicago, IL 60601 Tel.: 312-565-3300 Fax: 312-565-3871	Illinois Indiana Iowa Kansas Michigan Minnesota Missouri Nebraska North Dakota South Dakota Wisconsin
Consulate General 24 Greenway Plaza, Suite 1500 Houston, TX 77046 Tel.: 713-627-3780 Fax: 713-627-0149	Arkansas Louisiana New Mexico Oklahoma Texas
Consulate General 6380 Wilshire Boulevard, Suite 1700 Los Angeles, CA 90048 Tel.: 213-852-5500 Fax: 213-852-5555	Arizona California (Southern) Colorado Hawaii Nevada Utah Wyoming
Consulate General 100 North Biscayne Boulevard, # 1800 Miami, FL 33132 Tel.: 305-358-8111 Fax: 305-371-5034	Florida Puerto Rico

Address, Phone, Hours	*Jurisdiction*
Consulate General/Mission to UN 800 Second Avenue New York, NY 10017 Tel.: 212-499-5300 Fax: 212-499-5477 9:15 AM - 12:00 PM	Connecticut New Jersey (Northern) New York Virgin Islands
Consulate General 230 South 15th Street, Suite 8 Philadelphia, PA 19102 Tel.: 215-546-5556/7 Fax: 215-545-3986	Delaware Kentucky New Jersey (Southern) Ohio Pennsylvania West Virginia
Consulate General 456 Montgomery Street, Suite 2100 San Francisco, CA 94104 Tel.: 415-398-8885 Fax: 415-398-8589	Alaska California (Northern) Idaho Montana Oregon Washington

ITALY

National Holiday: Anniversary of the Republic, June 2

I. GENERAL INFORMATION

Italy is a party to the Hague Convention Abolishing the Requirement for Legalization for Foreign Public Documents.

A document should be sent to the appropriate authority in the state or territory in which the document is notarized in order to obtain the Apostille. For information on obtaining the Apostille for documents originating in the United States, see the procedures specified for each of the individual states under United States jurisdiction in Chapter 2. For the enumeration of Federal authorities competent to provide the Apostille, see Appendix D.

For the text of the Hague Convention, the Apostille, and a list of the parties to the Convention, see Appendix A.

For information purposes, the Embassy, Consulates General, Consulates and an Honorary Consulate of Italy having legalization authority are listed below.

II. EMBASSY, CONSULATES GENERAL, CONSULATES, AND HONORARY CONSULATE

Address, Phone, Hours	*Jurisdiction*
Embassy of Italy Chancery 1601 Fuller Street, NW Washington, DC 20009 Tel.: 202-328-5500	Maryland counties of: Montgomery, Prince George Virginia counties of: Arlington, Fairfax (Rest of Maryland and Virginia under jurisdiction of Philadelphia Consulate) Washington, DC

Address, Phone, Hours	*Jurisdiction*
Honorary Consulate 5 Light Street, Suite 600 Baltimore, MD 21202 Tel.: 410-727-6550 Fax: 410-727-6563	Maryland except for Montgomery and Prince George counties
Consulate General 100 Boylston Street, Suite 900 Boston, MA 02116 Tel.: 617-542-0483/4 Fax: 617-542-3998	Maine Massachusetts New Hampshire Rhode Island Vermont
Consulate General 500 No. Michigan Avenue, Suite 1850 Chicago, IL 60611 Tel.: 312-467-1550/1/2/3 Fax: 312-467-1335	Colorado Illinois Iowa Kansas Minnesota Missouri Nebraska North Dakota South Dakota Wisconsin Wyoming
Consulate 535 Griswold 1840 Buhl Building Detroit, MI 48226 Tel.: 313-963-8560 Fax: 313-963-8180	Indiana Kentucky Michigan Ohio Tennessee
Consulate General 1300 Post Oak Boulevard, Suite 660 Houston, TX 77056 Tel.: 713-850-7520 Fax: 713-850-9113	Arkansas Louisiana Oklahoma Texas

Address, Phone, Hours	*Jurisdiction*
Consulate General 12400 Wilshire Boulevard Suite 300 Los Angeles, CA 90025 Tel.: 213-820-0622 Tel.: 213-826-6207 Fax: 310-820-0727	Arizona California counties of: Imperial Valley, Kern, Los Angeles, Orange, Riverside, San Diego, San Bernadino, San Luis Obispo, Santa Barbara, Ventura Nevada New Mexico
Consulate General 1200 Brickell Avenue, 8th Floor Miami, FL 33131 Tel.: 305-374-6322 Fax: 305-374-7945	Alabama Florida Georgia Mississippi Puerto Rico South Carolina British Virgin Islands Cayman Islands St. Maarten St. Eustatius Turks and Caicos Virgin Islands
Consulate General 690 Park Avenue New York, NY 10021 Tel.: 212-737-9100 Fax: 212-249-4945	Connecticut New Jersey counties of: Bergen, Essex, Hudson, Morris, Passaic, Sussex, Union (for visa only; for other requests, contact Newark Vice Consulate) New York Bermuda
Vice Consulate 744 Broad Street, Suite 2800 Newark, NJ 07102 Tel.: 201-643-1448 Fax: 201-643-3043	New Jersey counties of: Bergen, Essex, Hudson, Morris, Passaic, Sussex, Union, Warren (for visas, residents should contact New York)

Address, Phone, Hours	*Jurisdiction*
Consulate General 1026 Public Ledger Building 100 South Sixth Street Philadelphia, PA 19106-3470 Tel.: 215-592-7329 Fax: 215-592-9808	Delaware Maryland (except for Montgomery and Prince George counties) New Jersey counties of: Atlantic, Burlington, Camden, Cape May, Cumberland, Gloucester, Hunterdon, Mercer, Middlesex, Monmouth, Ocean, Salem, Somerset Pennsylvania North Carolina Virginia (except Arlington and Fairfax counties) West Virginia
Consulate General 2590 Webster Street San Francisco, CA 94115 Tel.: 415-931-4924 Fax: 415-931-7205	Alaska California except for counties of: Imperial Valley, Kern, Los Angeles, Orange, Riverside, San Bernadino, San Diego, San Luis Obispo, Santa Barbara, Ventura Hawaii Idaho Montana Oregon Utah Washington American Samoa Caroline Islands Guam Marshall Islands Yap Palau Mariana Islands

JAMAICA

National Holiday: August 2

I. GENERAL INFORMATION

The Embassy and Consulates General have legalization functions. Each will legalize documents originating within its jurisdiction.

II. REQUIREMENTS FOR LEGALIZATION

Prior Authentications Required
The Embassy requires steps 1 through 4.
The New York Consulate requires steps 1 and 2.

1. Notarization
2. Authentication of Notary Signature (In most states this may be done directly by the State Secretary of State; if not, the County Clerk authenticates the signature.)
3. State Secretary of State Certification (In states where the Notary Signature may be authenticated directly by the State Secretary of State, steps 2 and 3 are combined.)
4. U.S. Secretary of State Certification

Materials to be Submitted with Request
1. Original document to be legalized
2. Photocopy of the document
3. Prepaid, self-addressed return envelope

Direct Registration of Notary Public: Not available

Direct Signing of Document Before Consular Official: The procedure of certifying the signature of a private person is available. No appointment is necessary; however, the signer should ensure that the Consul is available to certify the signature. The signer must have identification in the form of an official document issued by the government, its departments or agencies, preferably bearing a photograph.

Fee: $20 per document

Payment Method: Cash or money order payable to the Embassy of Jamaica

III. EMBASSY AND CONSULATES GENERAL

As noted above, for legalization purposes the offices are not necessarily limited to the jurisdictions indicated below.

Address, Phone, Hours	*Jurisdiction*
Embassy of Jamaica 1520 New Hampshire Avenue, NW Washington, DC 20036 Tel.: 202-452-0660 Fax: 202-452-0081 9:30 AM - 3:30 PM	Entire United States
Consulate General 842 Ingraham Building 25 SE Second Avenue Miami, FL 33131 Tel.: 305-374-8431/2 Fax: 305-577-4970	Alabama Florida Georgia Louisiana Mississippi Tennessee Texas
Consulate General 767 Third Avenue, Third Floor New York, NY 10017 Tel.: 212-935-9000 9:30 AM - 3:30 PM	Alaska Arizona Arkansas California Connecticut Delaware Hawaii Idaho Illinois Indiana Iowa Kansas Kentucky Louisiana Maine Massachusetts Michigan Minnesota Nevada New Hampshire

Address, Phone, Hours	*Jurisdiction*
	New Jersey New Mexico New York North Carolina North Dakota Ohio Oklahoma Oregon Pennsylvania Puerto Rico Rhode Island South Carolina South Dakota Utah Vermont Virginia Washington West Virginia Wisconsin Wyoming

JAPAN

National Holiday: Birthday of the Emperor, December 23

I. GENERAL INFORMATION

Japan is a party to the Hague Convention Abolishing the Requirement for Legalization for Foreign Public Documents.

A document should be sent to the appropriate authority in the state or territory in which the document is notarized in order to obtain the Apostille. See Chapter 2 for listings of individual states and U.S. territories; see Appendix C for Federal authorities competent to grant the Apostille.

For general information on the Hague Convention and the Apostille, see Appendix A.

For information purposes, the Embassy and Consulates General of Japan are listed below.

II. EMBASSY AND CONSULATES GENERAL

Address, Phone, Hours	*Jurisdiction*
Embassy of Japan Chancery 2520 Massachusetts Avenue, NW Washington, DC 20008 Tel.: 202-939-6700 Fax: 202-328-2187	Maryland Virginia Washington, DC
Consulate General 550 West 7th Avenue, Suite 701 Anchorage, AK 99501 Tel.: 907-279-8248/9 Fax: 907-279-9271	Alaska

Address, Phone, Hours	*Jurisdiction*
Consulate General Federal Reserve Plaza, 14th Floor 600 Atlantic Avenue Boston, MA 02210 Tel.: 617-973-9772/3/4 Fax: 617-542-1329	Connecticut (except Fairfield County) Maine Massachusetts New Hampshire Rhode Island Vermont
Consulate General 100 Colony Square Building 1175 Peachtree Street, NE Atlanta, GA 30361 Tel.: 404-892-2700 Fax: 404-881-6321	Alabama Georgia North Carolina South Carolina
Consulate General Olympia Centre, Suite 1100 737 N. Michigan Avenue Chicago, IL 60611 Tel.: 312-280-0400 Fax: 312-280-9568	Illinois Indiana Minnesota Wisconsin
Consulate General 200 Renaissance Center, Suite 3450 Detroit, MI 48243 Tel.: 313-567-0120 Fax: 313-567-0274	Michigan Ohio
Consulate General 1742 Nuuanu Avenue Honolulu, HI 06817-3294 Tel.: 808-536-2226 Fax: 808-527-3276	Hawaii U.S. possessions not covered by other offices
Consulate General 1000 Louisiana Street, Suite 5300 Houston, TX 77002 Tel.: 713-652-2977 Fax: 713-651-7822	Oklahoma Texas

Address, Phone, Hours	*Jurisdiction*
Consulate General 2519 Commerce Tower 911 Main Street Kansas City, MO 64105-2076 Tel.: 816-471-0111 Fax: 816-472-4248	Iowa Kansas Missouri Nebraska North Dakota South Dakota
Consulate General 350 South Grand Avenue, Suite 1700 Los Angeles, CA 90071 Tel.: 213-617-6700 Fax: 213-617-6727	Arizona California (south) New Mexico
Consulate General World Trade Center Bldg., Suite 3200 80 SW 8th Street Miami, FL 33139 Tel.: 305-530-9090 Fax: 305-530-0950	Florida
Consulate General One Poydras Plaza, Suite 2050 639 Loyola Avenue New Orleans, LA 70113 Tel.: 504-529-2101 Fax: 504-568-9847	Arkansas Kentucky Louisiana Mississippi Tennessee
Consulate General 299 Park Avenue New York, NY 10171 Tel.: 212-371-8222 Fax: 212-319-6357	Connecticut (Fairfield County) Delaware New Jersey New York Pennsylvania West Virginia

Address, Phone, Hours	*Jurisdiction*
Consulate General 2400 First Interstate Tower 1300 SW 5th Avenue Portland, OR 97201 Tel.: 503-221-1811 Fax: 503-224-8936	Idaho (south) Oregon Wyoming
Consulate General 50 Fremont Street, Suite 2300 San Francisco, CA 94105 Tel.: 415-777-3533 Fax: 415-974-3660	California (north) Colorado Nevada Utah
Consulate General 601 Union Street, Suite 500 Seattle, WA 98101 Tel.: 206-682-9107 Fax: 206-624-9097	Idaho (north) Montana Washington
Consulate General Guam Int'l. Trade Center Building 590 South Marine Drive Tamuning, Agana, Guam 96911 Tel.: 671-646-1290/5220	Guam U.S. Pacific Territories
Consular Office Horiguchi Building, Fifth Floor Broadway Street Garapan, Saipan Commonwealth of the Northern Marianas Islands, 96950 Tel.: 670-234-7201/2	Commonwealth of the Northern Marianas Islands

JORDAN

National Holiday: May 25

I. GENERAL INFORMATION

The Embassy and Consulate General have legalization functions. Consular fees are subject to change without notice.

All commercial invoices and shipping-related certificates must be certified by the U.S. Arab Chamber of Commerce. For information on National U.S.-Arab Chamber of Commerce procedures and addresses, see Appendix C.

II. REQUIREMENTS FOR LEGALIZATION

Prior Authentications Required
1. Notarization
2. Authentication of Notary Signature (In most states this may be done directly by the State Secretary of State; if not, the County Clerk authenticates the signature.)
3. State Secretary of State Certification (In states where the Notary Signature may be authenticated directly by the State Secretary of State, steps 2 and 3 are combined.)
4. U.S. Secretary of State Certification

Materials to be Submitted with Request
1. Original document to be legalized
2. Prepaid, self-addressed return envelope

Direct Registration of Notary Public: Not available

Direct Signing of Document Before Consular Official: Not available

Turn Around Time: If the document is personally delivered, there will be a delay of approximately three days before legalization.

Fee: $8.00 for certificates of origin et al., power of attorney, assignment of agent, trademark, article of incorporation, agreement, contract, affidavit
$8.00 to $20.00 for invoices, depending on amount of invoice
Consular fees are subject to change without notice, as noted.

Payment Method: Money order or certified check payable to the Consular Section, Embassy of Jordan

III. EMBASSY AND CONSULATE

Address, Phone, Hours	*Jurisdiction*
Embassy of Jordan 3504 International Drive, NW Washington, DC 20008 Tel.: 202-966-8757 10:00 AM - 1:30 PM	Entire United States
Consulate Permanent Mission to the United States 866 United Nations Plaza, Room 554 New York, NY 10017 Tel.: 212-355-9342 Fax: 212-826-0830	East Coast

REPUBLIC OF KAZAKSTAN

National Holidays: January 1, January 2, March 8, March 22, May 1, May 9, August 30, October 25, December 16

I. REQUIREMENTS FOR LEGALIZATION

Prior Authentications Required

1. Notarization
2. Authentication of Notary Signature (In most states this may be done directly by the State Secretary of State; if not, the County Clerk authenticates the signature.)
3. State Secretary of State Certification (In states where the Notary Signature may be authenticated directly by the State Secretary of State, steps 2 and 3 are combined.)
4. U.S. Secretary of State Certification

Materials to be Submitted with Request

1. Original document to be legalized
2. Photocopy of the document
3. Prepaid, self-addressed return envelope

Direct Registration of Notary Public: Not available

Direct Signing of Document Before Consular Official: The procedure of certifying the signature of a private person is available at the Embassy. An appointment should be made and the signer must present a valid passport as identification.

Turn Around Time: Documents must be left for seven days for legalization, whether they are personally delivered or mailed.

Fee: $50 per document or signature

Payment Method: Money order or company check, payable to the Embassy of Kazakstan

II. EMBASSY

Address, Phone, Hours	*Jurisdiction*
Embassy of the Republic of Kazakstan 3421 Massachusetts Avenue, NW Washington, DC 20007 Tel.: 202-333-4504 Fax: 202-333-4509 9:00 AM - 12:00 PM	Entire United States

KENYA

National Holiday: December 12

I. GENERAL INFORMATION

Only the Embassy has legalization functions.

II. REQUIREMENTS FOR LEGALIZATION

Prior Authentications Required
1. Notarization
2. Authentication of Notary Signature (In most states this may be done directly by the State Secretary of State; if not, the County Clerk authenticates the signature.)
3. State Secretary of State Certification (In states where the Notary Signature may be authenticated directly by the State Secretary of State, steps 2 and 3 are combined.)
4. U.S. Secretary of State Certification

Materials to be Submitted with Request
1. Original document to be legalized
2. Prepaid, self-addressed return envelope

Direct Registration of Notary Public: Not available

Direct Signing of Document Before Consular Official: The procedure of certifying the signature of a private person is available at the Embassy and Consulates General. An appointment should be made and the signer must present either a passport or a driver's license as identification.

Turn Around Time: If the document is personally delivered, it will be legalized immediately if the work load is not too great.

Fee: $8.00 per document or signature

Payment Method: Money order, certified check, company check payable to the Embassy of Kenya

III. EMBASSY AND CONSULATES GENERAL

Address, Phone, Hours	*Jurisdiction*
Embassy of Kenya 2249 R Street, NW Washington DC 20008 Tel.: 202-387-6101 Fax: 202-462-3829 9:00 AM - 1:00 PM 2:00 PM - 5:00 PM	Entire United States
Consulate General 424 Madison Avenue New York, NY 10017 Tel.: 212-486-1300 9:00 AM - 5:00 PM	Entire United States
Consulate General 9150 Wilshire Boulevard, Suite 160 Los Angeles, CA 90212 Tel.: 310-274-6635 9:00 AM - 5:00 PM	Entire United States

DEMOCRATIC PEOPLE'S REPUBLIC OF KOREA

I. GENERAL INFORMATION

The Democratic People's Republic of Korea does not have diplomatic relations with the United States and therefore has no U.S. Embassy. It does not legalize documents. It does have a permanent mission to the UN which is listed below for information purposes.

II. PERMANENT MISSION TO THE UN

Democratic People's Republic of Korea
Permanent Mission to the UN
820 Second Avenue, 13th Floor
New York, NY 10017
Tel.: 212-972-3105
Fax: 212-972-3154
9:00 AM - 5:00 PM

REPUBLIC OF KOREA

National Holiday: Independence Day, August 15

I. GENERAL INFORMATION

The Embassy does not legalize documents. The Consulates General have legalization functions. Each will legalize documents originating in its jurisdiction.

II. REQUIREMENTS FOR LEGALIZATION

Prior Authentications Required
1. Notarization

Materials to be Submitted with Request
1. Original document to be legalized
2. Photocopy of the document
3. Prepaid, self-addressed return envelope

Turn Around Time: If the document is personally delivered, there will be a delay of one day before legalization at the New York Consulate General.

Direct Registration of Notary Public: Not available

Direct Signing of Document Before Consular Official: The procedure of certifying the signature of a private person is available at the New York Consulate.

Fee: $3.00 per document or signature

Payment Method: Cash in person only, money order, certified check, company check payable to the Korean Consulate General

III. EMBASSY AND CONSULATES GENERAL

Address, Phone, Hours	*Jurisdiction*
Embassy of the Republic of Korea Consular Office 2320 Massachusetts Avenue, NW Washington, DC 20008 Tel.: 202-939-5600 Fax: 202-342-1597 9:30 AM - 12:00 PM 1:30 PM - 5:00 PM	Maryland Virginia Washington, DC
Consulate General GCIC Building, Suite 305 414 West Soledad Avenue Agana, Guam 96910 Tel.: 671-472-8076 Fax: 671-477-6391	Guam
Consulate General 101 Benson Building, Suite 304 Anchorage, AK 99503 Tel.: 907-561-5488 Fax: 907-563-0313	Alaska
Consulate General International Tower Suite 500 229 Peachtree Street Atlanta, GA 30303 Tel.: 404-522-1611 Fax: 404-521-3169	Alabama Georgia North Carolina South Carolina Tennessee
Consulate General One Financial Center, 15th Floor Boston, MA 02111 Tel.: 617-348-3660 Fax: 617-348-3670	Maine Massachusetts New Hampshire Rhode Island Vermont

Address, Phone, Hours	*Jurisdiction*
Consulate General NBC Tower, 27th Floor 455 North City Front Plaza Drive Chicago, IL 60611 Tel.: 312-822-9485 Fax: 312-822-9849	Illinois Indiana Iowa Kansas Kentucky Michigan Minnesota Missouri Nebraska North Dakota Ohio South Dakota Wisconsin
Consulate General 2756 Pali Highway Honolulu, HI 96817 Tel.: 808-595-6109 Fax: 808-595-3046	Hawaii Samoa
Consulate General Suite 1250 Three Post Oak Central Building 1990 Post Oak Boulevard Houston, TX 77056 Tel.: 713-961-0186/4866 Fax: 713-961-3340	Arkansas Louisiana Mississippi Oklahoma Texas Canal Zone
Consulate General 3243 Wilshire Boulevard Los Angeles, CA 90010 Tel.: 213-385-9300 Fax: 213-385-1849	Arizona Nevada New Mexico Southern California
Consulate General 201 South Biscayne Boulevard, Suite 800 Miami, FL 33131 Tel.: 305-372-1555 Fax: 305-371-6559	Florida Puerto Rico Virgin Islands

Address, Phone, Hours	*Jurisdiction*
Consulate General 460 Park Avenue, 5th Floor New York, NY 10022 Tel.: 212-752-1700 Fax: 212-888-6320 9:30 AM - 12:00 PM 1:30 PM - 4:00 PM	Connecticut Delaware New Jersey New York Pennsylvania West Virginia
Consulate General 3500 Clay Street San Francisco, CA 94118 Tel.: 415-921-2251 Fax: 415-931-6330	Colorado Northern California Utah Washington
Consulate General United Airlines Building, Suite 1125 2033 6th Avenue Seattle, WA 98121 Tel.: 206-441-1011/4 Fax: 206-441-7912	Idaho Montana Oregon Washington

STATE OF KUWAIT

National Holiday: February 25

I. GENERAL INFORMATION

The Embassy and the Consulate in New York legalize documents from anywhere in the United States. The Embassy will legalize documents certified by either the U.S. Secretary of State or the Secretary of the US-Arab Chamber of Commerce in San Francisco, New York, or Washington, DC. For information on National U.S.-Arab Chamber of Commerce procedures and addresses, see Appendix B.

The information in Section II below, for commercial documents such as Powers of Attorney, applies to the Embassy and to the New York Consulate.

Requirements for other types of documents, such as Certificates of Origin and other shipping documents, are covered in Section III.

II. REQUIREMENTS FOR LEGALIZATION FOR COMMERCIAL DOCUMENTS SUCH AS POWERS OF ATTORNEY, AGENCY AGREEMENTS, BOARD RESOLUTIONS, ETC.

Prior Authentication Required
The Embassy requires steps 1 through 4. (Personal documents, such as personal powers of attorney, diplomas, and marriage certificates require only notarization.)
The New York Consulate requires steps 1 through 3.

1. Notarization
2. Authentication of Notary Signature (In most states this may be done directly by the State Secretary of State; if not, the County Clerk authenticates the signature.)
3. State Secretary of State Certification (In states where the Notary Signature may be authenticated directly by the State Secretary of State, steps 2 and 3 are combined.)
4. U.S. Secretary of State Certification or Certification by a U.S. Arab Chamber of Commerce in the following cities only: Chicago, New York, San Francisco, Washington DC.

Materials to be Submitted with Request

1. Original document to be legalized; original copies to be legalized must be stapled together and marked "Originals to be returned."
2. Photocopy of the document; duplicate copies to be retained by the Consular office file must be marked "Consulate's Copies."
3. Prepaid, self-addressed return envelope

Direct Registration of Notary Public: Not available

Direct Signing of Document Before Consular Official: Not available

Turn Around Time: Not specified

Fee: $16.00

Payment Method: The Embassy will accept cash, money orders, or company checks; the New York Consulate requests money orders or certified checks. Personal checks are not accepted.

III. REQUIREMENTS FOR LEGALIZATION COMMERCIAL DOCUMENTS SUCH AS CERTIFICATES OF ORIGIN AND OTHER SHIPPING DOCUMENTS

The information given below covers the requirements for the New York Consulate.

Prior Authentications Required

All documents must be certified by a U.S. Arab Chamber of Commerce, following the requirements of those offices. For information on National U.S.-Arab Chamber of Commerce procedures and addresses, see Appendix B.

All certificates of origin and invoices must show the names of the manufacturers and the country of origin of the goods being shipped.

Other Requirements: See Section II above.

Fee: $24.00

IV. EMBASSY AND CONSULATE

Address, Phone, Hours	*Jurisdiction*
Embassy of the State of Kuwait 2940 Tilden Street, NW Washington, DC 20008 Tel.: 202-966-0702 9:30 AM - 1:00 PM	Entire United States
Consulate 321 East 44th Street New York, NY 10017 Tel.: 212-973-4318 9:30 AM - 5:00 PM	Entire United States

THE PEOPLE'S DEMOCRATIC REPUBLIC OF LAOS

National Holiday: December 2

I. REQUIREMENTS FOR LEGALIZATION

Prior Authentications Required

1. Notarization
2. Authentication of Notary Signature (In most states this may be done directly by the State Secretary of State; if not, the County Clerk authenticates the signature.)
3. State Secretary of State Certification (In states where the Notary Signature may be authenticated directly by the State Secretary of State, steps 2 and 3 are combined.)
4. U.S. Secretary of State Certification

Materials to be Submitted with Request

1. Original document to be legalized
2. Photocopy of the document
3. Prepaid, self-addressed return envelope

Direct Registration of Notary Public: Not available

Direct Signing of Document Before Consular Official: Not available

Turn Around Time: If the document is personally delivered, it must be left for three days for legalization. If the document is mailed, allow three days for legalization.

Fee: $10.00 per document or signature

Payment Method: Money order, certified check, company check payable to the Embassy of Laos

II. EMBASSY

Address, Phone, Hours	*Jurisdiction*
Embassy of the People's Democratic Republic of Laos 2222 S Street, NW Washington, DC 20008 Tel.: 202-332-6416 Fax: 202-332-4923 9:00 AM - 12:00 PM 1:00 PM - 4:30 PM	Entire United States

LATVIA

I. GENERAL INFORMATION

Latvia is a party to the Hague Convention Abolishing the Requirement for Legalization for Foreign Public Documents. Note, however, that documents executed by diplomatic or consular agents and administrative documents dealing directly with commercial or customs operations must be legalized if they are to be used in Latvia.

A document should be sent to the appropriate authority in the state or territory in which the document is notarized in order to obtain the Apostille. For information on obtaining the Apostille for documents originating in the United States, see the procedures specified for each of the individual states under United States jurisdiction in Chapter 2. For the enumeration of Federal authorities competent to provide the Apostille, see Appendix D.

For the text of the Hague Convention, the Apostille, and a list of the parties to the Convention, see Appendix A.

Documents executed by diplomatic or consular agents and administrative documents dealing directly with commercial or customs operations must be legalized if they are to be used in Latvia.

For information purposes, the Embassy of Latvia is listed below.

II. EMBASSY

Address, Phone, Hours

Embassy of Latvia
4325 17th Street, NW
Washington, DC 20011
Tel.: 202-726-8213
Fax: 202-726-6785
10:00 AM - 12:00 PM weekdays

LEBANON

I. GENERAL INFORMATION

The Embassy and Consulates General have legalization functions. Each will legalize documents originating in its jurisdiction. Requirements vary depending on the type of document involved.

II. REQUIREMENTS FOR LEGALIZATION

Prior Authentications Required

1. Notarization
2. Authentication of Notary Signature (In most states this may be done directly by the State Secretary of State; if not, the County Clerk authenticates the signature. Copies of witness{es}'s ID are required.)
3. State Secretary of State Certification (In states where the Notary Signature may be authenticated directly by the State Secretary of State, steps 2 and 3 are combined.)

Materials to be Submitted with Request

1. Original document to be legalized
2. Photocopy of the document
3. Prepaid, self-addressed return envelope

Direct Registration of Notary Public: Not available

Direct Signing of Document Before Consular Official: The procedure of certifying the signature of a private person is available at the Embassy and Consulates General. An appointment should be made and the signer must present identification such as a driver's license.

Turn Around Time: If the document is personally delivered, there will be a delay of three working days before legalization.

Fee: $15.00 to $125.00 depending on the type of document

Payment Method: Money order, certified check, company check

III. EMBASSY AND CONSULATES GENERAL

Address, Phone, Hours	*Jurisdiction*
Embassy of Lebanon 2560 28th Street, NW Washington DC 20008 Tel.: 202-939-6300 extensions 200, 201, 202 9:00 AM - 3:30 PM	Arkansas Delaware Florida Georgia Kansas Louisiana Maryland North Carolina Oklahoma South Carolina Tennessee Texas Virginia Washington, DC
Consulate General 1959 East Jefferson Street Detroit, MI 48207 Tel.: 313-567-0233	Illinois Indiana Iowa Kentucky Michigan Minnesota Missouri Nebraska North Dakota Ohio South Dakota West Virginia Wisconsin
Consulate General 7060 Hollywood Boulevard, Suite 510 Los Angeles, CA 90028 Tel.: 213-467-1253	Alaska Arizona California Colorado Hawaii Idaho Montana Nevada

Address, Phone, Hours	*Jurisdiction*
	New Mexico Oregon Utah Washington Wyoming
Consulate General 9 East 76th Street New York, NY 10021 Tel.: 212-744-7905 Fax: 212-794-1510 9:00 AM - 2:00 PM	Connecticut Delaware Maine Massachusetts New Hampshire New Jersey New York Pennsylvania Rhode Island Vermont

KINGDOM OF LESOTHO

National Holiday: October 4

I. GENERAL INFORMATION

The Embassy does not legalize documents. Documents to be authenticated must be sent to the Ministry of Law and Constitutional Affairs, P.O. Box 33, Maseru, Lesotho. The Ministry's telephone number in Maseru is 111-60.

II. EMBASSY

Embassy of the Kingdom of Lesotho
2511 Massachusetts Avenue, NW
Washington, DC 20008
Tel.: 202-797-6300

REPUBLIC OF LIBERIA

National Holidays: Independence Day, July 26; February 11, March 15, May 14, May 25, July 26, August 24, October 24, November 29, second Wednesday in March, second Friday in April, second Thursday in November

I. GENERAL INFORMATION

The Embassy and New York Consulate General have legalization functions. The information below pertains to the Embassy and the New York Consulate General. Trade documents for corporate and maritime programs should be sent to the administrative representative at:

International Registries, Inc.
11495 Commerce Park Drive
Reston, VA 20191
Tel.: 703-630-4880
Fax: 703-476-8522
9:00 AM - 5:00 PM

II. REQUIREMENTS FOR LEGALIZATION

Prior Authentications Required
The Embassy requires steps 1 through 4. The New York Consulate requires steps 1 and 2.

1. Notarization
2. Authentication of Notary Signature (In most states this may be done directly by the State Secretary of State; if not, the County Clerk authenticates the signature.)
3. State Secretary of State Certification (In states where the Notary Signature may be authenticated directly by the State Secretary of State, steps 2 and 3 are combined.)
4. U.S. Secretary of State Certification

Materials to be Submitted with Request
1. Original document to be legalized
2. Photocopy of the document
3. Prepaid, self-addressed return envelope

Direct Registration of Notary Public: Not available

Direct Signing of Document Before Consular Official: The procedure of certifying the signature of a private person is available at the New York Consulate General. An appointment is not required. The signer must present identification such as a passport.

Turn Around Time: If the document is personally delivered, there will be a delay of three days at the Embassy.

Fee: $30.00 per document or signature

Payment Method: Money order, certified check, company checks payable to the Embassy of Liberia or to the Consulate General of Liberia.

III. EMBASSY AND CONSULATE GENERAL

Address, Phone, Hours	*Jurisdiction*
Embassy of the Republic of Liberia 5201 16th Street Washington, DC 20011 Tel.: 202-723-0437/8/9/40 Fax: 202-723-0436 10:00 AM - 5:00 PM	Entire United States Canada
Consulate General 820 Second Avenue New York, NY 10017 Tel.: 212-687-1025/33 Fax: 212-687-1035 10:30 AM - 12:00 PM	Entire United States Canada

PRINCIPALITY OF LIECHTENSTEIN

The Principality of Liechtenstein is a party to the Hague Convention Abolishing the Requirement for Legalization for Foreign Public Documents.

A document should be sent to the appropriate authority in the state or territory in which the document is notarized in order to obtain the Apostille. For information on obtaining the Apostille for documents originating in the United States, see the procedures specified for each of the individual states under United States jurisdiction in Chapter 2. For the enumeration of Federal authorities competent to provide the Apostille, see Appendix D.

For the text of the Hague Convention, the Apostille, and a list of the parties to the Convention, see Appendix A.

For those instances in which legalization may be necessary, this service is provided for Liechtenstein by the Swiss Embassy or its consular offices for their jurisdiction. See the Swiss Confederation for specific information.

LITHUANIA

National Holidays: February 16, Easter Monday, July 6, November 1

I. GENERAL INFORMATION

The Embassy in Washington, DC does not exercise legalization functions. Only the Consulate General in New York has legalization functions. Requirements for legalization depend on the type of document involved.

II. REQUIREMENTS FOR LEGALIZATION

Prior Authentications Required

1. Notarization
2. Authentication of Notary Signature (In most states this may be done directly by the State Secretary of State; if not, the County Clerk authenticates the signature.)
3. State Secretary of State Certification (In states where the Notary Signature may be authenticated directly by the State Secretary of State, steps 2 and 3 are combined.)
4. U.S. Secretary of State Certification

Materials to be Submitted with Request

1. Original document to be legalized
2. Prepaid, self-addressed return envelope

Direct Registration of Notary Public: Not available

Direct Signing of Document Before Consular Official: Not available

Turn Around Time: If an appointment is made and an additional fee of $10 paid, the document may be legalized immediately.

Fee: $10.00 per document or signature

Payment Method: Cash, money order, certified check, company check, personal check

II. EMBASSY AND CONSULATE GENERAL

Address, Phone, Hours	*Jurisdiction*
Embassy of Lithuania 2622 16th Street, NW Washington, DC 20009 Tel.: 202-234-5860	Entire United States
Consulate General 420 Fifth Avenue, Third Floor New York, NY 10018 Tel.: 212-354-7849 Fax: 212-354-7911 10:00 AM - 3:00 PM Tuesday through Thursday	Entire United States

GRAND DUCHY OF LUXEMBOURG

National Holiday: National Day, June 23

I. GENERAL INFORMATION

The Grand Duchy of Luxembourg is a party to the Hague Convention Abolishing the Requirement for Legalization for Foreign Public Documents.

A document should be sent to the appropriate authority in the state or territory in which the document is notarized in order to obtain the Apostille. For information on obtaining the Apostille for documents originating in the United States, see the procedures specified for each of the individual states under United States jurisdiction in Chapter 2. For the enumeration of Federal authorities competent to provide the Apostille, see Appendix D.

For the text of the Hague Convention, the Apostille, and a list of the parties to the Convention, see Appendix A.

For information purposes, the Embassy and Consulates General of the Grand Duchy of Luxembourg are listed below.

II. EMBASSY AND CONSULATES GENERAL

Address, Phone, Hours	*Jurisdiction*
Embassy of the Grand Duchy of Liechtenstein 2200 Massachusetts Avenue, NW Washington, DC 20008 Tel.: 202-265-4171 Fax: 202-328-8270 By appointment only	States not covered by the San Francisco and New York Consulates General

Address, Phone, Hours	*Jurisdiction*
Consulate General 1 Sansome Street San Francisco, CA 94104 Tel.: 415-788-0816 Fax: 415-788-0985	Arizona Alaska California Colorado Hawaii Idaho Montana Nevada New Mexico Oregon Washington Utah
Consulate General 17 Beekman Place New York, NY 10022 Tel.: 212-888-6664	Connecticut Delaware Maine Massachusetts New Hampshire New Jersey New York Pennsylvania Rhode Island Vermont

DEMOCRATIC REPUBLIC OF MADAGASCAR

National Holidays: Easter Monday, March 29, May 1, June 26, November 1

I. GENERAL INFORMATION

Madagascar has an Embassy in the United States but no Consulates. Documents from anywhere in the United States may be sent to the Embassy for legalization.

II. REQUIREMENTS FOR LEGALIZATION

Prior Authentications Required
1. Notarization
2. Authentication of Notary Signature (In most states this may be done directly by the State Secretary of State; if not, the County Clerk authenticates the signature.)
3. State Secretary of State Certification (In states where the Notary Signature may be authenticated directly by the State Secretary of State, steps 2 and 3 are combined.)
4. U.S. Secretary of State Certification

Materials to be Submitted with Request
1. Original document to be legalized
2. Photocopy of the document
3. Prepaid, self-addressed return envelope

Direct Registration of Notary Public: Not available

Direct Signing of Document Before Consular Official: Not available

Turn Around Time: If the document is personally delivered, there will be a delay of 48 hours before legalization.

Fee: $0.87

Payment Method: Cash, money order, certified check, company check

III. EMBASSY

Address, Phone, Hours	*Jurisdiction*
Embassy of the Democratic Republic of Madagascar 2374 Massachusetts Avenue, NW Washington, DC 20008 Tel.: 202-265-5525 Fax: 202-265-3034 10:00 AM - 1:00 PM 2:00 PM - 4:00 PM	Entire United States

REPUBLIC OF MALAWI

National Holiday: Independence Day, July 6

I. GENERAL INFORMATION

The Republic of Malawi is a party to the Hague Convention Abolishing the Requirement for Legalization for Foreign Public Documents. The Hague Convention is given domestic effect in the Authentication of Documents Act Cap (4:06) of the Laws of Malawi.

A document should be sent to the appropriate authority in the state or territory in which the document is notarized in order to obtain the Apostille. For information on obtaining the Apostille for documents originating in the United States, see the procedures specified for each of the individual states under United States jurisdiction in Chapter 2. For the enumeration of Federal authorities competent to provide the Apostille, see Appendix D.

For the text of the Hague Convention, the Apostille, and a list of the parties to the Convention, see Appendix A.

For information purposes, the Embassy is listed below.

II. EMBASSY

Embassy of the Republic of Malawi
2408 Massachusetts Avenue, NW
Washington, DC 20008
Tel.: 202-797-1007
Fax: 202-265-0976

MALAYSIA

National Holiday: August 31

I. GENERAL INFORMATION

The Embassy and Consulates General have legalization functions. Each will legalize documents originating in its jurisdiction.

II. REQUIREMENTS FOR LEGALIZATION

Prior Authentications Required

1. Notarization
2. Authentication of Notary Signature (In most states this may be done directly by the State Secretary of State; if not, the County Clerk authenticates the signature.)
3. State Secretary of State Certification (In states where the Notary Signature may be authenticated directly by the State Secretary of State, steps 2 and 3 are combined.)
4. U.S. Secretary of State Certification

Materials to be Submitted with Request

1. Original document to be legalized
2. Cover letter
3. Prepaid, self-addressed return envelope

Direct Registration of Notary Public: Not available

Direct Signing of Document Before Consular Official: Not available

Fee: $5.00 per document or signature

Payment Method: Money order, certified check, company check payable to the Embassy or Consulate General of Malaysia

III. EMBASSY AND CONSULATES GENERAL

Address, Phone, Hours	*Jurisdiction*
Embassy of Malaysia 2401 Massachusetts Avenue, NW Washington, DC 20036 Tel.: 202-328-2700 Fax: 202-483-7661 9:00 AM - 1:00 PM 2:00 PM - 5:00 PM	Alabama Florida Georgia Illinois Indiana Kentucky Louisiana Maryland Massachusetts North Carolina Ohio South Carolina Tennessee Texas Virginia Washington, DC West Virginia
Consulate General 550 South Hope Street, Suite 400 Los Angeles, CA 90071 Tel.: 213-621-2991 Fax: 213-892-9031	Alaska Arizona California Colorado Hawaii Idaho Indiana Kansas Montana Nebraska Nevada New Mexico Oregon South Dakota Utah Washington Wyoming

Address, Phone, Hours	*Jurisdiction*
Consulate General 313 East 43rd Street New York, NY 10017 Tel.: 212-490-2722 Fax: 212-490-8676	Arizona Connecticut Delaware Iowa Maine Massachusetts Michigan Minnesota Missouri New Hampshire New Jersey New York Oklahoma Pennsylvania Rhode Island Vermont Wisconsin

MALI

National Holiday: September 22

I. REQUIREMENTS FOR LEGALIZATION

Prior Authentications Required
1. Notarization
2. Authentication of Notary Signature (In most states this may be done directly by the State Secretary of State; if not, the County Clerk authenticates the signature.)
3. State Secretary of State Certification (In states where the Notary Signature may be authenticated directly by the State Secretary of State, steps 2 and 3 are combined.)
4. U.S. Secretary of State Certification

Materials to be Submitted with Request
1. Original document to be legalized
2. Prepaid, self-addressed return envelope

Direct Registration of Notary Public: Not available

Direct Signing of Document Before Consular Official: Not available

Turn Around Time: If the document is personally delivered, there may be a delay of 24 to 48 hours before legalization.

Fee: $10.00 per page

Payment Method: Cash, money order payable to the Embassy of Mali

II. EMBASSY

Address, Phone, Hours	*Jurisdiction*
Embassy of Mali 2130 R Street, NW Washington, DC 20008 Tel.: 202-232-2249 Fax: 202-232-6603 9:00 AM - 5:00 PM	Entire United States

MALTA

National Holiday: Independence Day, September 21

I. GENERAL INFORMATION

Malta is a party to the Hague Convention Abolishing the Requirement for Legalization for Foreign Public Documents.

A document should be sent to the appropriate authority in the state or territory in which the document is notarized in order to obtain the Apostille. For information on obtaining the Apostille for documents originating in the United States, see the procedures specified for each of the individual states under United States jurisdiction in Chapter 2. For the enumeration of Federal authorities competent to provide the Apostille, see Appendix D.

For the text of the Hague Convention, the Apostille, and a list of the parties to the Convention, see Appendix A.

For information purposes, the Embassy and New York Consulate of Malta are listed below.

II. EMBASSY AND CONSULATE

Address, Phone, Hours	*Jurisdiction*
Embassy and Consulate 2017 Connecticut Avenue, NW Washington, DC 20008 Tel.: 202-462-3611/2 Fax: 202-387-5470 9:00 AM - 12:00 PM 1:30 PM - 5:00 PM	Entire United States except for New York Consulate jurisdiction
Consulate 249 East 35th Street New York, NY 10016 Tel.: 212-725-2345	Connecticut New Jersey counties: Bergen, Essex, Hunterdon, Mercer, Middlesex, Monmouth, Morris, Passaic, Somerset, Sussex, Union, Warren, New York

MARSHALL ISLANDS

National Holiday: May 1

I. GENERAL INFORMATION

The Embassy has legalization functions but does not legalize all types of documents. Trade documents for corporate and maritime programs should be sent to the administrative representative at:

International Registries, Inc.
11495 Commerce Park Drive
Reston, VA 20191
Tel.: 703-630-4880
Fax: 703-476-8522
9:00 AM - 5:00 PM

II. EMBASSY

Embassy of the Republic of the Marshall Islands
2433 Massachusetts Avenue, NW
Washington, DC 20008
Tel.: 202-234-5414
Fax: 202-232-3236
9:00 AM - 4:00 PM

MARTINIQUE

I. GENERAL INFORMATION

Martinique is an Overseas Department of France, covered by the Hague Convention Abolishing the Requirement for Legalization for Foreign Public Documents.

A document should be sent to the appropriate authority in the state or territory in which the document is notarized in order to obtain the Apostille. For information on obtaining the Apostille for documents originating in the United States, see the procedures specified for each of the individual states under United States jurisdiction in Chapter 2. For the enumeration of Federal authorities competent to provide the Apostille, see Appendix D.

For the text of the Hague Convention, the Apostille, and a list of the parties to the Convention, see Appendix A.

For information on French Consulates, see France.

THE ISLAMIC REPUBLIC OF MAURITANIA

I. GENERAL INFORMATION

The Embassy does not have legalization functions and was unable to provide additional information.

II. EMBASSY

Embassy of the Islamic Republic of Mauritania
2129 Leroy Place, NW
Washington, DC 20008
Tel.: 202-232-5700
Fax: 202-319-2623
9:00 AM - 5:00 PM

MAURITIUS

National Holiday: Independence Day, March 12

I. GENERAL INFORMATION

Mauritius is a party to the Hague Convention Abolishing the Requirement for Legalization for Foreign Public Documents.

A document should be sent to the appropriate authority in the state or territory in which the document is notarized in order to obtain the Apostille. For information on obtaining the Apostille for documents originating in the United States, see the procedures specified for each of the individual states under United States jurisdiction in Chapter 2. For the enumeration of Federal authorities competent to provide the Apostille, see Appendix D.

For the text of the Hague Convention, the Apostille, and a list of the parties to the Convention, see Appendix A.

For information purposes, the Embassy of Mauritius is listed below.

II. EMBASSY

Address, Phone, Hours	*Jurisdiction*
Embassy of Mauritius Chancery Suite 441 4301 Connecticut Avenue, NW Washington, DC 20008 Tel.: 202-244-1491/2 10:00 AM - 4:00 PM	Entire United States

MAYOTTE

I. GENERAL INFORMATION

Mayotte is an Overseas Department of France, covered by the Hague Convention Abolishing the Requirement for Legalization for Foreign Public Documents.

A document should be sent to the appropriate authority in the state or territory in which the document is notarized in order to obtain the Apostille. For information on obtaining the Apostille for documents originating in the United States, see the procedures specified for each of the individual states under United States jurisdiction in Chapter 2. For the enumeration of Federal authorities competent to provide the Apostille, see Appendix D.

For the text of the Hague Convention, the Apostille, and a list of the parties to the Convention, see Appendix A.

For information on French Consulates, see France.

MEXICO

National Holiday: Independence Day, September 16

I. GENERAL INFORMATION

Mexico is a party to the Hague Convention Abolishing the Requirement for Legalization for Foreign Public Documents.

A document should be sent to the appropriate authority in the state or territory in which the document is notarized in order to obtain the Apostille. For information on obtaining the Apostille for documents originating in the United States, see the procedures specified for each of the individual states under United States jurisdiction in Chapter 2. For the enumeration of Federal authorities competent to provide the Apostille, see Appendix D.

For the text of the Hague Convention, the Apostille, and a list of the parties to the Convention, see Appendix A.

For information purposes, the Embassy is listed below.

II. EMBASSY

Embassy of Mexico
Consular Section
2827 16th Street, NW
Washington, DC 20009
Tel.: 202-736-1000/1/2
Fax: 202-797-8438
9:00 AM - 2:00 PM

FEDERATED STATES OF MICRONESIA

National Holiday: November 3

I. GENERAL INFORMATION

The Embassy of the Federated States of Micronesia does not have legalization functions. These functions are handled by the Attorney General's Office of the Federated States of Micronesia, Palikir, Pohnpei, FM 96941.
Tel.: 691-320-2608
Fax: 691-320-6240

II. EMBASSY

Embassy of the Federated States of Micronesia
1725 N Street, NW
Washington, DC 20036
Tel.: 202-223-4383
Fax: 202-223-4391
9:00 AM - 5:00 PM

MOLDAVA

National Holidays: January 7; Easter; Independence Day, August 27

I. REQUIREMENTS FOR LEGALIZATION

Prior Authentications Required
1. Notarization
2. Authentication of Notary Signature (In most states this may be done directly by the State Secretary of State; if not, the County Clerk authenticates the signature.)
3. State Secretary of State Certification (In states where the Notary Signature may be authenticated directly by the State Secretary of State, steps 2 and 3 are combined.)
4. U.S. Secretary of State Certification

Materials to be Submitted with Request
1. Original document to be legalized
2. Prepaid, self-addressed return envelope

Direct Registration of Notary Public: Not available

Direct Signing of Document Before Consular Official: Not available

Turn Around Time: An appointment is necessary in order to deliver a document personally for authentication. If the document is mailed in, the average turn around time is 5 to 7 business days.

Fee: $35 per document or signature; $20 per set of documents for expedited service.

Payment Method: Money order, company check payable to the Embassy

II. EMBASSY

Embassy of Moldava
2101 S Street NW
Washington, DC 20008
Tel.: 202-667-1130, press 15
Fax: 202-667-1204
8:30 AM - 5:30 PM

MONGOLIA

National Holidays: July 11 - 13

I. GENERAL INFORMATION

Only the Embassy has legalization functions, although the Mission to the United Nations will authenticate documents signed at the mission as described below.

II. REQUIREMENTS FOR LEGALIZATION

Prior Authentications Required
1. Notarization

Materials to be Submitted with Request
1. Original document to be legalized
2. Photocopy of the document
3. Prepaid, self-addressed return envelope

Direct Registration of Notary Public: Not available

Direct Signing of Document Before Consular Official: The procedure of certifying the signature of a private person is available at the Embassy and the Mission to the UN. An appointment should be made and the signer must present identification such as photo ID, a passport or a driver's license.

Turn Around Time: If the document is personally delivered, it will be legalized immediately if the workload permits.

Fee: $10.00 per document or signature

Payment Method: Cash, money order, certified check, company check

III. EMBASSY AND UN MISSION

Address, Phone, Hours	*Jurisdiction*
Embassy of Mongolia 2833 M Street, NW Washington, DC 20007 Tel.: 202-333-7117 9:00 AM - 12:00 PM	Entire United States
Mission to the UN 6 East 77th Street New York, NY 10021 Tel.: 212-861-9460 Fax: 212-861-9464 9:00 AM - 1:00 PM 2:00 PM - 6:00 PM	New York only

MONTSERRAT

I. GENERAL INFORMATION

Montserrat is a dependency of the United Kingdom, covered by the Hague Convention Abolishing the Requirement for Legalization for Foreign Public Documents.

A document should be sent to the appropriate authority in the state or territory in which the document is notarized in order to obtain the Apostille. For information on obtaining the Apostille for documents originating in the United States, see the procedures specified for each of the individual states under United States jurisdiction in Chapter 2. For the enumeration of Federal authorities competent to provide the Apostille, see Appendix D.

For the text of the Hague Convention, the Apostille, and a list of the parties to the Convention, see Appendix A.

For information on United Kingdom Consulates, see the United Kingdom.

KINGDOM OF MOROCCO

National Holiday: March 3

I. GENERAL INFORMATION

The Embassy and the New York Consulate General have legalization functions.

II. REQUIREMENTS FOR LEGALIZATION

Prior Authentications Required
1. Notarization
2. Authentication of Notary Signature (In most states this may be done directly by the State Secretary of State; if not, the County Clerk authenticates the signature.)
3. State Secretary of State Certification (In states where the Notary Signature may be authenticated directly by the State Secretary of State, steps 2 and 3 are combined.)
4. U.S. Secretary of State Certification

Materials to be Submitted with Request
1. Original document to be legalized
2. Photocopy of the document
3. Prepaid, self-addressed return envelope

Direct Registration of Notary Public: Not available

Direct Signing of Document Before Consular Official: Not available

Turn Around Time: If the document is personally delivered, there will be a delay of one to two days before legalization.

Fee: U.S. $25.00 at current rate of exchange

Payment Method: Cash, money order, company check payable to the Embassy of Morocco

III. EMBASSY AND CONSULATE GENERAL

Address, Phone, Hours	*Jurisdiction*
Consulate General of Morocco 1821 Jefferson Place Washington, DC 20036 Tel: 202-462-7727/34 Fax: 202-452-0106 9:00 AM - 1:00 PM 9:00 AM - 5:00 PM telephone inquiries	Maryland Virginia Washington, DC
Consulate General 10 East 40th Street New York, NY 10006 Tel.: 212-213-9644 10:00 AM - 1:00 PM 10:00 AM - 5:00 PM telephone inquiries	Entire United States

REPUBLIC OF MOZAMBIQUE

National Holiday: June 25

I. GENERAL INFORMATION

Mozambique is a party to the Hague Convention Abolishing the Requirement for Legalization for Foreign Public Documents.

A document should be sent to the appropriate authority in the state or territory in which the document is notarized in order to obtain the Apostille. For information on obtaining the Apostille for documents originating in the United States, see the procedures specified for each of the individual states under United States jurisdiction in Chapter 2. For the enumeration of Federal authorities competent to provide the Apostille, see Appendix D.

For the text of the Hague Convention, the Apostille, and a list of the parties to the Convention, see Appendix A.

Mozambique has an Embassy but no Consulates.

II. EMBASSY

Address, Phone, Hours	*Jurisdiction*
Embassy of Mozambique 1990 M Street, NW Washington, DC 20036 Tel.: 202-293-7146 9:00 AM - 12:00 PM	Entire United States

UNION OF MYANMAR

I. GENERAL INFORMATION

The Embassy and Consulate General may legalize only documents originating in their jurisdiction.

II. REQUIREMENTS FOR LEGALIZATION

Prior Authentications Required
1. Notarization
2. Authentication of Notary Signature (In most states this may be done directly by the State Secretary of State; if not, the County Clerk authenticates the signature.)
3. State Secretary of State Certification (In states where the Notary Signature may be authenticated directly by the State Secretary of State, steps 2 and 3 are combined.)
4. U.S. Secretary of State Certification

Materials to be Submitted with Request
1. Original document to be legalized
2. Three photocopies of the document
3. Prepaid, self-addressed return envelope

Direct Registration of Notary Public: Not available

Direct Signing of Document Before Consular Official: The procedure of certification of a person's signature by a consular official is available. An appointment is necessary. The signer must present identification and authorization from the company to be signed.

Turn Around Time: If the document is personally delivered, there will be a delay of at least four days before legalization.

Fee: $15.00

Payment Method: Cash, money order, certified check, company check

III. EMBASSY AND CONSULATE GENERAL

Address, Phone, Hours	*Jurisdiction*
Embassy of the Union of Myanmar 2300 S Street, NW Washington, DC 20008-4089 Tel.: 202-332-9044/5 Fax: 202-332-9046 9:30 AM - 12:00 PM 1:00 PM - 5:00 PM	Entire United States
Consulate General 10 East 77th Street New York, NY 10021 Tel.: 212-535-1310/1 Fax: 212-737-2421 9:00 AM - 1:00 PM 2:00 PM - 5:00 PM	New York

KINGDOM OF NEPAL

National Holiday: December 28

I. REQUIREMENTS FOR LEGALIZATION

Prior Authentications Required
1. Notarization
2. Authentication of Notary Signature (In most states this may be done directly by the State Secretary of State; if not, the County Clerk authenticates the signature.)
3. State Secretary of State Certification (In states where the Notary Signature may be authenticated directly by the State Secretary of State, steps 2 and 3 are combined.)
4. U.S. Secretary of State Certification

Materials to be Submitted with Request
1. Original document to be legalized
2. Photocopy of the document
3. Prepaid, self-addressed return envelope

Direct Registration of Notary Public: Not available

Direct Signing of Document Before Consular Official: Not available

Turn Around Time: If the document is personally delivered, there will be a delay of 24 hours before legalization.

Fee: $15 per document or signature

Payment Method: Money order, company check

II. EMBASSY AND CONSULATE GENERAL

Address, Phone, Hours	*Jurisdiction*
Embassy of the Kingdom of Nepal 2131 Leroy Place, NW Washington, DC 20008 Tel.: 202-667-4550 Fax: 202-667-5534 10:00 AM - 12:30 PM 2:00 PM - 4:00 PM	Entire United States
Consulate General 820 Second Avenue, Suite 202 New York, NY 10017 Tel.: 212-370-4188 Fax: 212-953-2038 10:00 AM - 4:00 PM	Connecticut Maine Massachusetts New Hampshire New Jersey New York Pennsylvania Rhode Island

KINGDOM OF THE NETHERLANDS

National Holiday: Queen's Day, April 30

I. GENERAL INFORMATION

The Netherlands is a party to the Hague Convention Abolishing the Requirement for Legalization for Foreign Public Documents.

A document should be sent to the appropriate authority in the state or territory in which the document is notarized in order to obtain the Apostille. For information on obtaining the Apostille for documents originating in the United States, see the procedures specified for each of the individual states under United States jurisdiction in Chapter 2. For the enumeration of Federal authorities competent to provide the Apostille, see Appendix D.

For the text of the Hague Convention, the Apostille, and a list of the parties to the Convention, see Appendix A.

For information purposes, the Embassy, Consulates General and Consulates are listed below.

For those instances in which legalization by a Netherlands consulate official may still be necessary, the requirements for legalization are given below and are provided only for Netherlands citizens.

The independent governments of the Netherlands Antilles and Aruba both have a representative at the Royal Netherlands Embassy.

II. REQUIREMENTS FOR LEGALIZATION

Prior Authentications Required
1. Notarization
2. Authentication of Notary Signature (In most states this may be done directly by the State Secretary of State; if not, the County Clerk authenticates the signature.)

Materials to be Submitted with Request
1. Original document to be legalized
2. Prepaid, self-addressed return envelope

Direct Registration of Notary Public: Not available

Direct Signing of Document Before Consular Official: The procedure of certifying the signature of a private person is available. No appointment is necessary. The signer must present identification such as a driver's license or passport.

Turn Around Time: If the document is personally delivered, there may be a delay of a few hours before legalization.

Fee: Approximately $15.00; varies with the rate of exchange

Payment Method: Cash, check

III. EMBASSY, CONSULATES GENERAL AND CONSULATES

Address, Phone, Hours	*Jurisdiction*
Royal Netherlands Embassy 4200 Linnean Avenue, NW Washington, DC 20008 Tel.: 202-244-5300 Fax: 202-364-2410 9:30 AM - 4:30 PM	Delaware Maryland North Carolina Virginia Washington, DC West Virginia
Consulate c/o Arthur Anderson and Company Georgia Pacific Center 133 Peachtree Street, Suite 2500 Atlanta, GA 30303 Tel.: 404-525-4513 Fax: 404-223-7155	Georgia South Carolina
Consulate c/o Semmes, Bowen and Semmes 250 West Pratt Street, 15th Floor Baltimore, MD 21201 Tel.: 410-539-5040 Fax: 410-539-5223	Delaware Maryland West Virginia

Address, Phone, Hours	*Jurisdiction*
Consulate 6 James Avenue, Suite 1001 Boston, MA 02116-3800 Tel.: 617-542-8452 Fax: 617-542-3304	Maine Massachusetts New Hampshire Rhode Island Vermont
Consulate 21 Brantwood Road Snyder, NY 14226-4302 Tel.: 716-835-3174	New York counties of: Allegany, Chattaraugus, Chatauqua, Eric, Genesee, Livingston, Monroe, Niagara, Orleans, Wyoming
Consulate 303 East Wacker Drive, Suite 410 Chicago, IL 60601 Tel.: 312-856-0110 Fax: 312-856-9218	Illinois Indiana Iowa Kansas Kentucky Michigan (except for counties listed under Southfield) Minnesota Missouri Nebraska North Dakota Ohio South Dakota Tennessee Wisconsin
Consulate 7350 Young Drive Walton Hills Cleveland, OH 44146 Tel.: 216-232-5100 Fax: 216-439-2760	Ohio

Address, Phone, Hours	*Jurisdiction*
Consulate 6536 South Garfield Court Littleton, CO 80121 Tel.: 303-770-7747 Fax: 303-770-7747	Colorado New Mexico Wyoming
Consulate c/o New York Life Insurance Company 2000 Town Center, Suite 1200 Southfield, MI 48075-1135 Tel.: 810-352-0620	Michigan counties of: Macomb, Oakland, Wayne, Huron, Tuscola, Sanilac, Saginaw, Genesee, Lapeer, St. Clair, Ingham, Livingstone, Shiawassee, Jackson, Washtenaw, Lenawee, Monroe
Consulate 3250 28th Street SE Grand Rapids, MI 49512 Tel.: 616-285-9998 616-957-9716	Michigan counties of: Macomb, Oakland, Wayne, Huron, Tuscola, Sanilac, Saginaw, Genesee, Lapeer, St. Clair, Ingham, Livingstone, Shiawassee, Jackson, Washtenaw, Lenawee, Monroe
Consulate 345 Queen Street, Suite 600 Honolulu, HI 96813 Tel.: 808-537-1100 Fax: 808-536-2647	Hawaii

Address, Phone, Hours	*Jurisdiction*
Consulate General 2200 Post Oak Boulevard, Suite 610 Houston, TX 77056-4783 Tel.: 713-622-8000 Fax: 713-622-3581	Alabama Arkansas Florida Georgia Louisiana Mississippi Oklahoma South Carolina Texas
Consulate Suite 500 900 University Boulevard North Jacksonville, FL 32211 Tel.: 904-744-0275 Fax: 904-744-3547	Florida counties of: Alachua, Baker, Bay, Bradford, Brevard, Calhoun, Clay, Columbia, Dixie, Duval, Escambvia, Flagler, Franklin, Gadsden Gilchrist, Gulf, Hamilton, Homes, Jackson, Jefferson, Lafayette, Leon, Levy, Liberty, Madison, Nassau, Okaloosa, Putnam, Santa Rosa, Saint Johns, Suwannee, Taylor, Union, Volusia, Wakulla, Walton, Washington
Consulate 311 East 135th Street PO Box 480557 Kansas City, MO 64148-0557 Tel.: 816-941-4777 Fax: 816-941-4779	Kansas Missouri Nebraska

Address, Phone, Hours	*Jurisdiction*
Consulate General Central Plaza 11766 Wilshire Boulevard, Suite 1150 Los Angeles, CA 90025 Tel.: 310-268-1598 Fax: 310-312-0989	Alaska Arizona California Colorado Hawaii Idaho Montana Nevada New Mexico Oregon Utah Washington Wyoming
Consulate 562 North Woodlawn St. Louis, MO 63122 Tel.: 314-964-3533	Kentucky Tennessee
Consulate 801 Brickell Avenue, Suite 918 A/B Miami, FL 33131 Tel.: 305-789-6646 Fax: 305-372-0189	Florida counties of: Broward, Collier, Dade, Indian, River, Martin, Monroe, Palm Beach, Saint Lucie
Consulate 4131 Pipewood Curve Excelsior, MN 55331 Tel.: 612-474-1475 Fax: 612-430-1437	Minnesota
Consulate 643 Magazine Street New Orleans, LA 70130 Tel.: 504-596-2838 Fax: 504-596-2800	Alabama Louisiana Mississippi

Address, Phone, Hours	*Jurisdiction*
Consulate General 1 Rockefeller Plaza, 11th Floor New York, NY 10020-2094 Tel.: 212-246-1429 Fax: 212-333-3603	Connecticut Maine Massachusetts New Hampshire New Jersey New York Pennsylvania Rhode Island Vermont Puerto Rico St. John St. Tomas St. Croix
Consulate 1128 West Olney Road Norfolk, VA 23507-1390 Tel.: 804-625-3658 Fax: 804-524-8154	Virginia South Carolina
Consulate 45 Brennan Drive Bryn Mawr, PA 19010 PO Box 8047 Philadelphia, PA 19101-8047 Tel.: 610-520-1614 Fax: 610-520-9591	Pennsylvania
Consulate 10089 East Becker Scottsdale, AZ 85260 Tel.: 602-661-9159 Fax: 602-451-7701	Arizona
Consulate 4555 North Channel Avenue Portland, OR 97217 Tel.: 503-285-9111 ext. 419 Fax: 503-240-2256	Oregon

Address, Phone, Hours	*Jurisdiction*
Consulate 230 West 700 South Salt Lake City, UT 84101 Tel.: 801-364-1981 Fax: 801-355-2029	Utah
Consulate Chamber Building, Suite 711 110 West C Street San Diego, CA 92101 Tel.: 619-696-7941 Fax: 619-234-1606	
Consulate 1 Maritime Plaza, Suite 316 San Francisco, CA 94111 Tel.: 415-981-6454/5 Fax: 415-956-3014	
Consulate 10051 NE 112th Street Kirkland, WA 98033 Tel.: 206-861-4437 Fax: 206-861-4437	Idaho Montana Washington
Consulate City Hall, One City Commons 400 South Orange Avenue, 9th Floor Orlando, FL 32801-3302 Tel.: 407-425-800 Fax: 407-843-6161	

NETHERLANDS ANTILLES

I. GENERAL INFORMATION

The Netherlands Antilles is a party to the Hague Convention Abolishing the Requirement for Legalization for Foreign Public Documents.

A document should be sent to the appropriate authority in the state or territory in which the document is notarized in order to obtain the Apostille. For information on obtaining the Apostille for documents originating in the United States, see the procedures specified for each of the individual states under United States jurisdiction in Chapter 2. For the enumeration of Federal authorities competent to provide the Apostille, see Appendix D.

For the text of the Hague Convention, the Apostille, and a list of the parties to the Convention, see Appendix A.

The Netherlands Antilles is represented at the Royal Netherlands Embassy.

NETHERLANDS/ARUBA

I. GENERAL INFORMATION

The Netherlands Antilles is a party to the Hague Convention Abolishing the Requirement for Legalization for Foreign Public Documents.

A document should be sent to the appropriate authority in the state or territory in which the document is notarized in order to obtain the Apostille. For information on obtaining the Apostille for documents originating in the United States, see the procedures specified for each of the individual states under United States jurisdiction in Chapter 2. For the enumeration of Federal authorities competent to provide the Apostille, see Appendix D.

For the text of the Hague Convention, the Apostille, and a list of the parties to the Convention, see Appendix A.

Aruba is represented at the Royal Netherlands Embassy.

NEW CALEDONIA

I. GENERAL INFORMATION

New Caledonia is an Overseas Territory of France, covered by the Hague Convention Abolishing the Requirement for Legalization for Foreign Public Documents.

A document should be sent to the appropriate authority in the state or territory in which the document is notarized in order to obtain the Apostille. For information on obtaining the Apostille for documents originating in the United States, see the procedures specified for each of the individual states under United States jurisdiction in Chapter 2. For the enumeration of Federal authorities competent to provide the Apostille, see Appendix D.

For the text of the Hague Convention, the Apostille, and a list of the parties to the Convention, see Appendix A.

For information on French Consulates, see France.

DOMINION OF NEW ZEALAND

National Holidays: January 2 and 5, February 6, April 10 and 25, June 5, October 26, December 28

I. GENERAL INFORMATION

The Embassy and Consulates General have legalization functions. Each will legalize documents originating in its jurisdiction.

New Zealand handles legalizations for Western Samoa.

II. REQUIREMENTS FOR LEGALIZATION

Prior Authentications Required

1. Notarization
2. Authentication of Notary Signature (In most states this may be done directly by the State Secretary of State; if not, the County Clerk authenticates the signature.)
3. State Secretary of State Certification (In states where the Notary Signature may be authenticated directly by the State Secretary of State, steps 2 and 3 are combined.)
4. U.S. Secretary of State Certification

Materials to be Submitted with Request

1. Original document to be legalized
2. Photocopy of the document
3. Prepaid, self-addressed return envelope not required but appreciated

Direct Registration of Notary Public: Not available

Direct Signing of Document Before Consular Official: The procedure of certifying the signature of a private person is available at the Embassy and Consulates General. An appointment should be made and the signer must present a driver's license or passport as identification.

Turn Around Time: Documents will be authenticated within three working days of receipt.

Fee: $20.00 per document or signature

Payment Method: Cash, money order, certified check, company check payable to the Embassy of New Zealand

III. EMBASSY AND CONSULATES GENERAL

Address, Phone, Hours	*Jurisdiction*
Embassy of New Zealand 37 Observatory Circle, NW Washington, DC 20008 Tel.: 202-328-4885 Fax: 202-667-5227 9:00 AM - 5:00 PM	Entire United States for government matters All states not covered by Los Angeles and New York Consulates
Consulate General 12400 Wilshire Boulevard, Suite 1150 Los Angeles, CA 90025 Tel.: 310-207-1605 9:00 AM - 3:00 PM	Alaska Arizona California Colorado Hawaii Idaho Montana Nevada New Mexico Oregon Utah Washington Wyoming
Consulate General 780 Third Avenue, Suite 1904 New York, NY 10017-2024 Tel.: 212-832-4038 Fax: 212-832-7602 9:00 AM - 4:00 PM	New York

NICARAGUA

National Holiday: September 15

I. GENERAL INFORMATION

The Embassy and Consulates have legalization functions. Each will legalize documents originating in its jurisdiction.

II. REQUIREMENTS FOR AUTHENTICATION

Prior Authentications Required
1. Notarization
2. Authentication of Notary Signature (In most states this may be done directly by the State Secretary of State; if not, the County Clerk authenticates the signature.)
3. State Secretary of State Certification (In states where the Notary Signature may be authenticated directly by the State Secretary of State, steps 2 and 3 are combined.)

NOTE: Nicaragua requires authentication by the County Clerk OR the Secretary of State OR the U.S. Secretary of State, i.e., only one authentication.

Materials to be Submitted with Request
1. Original document to be legalized
2. Photocopy of the document
3. Prepaid, self-addressed return envelope
4. Cover letter or business card

Direct Registration of Notary Public: Not available

Direct Signing of Document Before Consular Official: Not available unless the signer is a citizen of Nicaragua, in which case he or she may sign the document in the presence of a consular official provided he or she can provide proof of Nicaraguan citizenship.

Turn Around Time: If the document is personally delivered, there will be a delay of three days before legalization.

Fee: $25.00 per document or signature for most documents; invoices, bills of lading and other documents are subject to other fees and a copy of the scale for these fees is appended to this entry; $5.00 additional for rush (expedited service)

Payment Method: Money order, certified check, company check payable to the Embassy or Consulate of Nicaragua

III. EMBASSY AND CONSULATES

Address, Phone, Hours	*Jurisdiction*
Consulate of Nicaragua 1627 New Hampshire Avenue, NW Washington, DC 20009 Tel.: 202-939-6531/32/70 Fax: 202-939-6574 9:00 AM - 1:00 PM	Illinois Indiana Kentucky Maryland Michigan North Carolina Ohio Pennsylvania Tennessee Virginia Washington, DC West Virginia Wisconsin Canada
Consulate 3300 Wilshire Boulevard, Suite 410 Los Angeles, CA 90057 Tel.: 213-252-1170 Fax: 213-252-1177	Arizona California Idaho Oregon Utah Washington
Consulate 8370 West Flagler Street, Suite 220 Miami, FL 33144 Tel.: 305-220-6900 Fax: 305-220-8794	Alabama Florida Georgia South Carolina

Address, Phone, Hours	*Jurisdiction*
Consulate World Trade Center 2 Canal Street, Suite 1937 New Orleans, LA 70130 Tel.: 504-523-1507 Fax: 504-523-2359	Arkansas Iowa Louisiana Minnesota Mississippi Missouri
Consulate 820 Second Avenue, Suite 802 New York, NY 10017 Tel.: 212-983-1981 Fax: 212-983-2646	Connecticut Maine Massachusetts New Hampshire New Jersey New York Pennsylvania Rhode Island Vermont
Consulate 6300 Hillcroft, Suite 470 Houston, TX 77081 Tel.: 713-272-9628 Fax: 713-272-7131	Colorado Kansas Montana Nebraska New Mexico North Dakota Oklahoma South Dakota Texas Wyoming

IV. APPENDED FEES AND ADDITIONAL INFORMATION

<u>Costos y servicios del consulado de Nicaragua en Washington</u>

Actividad commercial

Legalizaciones*.......................................Referirse a documento adjunto

Actividad legal

Autenticaciones* ....US $ 25.00 por documento
Decl. jurada..US $ 20.00
Poder...US $ 75.00
Traduccion de partida de nacimiento............US $ 10.00

Carta de autorizacion	US $ 10.00
Constancia	US $ 10.00
Fe de vida	US $ 10.00
Carta de identificacion	US $ 10.00
Inscripcion/certificado de nacimiento	US $ 50.00
Inscripcion/certificado de matrimonio	US $ 50.00
Inscripcion/certificado de divorcio	US $ 50.00
* Servicio immediato/ hasta 5 documentos	US $ 5.00

Actividad migratoria

Visas	US $ 25.00
Pasaportes provisionales	US $ 25.00
(Cuando NO esta tramitando pasaporte nuevo)	
Pasaportes nuevos	US $ 50.00

Requirements for the legalization of documents

A. Commercial invoice: one original and three copies
The commercial invoice must indicate the country of origin in Spanish, e.g., "Esta mercancia es procedente de los Estados Unidos de Norteamérica." It must also contain a detailed description of the merchandise and an itemized account of all charges up to the C.I.F. value.
B. Bill of lading: three originals and two copies
C. Airway bill: one original and two copies.
We only legalize the airway bill when a letter of credit requests it.
D. Copy of the letter of credit
You should always send us a copy of the letter of credit.

Order in which the documents should be arranged

FOR SHIPPER: One set with one original and one copy of the commercial invoice and three originals of the bill of lading

FOR CONSULATE: Two sets with one copy of the commercial invoice and one copy of the bill of lading

Consular fees: C.I.F. value of shipment based on Decrey 880

From $	00.00	to	49.00	$10.00 por/set
	50.00	to	500.00	20.00 por/set
	501.00	to	1,000.00	25.00 por/set
	1,001.00	to	10,000.00	35.00 por/set
	10,001.00	to	100,000.00	50.00 por/set

If the C.I.F. value is higher than $100,000.00, the consular fee would be in fractions at a charge of $50.00 per fraction. For example, if the C.I.F. value of the shipment is $100,000.00 the fee would be $50.00; if it is $118,000.00 it would be $100.00; if it is $225,000.00, it would be $150.00.

Please send money order or cashier's check.

<u>Legalizations consular fees</u>

Pasavantes	$ 500.00
Shipping manifesto	$ 100.00
Certificate - fitosanitario	$ 25.00
Certificate of origin	$ 25.00
Certificate of fumigation	$ 25.00
Packing list	$ 25.00
Ship's personnel list	$ 25.00
Storage list	$ 25.00
Rush/Next day service/per document	$ 5.00**
Correction letter	$ 15.00*
Duplicate of the original	$ 10.00

* Readjusted consular fee as of September 14, 1994
**Readjusted rush/next day service as of July 1996

REPUBLIC OF NIGER

I. GENERAL INFORMATION

The Embassy has legalization functions.

II. REQUIREMENTS FOR LEGALIZATION

Prior Authentications Required
1. Notarization
2. Authentication of Notary Signature (In most states this may be done directly by the State Secretary of State; if not, the County Clerk authenticates the signature.)
3. State Secretary of State Certification (In states where the Notary Signature may be authenticated directly by the State Secretary of State, steps 2 and 3 are combined.)
4. U.S. Secretary of State Certification

Materials to be Submitted with Request
1. Original document to be legalized
2. Photocopy of the document
3. Prepaid, self-addressed return envelope

Direct Registration of Notary Public: Not available

Direct Signing of Document Before Consular Official: The procedure of certifying the signature of a private person is available at the Embassy. An appointment should be made.

Turn Around Time: If the document is personally delivered, there will be a delay of three days before legalization.

Fee: None

III. EMBASSY

Embassy of the Republic of Niger
2204 R Street, NW
Washington, DC 20008
Tel.: 202-483-4224
Fax: 202-483-3169
9:00 AM - 5:00 PM

Entire United States

FEDERAL REPUBLIC OF NIGERIA

National Holiday: October 1

I. GENERAL INFORMATION

The Embassy does not legalize American documents. For information purposes, the Embassy and Consulate General are listed below.

II. EMBASSY AND CONSULATE GENERAL

Embassy of the Federal Republic of Nigeria
Consular Section
2201 M Street NW
Washington DC
Tel.: 202-822-1513
9:00 AM - 1:00 PM
2:00 PM - 5:00 PM

Consulate General
828 Second Avenue
New York, NY 10017
Tel.: 212-715-7200

KINGDOM OF NORWAY

National Holiday: Constitution Day, May 17

I. GENERAL INFORMATION

Norway is a party to the Hague Convention Abolishing the Requirement for Legalization for Foreign Public Documents.

A document should be sent to the appropriate authority in the state or territory in which the document is notarized in order to obtain the Apostille. For information on obtaining the Apostille for documents originating in the United States, see the procedures specified for each of the individual states under United States jurisdiction in Chapter 2. For the enumeration of Federal authorities competent to provide the Apostille, see Appendix D.

For the text of the Hague Convention, the Apostille, and a list of the parties to the Convention, see Appendix A.

For information purposes, the Embassy and Consulates General of Norway are listed below.

II. EMBASSY AND CONSULATES GENERAL

Address, Phone, Hours	*Jurisdiction*
Royal Norwegian Embassy 2720 34th Street, NW Washington, DC 20008-2714 Tel.: 202-333-6000 Fax: 202-337-0870	Entire United States

Address, Phone, Hours	*Jurisdiction*
Consulate General 2777 Allen Parkway, Suite 1185 Houston, TX 77019-2136 Tel.: 713-521-2900 Fax: 713-521-9473	Alabama Arkansas Kansas Louisiana Mississippi Missouri Oklahoma Puerto Rico Texas Virgin Islands
Consulate General 1007 North America Way, Suite 305 Miami, FL 33132-2092 Tel.: 305-358-4386 Fax: 305-374-4369	Florida
Consulate General 800 Foshay Tower 821 Marquette Avenue Minneapolis, MN 55402-2916 Tel.: 612-332-3338 Fax: 612-332-1386	Iowa Michigan Minnesota Montana Nebraska North Dakota South Dakota Wisconsin
Consulate General 825 Third Avenue, 38th Floor New York, NY 10022-7584 Tel.: 212-421-7333 Fax: 212-754-0583	Connecticut Delaware Georgia Illinois Indiana Kentucky Maine Maryland Massachusetts New Hampshire New Jersey New York North Carolina

Address, Phone, Hours	*Jurisdiction*
	Ohio Pennsylvania Rhode Island South Carolina Tennessee Vermont Virginia West Virginia
Consulate General 20 California Street, 6th Floor San Francisco, CA 94111-4803 Tel.: 415-986-0766/7/8 Fax: 415-986-3318	Alaska Arizona California Colorado Hawaii Idaho Nevada New Mexico Oregon Utah Washington Wyoming

SULTANATE OF OMAN

National Holiday: National Day, November 18

I. GENERAL INFORMATION

Oman has an Embassy in the United States but no Consulates. Documents from anywhere in the United States may be sent to the Embassy for legalization.

II. REQUIREMENTS FOR LEGALIZATION

Prior Authentications Required
1. Notarization
2. Authentication of Notary Signature (In most states this may be done directly by the State Secretary of State; if not, the County Clerk authenticates the signature.)
3. State Secretary of State Certification (In states where the Notary Signature may be authenticated directly by the State Secretary of State, steps 2 and 3 are combined.)
4. U.S. Secretary of State Certification

Materials to be Submitted with Request
1. Original document to be legalized
2. Prepaid, self-addressed return envelope

Direct Registration of Notary Public: Not available

Direct Signing of Document Before Consular Official: Not available

Turn Around Time: If the document is personally delivered, there will be a delay of two to three days before legalization.

Fees

Legalization of Power of Attorney: $30.00
  Duplicate or copy: $15.00

Legalization of Commercial Invoice in the Amount of $1.00 - $10,000: $45.00
  Duplicate or copy: $30.00

Legalization of Commercial Invoice in the Amount of $10,000 and up: $60.00
  Duplicate or copy: $30.00

Bill of Lading, Airway Bill: $15.00
Duplicate or copy: $9.00
Legalization of Financial Statement: $15.00

Payment Method: Cash, money order, certified check payable to the Embassy of Oman

III. EMBASSY

Address, Phone, Hours	*Jurisdiction*
Embassy of the Sultanate of Oman 2535 Belmont Road, NW Washington, DC 20008 Tel.: 202-387-1980 Fax: 202-745-4933 9:30 AM - 12:30 PM	Entire United States

PALAU

National Holiday: October 1

I. GENERAL INFORMATION

The Embassy does not legalize documents but will provide applications and submit them to the Foreign Investment Board in Palau.

For information purposes, the Embassy is listed below. An answering machine will record messages after office hours.

II. EMBASSY

Address, Phone, Hours	*Jurisdiction*
Embassy of Palau 1150 18th Street, NW Washington, DC 20036 Tel.: 202-452-6814 Fax: 202-452-6281 9:00 AM - 5:00 PM	Entire United States

PANAMA

National Holiday: November 3

I. GENERAL INFORMATION

Panama is a party to the Hague Convention Abolishing the Requirement for Legalization for Foreign Public Documents. The Embassy has stated that documents bearing an Apostille must nevertheless by submitted to the Embassy or an appropriate Consulate General for authentication.

A document should be sent to the appropriate authority in the state or territory in which the document is notarized in order to obtain the Apostille. For information on obtaining the Apostille for documents originating in the United States, see the procedures specified for each of the individual states under United States jurisdiction in Chapter 2. For the enumeration of Federal authorities competent to provide the Apostille, see Appendix D.

For the text of the Hague Convention, the Apostille, and a list of the parties to the Convention, see Appendix A.

For information purposes, the Embassy is listed below.

For instances in which legalization by a Panamanian consular official is still necessary, the requirements for legalization by the Embassy are given below.

II. REQUIREMENTS FOR LEGALIZATION

Prior Authentications Required
1. Notarization

Materials to be Submitted with Request
1. Original document to be legalized
2. Prepaid, self-addressed return envelope

Direct Registration of Notary Public: Not available.

Direct Signing of Document Before Consular Official: The procedure of certifying the signature of a private person is available at the

Embassy. An appointment should be made and the signer must present identification with a photo such as a driver's license or passport.

Turn Around Time: If the document is personally delivered, there will be a delay of 24 hours before legalization. If an appointment is made, the document will be legalized the same day.

Fees
Certification $30.00
Notarization $40.00
Authentication $30.00

Payment Method: Cash, money order, certified check, company check payable to the Consulate of Panama

III. EMBASSY

Embassy of Panama
Consulate
2862 McGill Terrace, NW, First Floor
Washington, DC 20008
Tel.: 202-387-6154
Fax: 202-387-6141
9:30 AM - 12:30 PM
2:00 PM - 4:00 PM

Delaware
Maryland
North Carolina
Virginia
Washington, DC
West Virginia

Note: The Consulate of Panama in Washington, DC will legalize documents from any state without a Consulate.

PAPUA NEW GUINEA

National Holidays: Easter Monday, June 10, July 23, September 16, December 26

I. GENERAL INFORMATION

The queen of Papua New Guinea is the head of state and the Resident Representative as in each country belonging to the Commonwealth.

II. REQUIREMENTS FOR LEGALIZATION

Prior Authentications Required

1. Notarization
2. Authentication of Notary Signature (In most states this may be done directly by the State Secretary of State; if not, the County Clerk authenticates the signature.)
3. State Secretary of State Certification (In states where the Notary Signature may be authenticated directly by the State Secretary of State, steps 2 and 3 are combined.)
4. U.S. Secretary of State Certification

Materials to be Submitted with Request

1. Original document to be legalized
2. Photocopy of the document
3. Prepaid, self-addressed return envelope

Direct Registration of Notary Public: Not available

Direct Signing of Document Before Consular Official: The procedure of certifying the signature of a private person is available at the Embassy. An appointment should be made and the signer must present identification in the form of a photo ID.

Turn Around Time: If the document is personally delivered, there will be a delay of five business days before legalization.

Fee: Variable

Payment Method: Money order, certified check, company check

III. EMBASSY

Address, Phone, Hours	*Jurisdiction*
Embassy of Papua New Guinea 1615 New Hampshire Avenue, NW Washington, DC 20009 Tel.: 202-745-3680 Fax: 202-745-3679 9:00 AM - 5:00 PM	Entire United States

REPUBLIC OF PARAGUAY

National Holiday: Independence Day, May 14 and 15

I. GENERAL INFORMATION

The Embassy and Consulates General have legalization functions. Each will legalize documents originating in its jurisdiction; some may legalize documents originating anywhere in the United States.

II. REQUIREMENTS FOR LEGALIZATION

Prior Authentications Required

1. Notarization
2. Authentication of Notary Signature (In most states this may be done directly by the State Secretary of State; if not, the County Clerk authenticates the signature.)
3. State Secretary of State Certification (In states where the Notary Signature may be authenticated directly by the State Secretary of State, steps 2 and 3 are combined.)
4. U.S. Secretary of State Certification

Materials to be Submitted with Request

1. Original document to be legalized
2. Two photocopies of the document
3. Prepaid, self-addressed return envelope

Direct Registration of Notary Public: Not available

Direct Signing of Document Before Consular Official: Not available

Turn Around Time: If the document is personally delivered, there will be a delay of 24 to 48 hours before legalization.

Fee:
$1.00 to $105.00 per document or signature, depending on document(s)
$30.00 for power of attorney

Payment Method: Cash, money order, company check, personal check payable to the Embassy of Paraguay

III. EMBASSY AND CONSULATES GENERAL

Address, Phone, Hours	*Jurisdiction*
Embassy of the Republic of Paraguay 2400 Massachusetts Avenue, NW Washington, DC 20008 Tel.: 202-483-6960 Fax: 202-234-4508 10:00 AM - 2:00 PM	Entire United States
Consulate General 18377 Beach Boulevard Huntington Beach, CA 92648 Tel.: 714-848-3168 Fax: 714-841-4739 9:00 AM - 3:00 PM	
Consulate General DuPont Plaza Center 300 Biscayne Boulevard Way, Suite 907 Miami, FL 33131 Tel.: 305-374-9090 Fax: 305-374-5522 10:00 AM - 3:00 PM	Alabama Florida Georgia Kentucky Mississippi North Carolina South Carolina Tennessee Virginia
Consulate General 675 Third Avenue, Suite 1604 New York, NY 10017 Tel.: 212-682-9441 Fax: 212-682-9943	Connecticut Maine Massachusetts New Hampshire New Jersey New York Pennsylvania Rhode Island Vermont

PERU

National Holiday: Independence Day, July 28

I. GENERAL INFORMATION

The Embassy and Consulates General have legalization functions. Each will legalize documents originating in its jurisdiction. The specific requirements for the Embassy and New York Consulate General are given below.

II. REQUIREMENTS FOR LEGALIZATION

Prior Authentications Required
The Embassy and the New York Consulate General require steps 1 and 2. For commercial documents, the Embassy only requires the signature of the State Secretary of State under its jurisdiction. Personal documents appear to require all four steps.

1. Notarization
2. Authentication of Notary Signature by the State Secretary of State
3. State Secretary of State Certification (In states where the Notary Signature may be authenticated directly by the State Secretary of State, steps 2 and 3 are combined.)
4. U.S. Secretary of State Certification

Materials to be Submitted with Request
1. Original document to be legalized
2. Prepaid, self-addressed return envelope

Direct Registration of Notary Public: Not available

Direct Signing of Document Before Consular Official: The procedure of certifying the signature of a private person is available at the New York Consulate. An appointment is not necessary. The signer must present identification which includes a picture, such as a passport.

Time Delay: If the document is presented by hand for legalization, the legalization can be done immediately if an official is available. Otherwise, there will be a delay of one or two days.

Fee: $82.00 for company documents such as patents and trademarks, power of attorney, authorizations and representations
$32.00 for personal documents such as birth certificates, death certificates, health certificates etc.

Payment Method: Cash, company check, money order payable to the Consulate General of Peru

III. EMBASSY AND CONSULATES GENERAL

Address, Phone, Hours	*Jurisdiction*
Consular Section of Peru 1625 Massachusetts Avenue, NW Sixth Floor Washington, DC 20036 Tel.: 202-462-1084/5 Fax: 202-462-1086 9:00 AM - 1:00 PM	Delaware Kentucky Maryland North Carolina Tennessee Washington, DC West Virginia Virginia
Consulate General 180 N. Michigan Avenue, Suite 1830 Chicago, IL 60601 Tel.: 312-853-6174/0	Arkansas Illinois Indiana Iowa Michigan Minnesota Missouri Ohio Wisconsin
Consulate General 5847 San Felipe Avenue, Suite 1481 Houston, TX 77057 Tel.: 713-781-6145/5000	Kansas Nebraska Oklahoma Texas
Consulate General 3460 Wilshire Boulevard, Suite 1005 Los Angeles, CA 90010 Tel.: 213-383-9895/6	Alaska Arizona California Colorado

Address, Phone, Hours	*Jurisdiction*
	Hawaii New Mexico Utah
Consulate General 444 Brickell Avenue, Suite M-135 Miami, FL 33131 Tel.: 305-374-1407/1305	Alabama Florida Georgia Louisiana Mississippi South Carolina
Consulate General 215 Lexington Avenue, 21st Floor New York, NY 10016 Tel.: 212-481-7410 ext. 310 Fax: 212-481-8607/6 9:00 AM - 3:00 PM 9:00 AM - 5:00 PM Wednesday	Connecticut Maine Massachusetts New Hampshire New York Rhode Island Vermont
Consulate General 100 Hamilton Plaza, Suite 1221 Paterson, NJ 07050 Tel.: 201-278-3324	New Jersey Pennsylvania
Consulate General 870 Market Street, Suite 579 San Francisco, CA 94102 Tel.: 415-362-5185/7136	California Idaho Montana Nevada North Dakota Oregon South Dakota Washington Wyoming
Consulate General Home Mortgage Place, 268 Ave Ponce de Leon Suite 1009 San Juan, Puerto Rico Tel.: 809-250-0391	Puerto Rico

THE PHILIPPINES

National Holiday: Independence Day, June 12

I. GENERAL INFORMATION

The Embassy and Consulates General have legalization functions.

II. REQUIREMENTS FOR LEGALIZATION

Prior Authentications Required
Steps 1 - 4, listed below, are required for the Embassy and most Consulates General. The New York Consulate General does not require step 4. Only if the document is signed in the presence of the Consular Officer at the Philippine Embassy are these steps not required.

1. Notarization
2. Authentication of Notary Signature by the County Clerk
3. State Secretary of State Certification
4. U.S. Secretary of State Certification required for Trademark, Patent Application, Combined Oath, Power of Attorney and Petition, Affidavit of Use/Non Use, Appointment or Resident Agent, Assignment of Letters Patent

Materials to be Submitted with Request
1. Original document to be legalized
2. Photocopy of document
3. Prepaid, self-addressed return envelope, preferably certified mail postage

Direct Registration of Notary Public: Not available

Direct Signing of Document Before Consular Official: Available at Embassy

Turn Around Time: If the document is personally delivered, there may be a delay of up to 24 hours before legalization, although the Chicago Consulate indicated that in most cases it can legalize a document immediately.

Fee: $20.00

Payment Method: Cash, money order, certified check, company check payable to the Philippine Embassy, Consulate General or Honorary Consulate of the Philippines

III. EMBASSY, CONSULATES GENERAL

Address, Phone, Hours	*Jurisdiction*
Embassy of the Philippines Authorization Office 1600 Massachusetts Avenue, NW Washington, DC 20036 Tel.: 202-467-9300 Fax: 202-467-9417 9:00 AM - 12:00 PM, Mon. - Fri. 2:00 PM - 5:00 PM, except Wednesday 2:00 PM - 7:00 PM, Wednesday	Alabama Florida Georgia Kentucky Maryland North Carolina South Carolina Tennessee Washington DC West Virginia Virginia Virgin Islands
Consulate General 30 N. Michigan Avenue, Suite 2100 Chicago, IL 60602 Tel.: 312-332-6458/9 Fax: 312-332-3657 9:00 AM - 4:00 PM	Illinois Indiana Iowa Kansas Michigan Minnesota Missouri Nebraska North Dakota Ohio South Dakota Wisconsin
Consulate General 2433 Pali Highway Honolulu, HI 96817 Tel.: 808-595-6316 Fax: 808-595-2581	Hawaii

Address, Phone, Hours	*Jurisdiction*
Consulate General 3660 Wilshire Boulevard, Suite 900 Los Angeles, CA 90010 Tel.: 213-387-5321 Fax: 213-387-6664	Arkansas Arizona California (south of Fresno) Nevada Las Vegas New Mexico Oklahoma Texas
Consulate General 556 Fifth Avenue New York, NY 10036 Tel.: 212-764-1330/4 Fax: 212-382-1146 9:00 AM - 4:00 PM	Connecticut Delaware Louisiana Maine Massachusetts Mississippi New Hampshire New Jersey New York Pennsylvania Rhode Island Vermont
Consulate General 447 Sutter Street, Sixth Floor San Francisco, CA 94108 Tel.: 415-433-6666/9 Fax: 415-421-2641 9:00 AM - 4:00 PM	Alaska California (north of Fresno) Colorado Idaho Montana Oregon Utah Washington Wyoming
Consulate General GITC Building, Suite 406 Marine Drive Tamuning, Agana, Guam 96911 Tel.: 671-646-4620 Fax: 671-649-1868	Caroline Islands Marshall Islands Saipan Wake Island

Address, Phone, Hours	*Jurisdiction*
Consulate General CTC Building PO Box 731 Beach Road, San Jose, Saipan Commonwealth of Northern Mariana Islands MP 96950 Tel.: 670-234-1848 Fax: 670-234-1849	

REPUBLIC OF POLAND

National Holiday: May 3

I. GENERAL INFORMATION

The Embassy and Consulates General have legalization functions. Each will legalize documents originating in its jurisdiction.

Requirements for different types of documents vary.

II. REQUIREMENTS FOR LEGALIZATION

Prior Authentications Required
1. Notarization
2. Authentication of Notary Signature (In most states this may be done directly by the State Secretary of State; if not, the County Clerk authenticates the signature.)
3. State Secretary of State Certification (In states where the Notary Signature may be authenticated directly by the State Secretary of State, steps 2 and 3 are combined.)
4. U.S. Secretary of State Certification

Materials to be Submitted with Request
1. Original document to be legalized
2. Photocopy of the document
3. Prepaid, self-addressed return envelope

Direct Signing of Document Before Consular Official: The procedure of certifying the signature of a private person is available. The signer must present identification with a photo, such as a passport. Consult the Embassy when the document relates to real estate located in Poland.

Turn Around Time: If the document is personally delivered, it will be legalized immediately in most cases for an additional fee of $35.00. If the document is mailed, there may be a delay of up to ten working days before legalization, but in most cases documents are legalized within two or three days.

Fee: $35.00 except for the following: $115 for power of attorney for conveyance of real estate and some other proprietary interests located in

Poland; $55.00 for assignment of priority right and other patent-related documents

Payment Method: Cash, money order, cashier's check, certified check payable to the Embassy of Poland

III. EMBASSY AND CONSULATES GENERAL

Address, Phone, Hours	*Jurisdiction*
Embassy of the Republic of Poland Consular Division 2224 Wyoming Avenue, NW Washington, DC 20008 Tel.: 202-232-4517 Fax: 202-328-2152 9:00 AM - 1:00 PM 2:00 PM - 6:00 PM, Wednesday	Alabama Florida Georgia Kentucky Maryland Mississippi North Carolina South Carolina Tennessee Virginia Washington, DC West Virginia American Virgin Islands America Samoa Guam Puerto Rico
Consulate General 1530 North Lake Shore Drive Chicago, IL 60610 Tel.: 312-337-8166 Fax: 312-337-7841	Arkansas Illinois Indiana Iowa Kansas Louisiana Michigan Minnesota Missouri Nebraska North Dakota South Dakota Wisconsin

Address, Phone, Hours	*Jurisdiction*
Consulate General 12400 Wilshire Boulevard, Suite 555 Los Angeles, CA 90025 Tel.: 310-442-8500 Fax: 310-442-8515	Alaska Arizona California Colorado Hawaii Idaho Montana Nevada New Mexico Oklahoma Oregon Texas Utah Washington Wyoming
Consulate General 233 Madison Avenue New York, NY 10016 Tel.: 212-889-8360 Fax: 212-779-3062	Connecticut Delaware Maine Massachusetts New Hampshire New Jersey New York Ohio Pennsylvania Rhode Island Vermont

PORTUGAL

National Holiday: Day of Portugal, June 10

I. GENERAL INFORMATION

Portugal is a party to the Hague Convention Abolishing the Requirement for Legalization for Foreign Public Documents.

A document should be sent to the appropriate authority in the state or territory in which the document is notarized in order to obtain the Apostille. For information on obtaining the Apostille for documents originating in the United States, see the procedures specified for each of the individual states under United States jurisdiction in Chapter 2. For the enumeration of Federal authorities competent to provide the Apostille, see Appendix D.

For the text of the Hague Convention, the Apostille, and a list of the parties to the Convention, see Appendix A.

For those instances in which legalization by a Portuguese Consulate official may still be necessary, the requirements for legalization by the Embassy are given below. The Embassy, Consulates General, Consulates and Honorary Consulates have legalization functions.

For information purposes, the Embassy, Consulates General, Consulates, and Honorary Consulates of Portugal are listed below.

II. REQUIREMENTS FOR LEGALIZATION

Prior Authentications Required
1. Notarization
2. Authentication of Notary Signature (In most states this may be done directly by the State Secretary of State; if not, the County Clerk authenticates the signature.)

Materials to be Submitted with Request
1. Original document to be legalized
2. Prepaid, self-addressed return envelope

Turn Around Time: If the document is personally delivered, it can be legalized immediately.

Direct Registration of Notary Public: Not available

Direct Signing of Document Before Consular Official: The procedure of certifying the signature of a private appointment is available. No appointment is necessary.

Fee: Check with the consulate in your area.

Payment Method: Cash, company check, money order payable to the Consulate of Portugal in Washington

III. EMBASSY, CONSULATES GENERAL, CONSULATES AND HONORARY CONSULATES

Address, Phone, Hours	*Jurisdiction*
Consular Section Embassy of Portugal 2310 Tracy Place, NW Washington, DC 20008 Tel.: 202-332-3007 Fax: 202-387-2768 9:00 AM - 1:00 PM	Alabama Arkansas Delaware Georgia Indiana Iowa Kansas Kentucky Louisiana Maryland Michigan Minnesota Mississippi Missouri Nebraska North Carolina North Dakota Ohio Oklahoma South Carolina South Dakota Tennessee Virginia Washington, DC

Address, Phone, Hours	*Jurisdiction*
Consulate General 899 Boylston Street Boston, MA 02115 Tel.: 617-536-8740	Maine Massachusetts (except area covered by New Beford) New Hampshire Vermont
Honorary Consulate 1955 N. New England Avenue Chicago, IL 60635 Tel.: 313-889-7405	Illinois
Honorary Consulate 1901 Ponce de Leon Boulevard, 2nd Floor Coral Gables, FL 33134 Tel.: 305-444-8111	Florida
Honorary Consulate 700 Louisiana Street, Suite 4800 Houston, TX 77002 Tel.: 713-759-1188	Notarizations only
Honorary Consulate PO Box 1246 Kaneohe, HI 96744 Tel.: 808-233-4433	Hawaii
Consulate 1801 Avenue of the Stars - 400 Los Angeles, CA 90067 Tel.: 213-277-1491	Arizona California counties of: Imperial, Kern, Los Angeles, Riverside, San Bernadino, San Diego, San Luis Obispo, Santa Barbara, Ventura New Mexico
Consulate 628 Pleasant Street, Room 201-204 New Bedford, MA 02740 Tel.: 508-997-6151	Massachusetts cities of: Acushnet, Dartmouth, New Bedford, Fall River

Address, Phone, Hours	*Jurisdiction*
	Massachusetts counties of: Barnstable, Bristol, Dukes, Nantucket, Plymouth
Consulate General 630 Fifth Avenue, Suite 378 New York, NY 10111 Tel.: 212-246-4580	New York Puerto Rico Virgin Islands
Consulate 1180 Raymond Boulevard, Suite 222 Newark, NJ 07102 Tel.: 201-622-7300	New Jersey
Honorary Consulate 2001 Welsh Road Philadelphia, PA 19115 Tel.: 215-464-3335	Pennsylvania
Consulate 56 Pine Street, 6th Floor Providence, RI 02903 Tel.: 401-272-2003	Rhode Island
Consulate General 3298 Washington Street San Francisco, CA 94115 Tel.: 415-346-3400	Alaska California (except for area covered by LA Consulate) Colorado Idaho Montana Nevada Oregon Utah Washington Wyoming

Address, Phone, Hours	*Jurisdiction*
Honorary Consulate 20 E. Main Street, Room 220 Waterbury, CT 06702 Tel.: 203-755-4111 9:00 AM - 4:00 PM Mon. - Thurs. 9:00 AM - 5:00 PM Friday	Connecticut

STATE OF QATAR

National Holiday: Independence Day, September 3

I. GENERAL INFORMATION

Qatar has an Embassy in the United States but no Consulates. Documents from anywhere in the United States may be sent to the Embassy for legalization. Commercial documents must be processed by the U.S.-Arab Chamber of Commerce before being submitted to the Embassy. See Appendix C for information on the U.S.-Arab Chamber of Commerce.

II. REQUIREMENTS FOR LEGALIZATION

Prior Authentications Required

1. Notarization
2. Authentication of Notary Signature (In most states this may be done directly by the State Secretary of State; if not, the County Clerk authenticates the signature.)
3. State Secretary of State Certification (In states where the Notary Signature may be authenticated directly by the State Secretary of State, steps 2 and 3 are combined.)
4. U.S. Secretary of State Certification
5. Commercial documents must be submitted to the U.S.-National Arab Chamber of Commerce.

Materials to be Submitted with Request

1. Original document to be legalized
2. Photocopy of the document; two copies of commercial invoices, one copy of a certificate of origin and one copy of any other document that requires authentication such as a health certificate
3. Prepaid, self-addressed return envelope

Fees

Legalization of Certificates of Origin, Bill of Lading Airway Bill: $42.00

Legalization of Commercial Invoices: fee depends on amount stated on invoice and ranges from $28.00 to $825 and more, with fees of 0.4% of the value of the invoice charged for invoices valued at $274,725.01 and more.

Legalization of commercial documents other than those listed above, e.g., Commercial Contract: $28.00

Legalization of Powers of Attorney (general or special), Agency Deeds, Real Estate Sales and Leasing Contracts, Guaranty Contracts and Trusteeship Deeds: $14.00
Legalization of any other civil documents: $6.00

III. EMBASSY

Address, Phone, Hours	*Jurisdiction*
Embassy of the State of Qatar Suite 200 4200 Wisconsin Avenue, NW Washington, DC 20016 Tel.: 202-274-1646 Fax: 202-237-0061 9:00 AM - 1:00 PM 2:00 PM - 5:00 PM	Entire United States

REUNION

I. GENERAL INFORMATION

Reunion is an Overseas Department of France, covered by the Hague Convention Abolishing the Requirement for Legalization for Foreign Public Documents.

A document should be sent to the appropriate authority in the state or territory in which the document is notarized in order to obtain the Apostille. For information on obtaining the Apostille for documents originating in the United States, see the procedures specified for each of the individual states under United States jurisdiction in Chapter 2. For the enumeration of Federal authorities competent to provide the Apostille, see Appendix D.

For the text of the Hague Convention, the Apostille, and a list of the parties to the Convention, see Appendix A.

For information on French Consulates, see France.

ROMANIA

National Holiday: December 1

I. GENERAL INFORMATION

The Embassy and Consulates General have legalization functions. Each will legalize documents originating in its jurisdiction.

II. REQUIREMENTS FOR LEGALIZATION

Prior Authentications Required
1. Notarization
2. Authentication of Notary Signature (In most states this may be done directly by the State Secretary of State; if not, the County Clerk authenticates the signature.)
3. State Secretary of State Certification (In states where the Notary Signature may be authenticated directly by the State Secretary of State, steps 2 and 3 are combined.)
4. U.S. Secretary of State Certification

Materials to be Submitted with Request
1. Original document to be legalized
2. Prepaid, self-addressed return envelope

Direct Registration of Notary Public: Not available

Direct Signing of Document Before Consular Official: The procedure of certifying the signature of a private person is available at the Embassy and Consulates General for power of attorney for sales, purchases, pensions, judicial representation or general administration. Identity papers must be presented.

Turn Around Time: If the document is personally delivered, it will generally be legalized immediately.

Fee: $30.00 per document or signature if submitted by mail; $45.00 per document or signature if document is signed in the presence of a Consular official.

Payment Method: Cash, money order, certified check, company check payable to the Embassy or Consulate General of Romania

III. EMBASSY AND CONSULATES GENERAL

Address, Phone, Hours	*Jurisdiction*
Embassy of Romania 1607 23rd Street, NW Washington, DC 20008 Tel.: 202-332-4846/8/52, ext. 117/8 Fax: 202-232-4748 8:30 AM - 5:30 PM	Alabama Alaska Arkansas Florida Georgia Hawaii Illinois Indiana Iowa Kansas Kentucky Louisiana Maryland Michigan Minnesota Mississippi Missouri Nebraska North Carolina North Dakota Ohio Oklahoma Puerto Rico South Carolina South Dakota Tennesse Texas Virginia Washington, DC West Virginia Wisconsin

Address, Phone, Hours	*Jurisdiction*
Consulate General 573-577 Third Avenue New York, NY 10016 Tel.: 212-682-9120 Fax: 212-972-8463	Connecticut Delaware Maine Massachusetts New Hampshire New Jersey New York Pennsylvania Rhode Island Vermont
Consulate General 11766 Wilshire Boulevard, Suite 560 Los Angeles, CA 90025 Tel.: 310-444-0043 Fax: 310-445-0043	Arizona California Colorado Idaho Montana Nevada New Mexico Oregon Utah Washington Wyoming

RUSSIAN FEDERATION

National Holidays: January 7; May 1; May 2; Victory Day, May 9 and May 10; and others

I. GENERAL INFORMATION

The Russian Federation is a party to the Hague Convention Abolishing the Requirement for Legalization for Foreign Public Documents.

A document should be sent to the appropriate authority in the state or territory in which the document is notarized in order to obtain the Apostille. For information on obtaining the Apostille for documents originating in the United States, see the procedures specified for each of the individual states under United States jurisdiction in Chapter 2. For the enumeration of Federal authorities competent to provide the Apostille, see Appendix D.

For the text of the Hague Convention, the Apostille, and a list of the parties to the Convention, see Appendix A.

For information purposes, the Embassy of the Russian Federation is listed below.

For instances in which legalization by a Russian Consular official is still necessary, the requirements for legalization by the Embassy are given below.

II. REQUIREMENTS FOR LEGALIZATION

Prior Authentications Required

1. Notarization

Materials to be Submitted with Request

1. Original document to be legalized

III. EMBASSY AND CONSULATES

Address, Phone, Hours	*Jurisdiction*
Embassy of the Russian Federation Consular Division 1825 Phelps Place Washington, DC 10008 Tel.: 202-939-8910 Fax: 202-939-8909	Entire United States
Consulate 9 East 91st Street New York, NY 10128 Tel.: 212-348-0096	New York
Consulate 2790 Green Street San Francisco, CA 94123 Tel.: 415-928-6878	California
Consulate 2323 Westin Building 2001 Sixth Avenue Seattle, WA 98121 Tel.: 206-728-1910	Washington

REPUBLIC OF RWANDA

National Holiday: Independence Day, July 1

I. GENERAL INFORMATION

Please communicate directly with the Embassy for information about legalization procedures.

II. EMBASSY

Embassy of the Republic of Rwanda
1714 New Hampshire Avenue, NW
Washington, DC 20009
Tel.: 202-232-2882
Fax: 202-232-4544
9:00 AM - 5:00 PM

KINGDOM OF SAUDI ARABIA

National Holiday: Unification of the Kingdom, September 23

I. GENERAL INFORMATION

Commercial documents, i.e., shipment of goods certificates, bills of lading, certificates of origin, invoices, etc., must be legalized by the National-U.S. Arab Chamber of Commerce and then by the Consular Section of The Royal Embassy of Saudi Arabia. For information on the National-U.S. Arab Chamber of Commerce, see Appendix C.

Company documents, such as power of attorney, commercial and corporation agreements and birth and death certificates, must be notarized, authenticated by the County Clerk, certified by the Secretary of State and then by the U.S. State Department Authentication Division before being submitted to the Embassy.

Islamic documents issued in Washington, DC must be notarized and authenticated by the Office of the Secretary of State.

II. REQUIREMENTS FOR LEGALIZATION

Prior Authentications Required

1. Notarization
2. Authentication of Notary Signature (In most states this may be done directly by the State Secretary of State; if not, the County Clerk authenticates the signature.)
3. State Secretary of State Certification (In states where the Notary Signature may be authenticated directly by the State Secretary of State, steps 2 and 3 are combined.)
4. U.S. Secretary of State Certification

Materials to be Submitted with Request

1. Original document to be legalized
2. Photocopy of the document
3. Prepaid, self-addressed return envelope

Fees

Legalization of certificates/commercial documents by National-U.S. Arab Chamber of Commerce: $15.00 per original certification, $2.00 per copy

Legalization of commercial documents by Embassy: $8.50 per page
Legalization of company and corporation documents by Embassy: $8.50 per set
Legalization by the U.S. State Department: $4.00 per document

Payment Method: Money order payable to the Royal Embassy of Saudi Arabia

III. EMBASSY, NATIONAL U.S.-ARAB CHAMBER OF COMMERCE, U.S. STATE DEPARTMENT

Address, Phone, Hours	*Jurisdiction*
Royal Embassy of Saudi Arabia Consular Section 601 New Hampshire Avenue, NW Washington, DC 20037 Tel.: 202-944-3126 Fax: 202-337-4084 9:30 AM - 12:00 PM 2:00 PM - 3:00 PM	Entire United States
National U.S.-Arab Chamber of Commerce 1825 K Street NW, Suite 1107 Washington, DC 20006 Tel.: 202-289-5920 Fax: 202-331-8297	
U.S. State Department Authentication Division 2400 N. Street, NW Washington, DC 20037 Tel.: 202-647-5002	

SENEGAL

National Holiday: Independence Day, April 4

I. REQUIREMENTS FOR LEGALIZATION

Prior Authentications Required
1. Notarization
2. Authentication of Notary Signature (In most states this may be done directly by the State Secretary of State; if not, the County Clerk authenticates the signature.)
3. State Secretary of State Certification (In states where the Notary Signature may be authenticated directly by the State Secretary of State, steps 2 and 3 are combined.)
4. U.S. Secretary of State Certification

Materials to be Submitted with Request
1. Original document to be legalized
2. Photocopy of the document
3. Prepaid, self-addressed return envelope

Direct Registration of Notary Public: Not available

Direct Signing of Document Before Consular Official: The procedure of certifying the signature of a private person is available at the Embassy if a Senegalese Consular Officer is on hand.

Fee: $1.78 per document, subject to change without notice

Payment Method: Money order payable to the Embassy of Senegal

II. EMBASSY

Address, Phone, Hours	*Jurisdiction*
Embassy of Senegal 2112 Wyoming Avenue, NW Washington, DC 20008 Tel.: 202-234-0540 Fax: 202-332-6315 9:00 - 4:00 AM	Entire United States

REPUBLIC OF SEYCHELLES

National Holiday: Constitution Day, June 18

I. GENERAL INFORMATION

The Republic of Seychelles is a party to the Hague Convention Abolishing the Requirement for Legalization for Foreign Public Documents.

A document should be sent to the appropriate authority in the state or territory in which the document is notarized in order to obtain the Apostille. For information on obtaining the Apostille for documents originating in the United States, see the procedures specified for each of the individual states under United States jurisdiction in Chapter 2. For the enumeration of Federal authorities competent to provide the Apostille, see Appendix D.

For the text of the Hague Convention, the Apostille, and a list of the parties to the Convention, see Appendix A.

For information purposes, the Embassy Chancery, situated at the United Nations Mission, is listed below.

II. EMBASSY

Address, Phone, Hours	*Jurisdiction*
Embassy of the Republic of Seychelles Chancery c/o Permanent Mission of Seychelles 820 Second Avenue, Suite 900 F New York, NY 10017 Tel.: 212-972-1785 Fax: 212-972-1786 9:30 AM - 5:30 PM	Entire United States and Canada

SIERRA LEONE

National Holiday: Independence Day, April 28

I. GENERAL INFORMATION

The Embassy legalizes only visas and other documents pertaining to citizens of Sierra Leone.

II. EMBASSY

Embassy of Sierra Leone
1701 19th Street, NW
Washington, DC 20009
Tel.: 202-939-9261
Fax: 202-483-1793
9:00 AM - 5:00 PM

REPUBLIC OF SINGAPORE

National Holiday: August 9

I. GENERAL INFORMATION

The Republic of Singapore has an Embassy in the United States but no Consulates. Documents from anywhere in the United States may be sent to the Embassy for legalization.

II. REQUIREMENTS FOR LEGALIZATION

Prior Authentications Required

1. Notarization
2. Authentication of Notary Signature (In most states this may be done directly by the State Secretary of State; if not, the County Clerk authenticates the signature.)
3. State Secretary of State Certification (In states where the Notary Signature may be authenticated directly by the State Secretary of State, steps 2 and 3 are combined.)
4. U.S. Secretary of State Certification

Materials to be Submitted with Request

1. Original document to be legalized
2. Photocopy of the document
3. Prepaid, self-addressed return envelope

Direct Registration of Notary Public: Not available

Direct Signing of Document Before Consular Official: The procedure of certifying the signature of a private person is available only for documents originating in Singapore.

Turn Around Time: If the document is personally delivered, there will be a delay of four days for legalization.

Fee: $8.00 per document

Payment Method: Cash, money order, certified check, company check payable to the Embassy of Singapore.

III. EMBASSY

Embassy of the Republic of Singapore 3501 International Place, NW Washington, DC 20008 Tel.: 202-537-3100 Fax: 202-537-0876 9:00 AM - 12:00 PM 2:00 PM - 5:00 PM	Entire United States

SLOVAK REPUBLIC

National Holidays: None; American holidays observed

I. GENERAL INFORMATION

The Slovak Republic has an Embassy in the United States but no Consulates. Documents from anywhere in the United States may be sent to the Embassy for legalization.

II. REQUIREMENTS FOR LEGALIZATION

Prior Authentications Required

1. Notarization
2. Authentication of Notary Signature (In most states this may be done directly by the State Secretary of State; if not, the County Clerk authenticates the signature.)
3. State Secretary of State Certification (In states where the Notary Signature may be authenticated directly by the State Secretary of State, steps 2 and 3 are combined.)
4. U.S. Secretary of State Certification

Materials to be Submitted with Request

1. Original document to be legalized
2. Photocopy of the document
3. Prepaid, self-addressed return envelope

Direct Registration of Notary Public: Not available

Direct Signing of Document Before Consular Official: The procedure of certifying the signature of a private person is available. An appointment should be made and the signer must present identification such as a driver's license or passport.

Turn Around Time: If the document is personally delivered, there may be a delay of 24 hours before legalization.

Fee: $12.00 per document or signature

Payment Method: Cash, money order, certified check, company check

III. EMBASSY

Address, Phone, Hours	*Jurisdiction*
Embassy of the Slovak Republic Suite 250 2201 Wisconsin Avenue, NW Washington, DC 20007 Tel.: 202-965-5160 Fax: 202-965-5166 9:00 AM - 12:00 PM	Entire United States

REPUBLIC OF SLOVENIA

National Holiday: June 25

I. GENERAL INFORMATION

Slovenia is a party to the Hague Convention Abolishing the Requirement for Legalization for Foreign Public Documents.

A document should be sent to the appropriate authority in the state or territory in which the document is notarized in order to obtain the Apostille. For information on obtaining the Apostille for documents originating in the United States, see the procedures specified for each of the individual states under United States jurisdiction in Chapter 2. For the enumeration of Federal authorities competent to provide the Apostille, see Appendix D.

For the text of the Hague Convention, the Apostille, and a list of the parties to the Convention, see Appendix A.

For information purposes, the Embassy and Consulate General are listed below.

II. EMBASSY AND CONSULATE GENERAL

Address, Phone, Hours	*Jurisdiction*
Embassy of the Republic of Slovenia 1525 New Hampshire Avenue, NW Washington, DC 20036 Tel.: 202-667-5363 Fax: 202-667-4563 9:00 AM - 5:00 PM	Entire United States
Consulate General 600 Third Avenue, 24th Floor New York, NY 10016 Tel.: 212-370-3006 Fax: 212-370-3581	Connecticut Maine Massachusetts New Hampshire New Jersey New York Rhode Island Vermont

REPUBLIC OF SOUTH AFRICA

National Holiday: Freedom Day, April 27

I. GENERAL INFORMATION

South Africa is a party to the Hague Convention Abolishing the Requirement for Legalization for Foreign Public Documents.

A document should be sent to the appropriate authority in the state or territory in which the document is notarized in order to obtain the Apostille. For information on obtaining the Apostille for documents originating in the United States, see the procedures specified for each of the individual states under United States jurisdiction in Chapter 2. For the enumeration of Federal authorities competent to provide the Apostille, see Appendix D.

For the text of the Hague Convention, the Apostille, and a list of the parties to the Convention, see Appendix A.

For information purposes, the Embassy and Consulates General are listed below.

II. EMBASSY AND CONSULATES GENERAL

Address, Phone, Hours	*Jurisdiction*
Embassy of the Republic of South Africa 3051 Massachusetts Avenue, NW Washington, DC 20008 Tel.: 202-232-4400 9:00 AM - 12:00 PM 2:00 PM - 3:00 PM	Alabama Florida Georgia Louisiana Maryland Mississippi Puerto Rico Texas Virginia Washington, DC Virgin Islands

Address, Phone, Hours	*Jurisdiction*
Consulate General 50 North La Cienega Boulevard, Suite 300 Beverly Hills, CA 90211 Tel.: 310-657-9200 9:00 AM - 12:00 PM 1:00 PM - 3:00 PM Monday through Friday	Alabama Arizona California Colorado Hawaii Idaho Montana New Mexico Nevada Oregon Vermont Washington Wyoming American Samoa Guam
Consulate General 200 South Michigan Avenue Chicago, IL 60604 Tel.: 312-939-7929 Fax: 312-939-8748	Arkansas Idaho Illinois Indiana Kentucky Michigan Minnesota Missouri Nebraska North Dakota Ohio Oklahoma South Dakota Wisconsin

Address, Phone, Hours	*Jurisdiction*
Consulate General 333 East 38th Street, 9th Floor New York, NY 10016 Tel.: 212-213-4880	Connecticut Delaware Kentucky Maine Massachusetts New Hampshire New Jersey New York North Carolina Pennsylvania Rhode Island South Carolina Tennessee Vermont West Virginia

SPAIN

National Holidays: October 12, December 7

I. GENERAL INFORMATION

Spain is a party to the Hague Convention Abolishing the Requirement for Legalization for Foreign Public Documents.

A document should be sent to the appropriate authority in the state or territory in which the document is notarized in order to obtain the Apostille. For information on obtaining the Apostille for documents originating in the United States, see the procedures specified for each of the individual states under United States jurisdiction in Chapter 2. For the enumeration of Federal authorities competent to provide the Apostille, see Appendix D.

For the text of the Hague Convention, the Apostille, and a list of the parties to the Convention, see Appendix A.

For information purposes, the Embassy and Consulates General of Spain are listed below.

II. EMBASSY AND CONSULATES GENERAL

Address, Phone, Hours	*Jurisdiction*
Embassy of Spain Consulate General 2375 Pennsylvania Avenue, NW Washington, DC 20037 Tel.: 202-728-2330 Fax: 202-728-2302 9:00 AM - 1:30 PM	Maryland Virginia Washington, DC West Virginia
Consulate General 545 Boylston Street, Suite 803 Boston, MA 02116 Tel.: 617-536-2506/2527 Fax: 617-536-8512	Maine Massachusetts New Hampshire Rhode Island Vermont

Address, Phone, Hours	*Jurisdiction*
Consulate General 180 North Michigan Avenue, Suite 1500 Chicago, IL 60601 Tel.: 312-782-4588/9 Fax: 312-782-1635	Illinois Indiana Iowa Kansas Kentucky Michigan Minnesota Missouri Nebraska North Dakota Ohio South Dakota Wisconsin
Consulate General 2655 Le Jeune Road, Suite 203 Coral Gables, FL 33134 Tel.: 305-446-5511/2/3 Fax: 305-446-0585	Florida Georgia North Carolina South Carolina
Consulate General 1800 Bering Drive, Suite 660 Houston, TX 77057 Tel.: 713-783-6200/05/14 Fax: 713-783-6166	New Mexico Oklahoma Texas
Consulate General 5055 Wilshire Boulevard, Suite 960 Los Angeles, CA 90036 Tel.: 213-938-0158 Fax: 213-938-2502	Arizona California counties of: Imperial, Inyo, Kern, Los Angeles, Orange, Riverside, San Bernardino, San Diego, San Luis Obispo, Santa Barbara, Ventura Colorado Utah

Address, Phone, Hours	*Jurisdiction*
Consulate General 2102 World Trade Center 2 Canal Street New Orleans, LA 70130 Tel.: 504-525-4951/7920 Fax: 504-525-4955	Alabama Arkansas Louisiana Mississippi Tennessee
Consulate General 150 East 58th Street, 30th Floor New York, NY 10155 Tel.: 212-355-4080/81/82/85/90 Fax: 212-644-3751	Connecticut Delaware New Jersey New York Pennsylvania
Consulate General Edificio Mercantil Plaza Piso 11 - Suite 1101 Avenida Ponce de Leon Hato Rey, Puerto Rico 00918 Tel.: 787-758-6090 Fax: 787-758-6948	Puerto Rico Culebra Island Vieques Island Virgin Islands
Consulate General 1405 Sutter Street San Francisco, CA 94109 Tel.: 415-922-2995/6 Fax: 415-931-9706	Alaska California (except area covered by Los Angeles office) Hawaii Idaho Montana Nevada Oregon Washington Wyoming U.S. Pacific Territories

DEMOCRATIC SOCIALIST REPUBLIC OF SRI LANKA

National Holidays: Thai Pongal Day, January 14; Independence Day, February 4; Ramazan, June 20; Esala Full Moon, July 1; Deepavali, November 11; Mohammed's Birthday, November 25; Unduwap Poya, December 26

I. GENERAL INFORMATION

The Embassy and Consulate have legalization functions. Each will legalize documents originating in its jurisdiction.

II. REQUIREMENTS FOR LEGALIZATION

Prior Authentications Required

1. Notarization
2. Authentication of Notary Signature (In most states this may be done directly by the State Secretary of State; if not, the County Clerk authenticates the signature.)
3. State Secretary of State Certification (In states where the Notary Signature may be authenticated directly by the State Secretary of State, steps 2 and 3 are combined.)
4. U.S. Secretary of State Certification

Materials to be Submitted with Request

1. Original document to be legalized
2. Photocopy of the document
3. Prepaid, self-addressed return envelope

Direct Registration of Notary Public: Not available

Direct Signing of Document Before Consular Official: Not available

Turn Around Time: If the document is personally delivered, there will be a delay of two working days before legalization.

Fee: $19.00 per document or signature

Payment Method: Money order, certified check payable to the Embassy or Consulate of the Democratic Socialist Republic of Sri Lanka

III. EMBASSY AND CONSULATE

Address, Phone, Hours	*Jurisdiction*
Embassy of the Democratic Socialist Republic of Sri Lanka 2148 Wyoming Avenue, NW Washington, DC 20008 Tel.: 202-483-4025, information Tel.: 202-483-4026/8 staff Fax: 202-232-7181 9:00 AM - 12:00 PM (drop off documents) 3:00 PM - 4:30 PM (pick up documents)	Entire United States
Consulate 630 Third Avenue, 20th Floor New York, NY 10017 Tel.: 212-986-7040 Fax: 212-986-1838 9:30 AM - 1:00 PM	Connecticut New Jersey New York

ST. HELENA

I. GENERAL INFORMATION

St. Helena is a dependency of the United Kingdom, covered by the Hague Convention Abolishing the Requirement for Legalization for Foreign Public Documents.

A document should be sent to the appropriate authority in the state or territory in which the document is notarized in order to obtain the Apostille. For information on obtaining the Apostille for documents originating in the United States, see the procedures specified for each of the individual states under United States jurisdiction in Chapter 2. For the enumeration of Federal authorities competent to provide the Apostille, see Appendix D.

For the text of the Hague Convention, the Apostille, and a list of the parties to the Convention, see Appendix A.

For information on United Kingdom Consulates, see the United Kingdom.

ST. KITTS & NEVIS

I. GENERAL INFORMATION

St. Kitts & Nevis is a party to the Hague Convention Abolishing the Requirement for Legalization for Foreign Public Documents.

A document should be sent to the appropriate authority in the state or territory in which the document is notarized in order to obtain the Apostille. For information on obtaining the Apostille for documents originating in the United States, see the procedures specified for each of the individual states under United States jurisdiction in Chapter 2. For the enumeration of Federal authorities competent to provide the Apostille, see Appendix D.

For the text of the Hague Convention, the Apostille, and a list of the parties to the Convention, see Appendix A.

For information purposes, the Embassy of St. Kitts & Nevis is listed below.

II. EMBASSY

Embassy of St. Kitts & Nevis
3216 New Mexico Avenue, NW
Washington, DC 20016
Tel.: 202-833-3500

ST. LUCIA

St. Lucia is a party to the Hague Convention Abolishing the Requirement for Legalization for Foreign Public Documents.

A document should be sent to the appropriate authority in the state or territory in which the document is notarized in order to obtain the Apostille. For information on obtaining the Apostille for documents originating in the United States, see the procedures specified for each of the individual states under United States jurisdiction in Chapter 2. For the enumeration of Federal authorities competent to provide the Apostille, see Appendix D.

For the text of the Hague Convention, the Apostille, and a list of the parties to the Convention, see Appendix A.

For information purposes, the Embassy of St. Lucia is listed below.

II. EMBASSY

Embassy of St. Lucia
3216 New Mexico Avenue, NW
Washington, DC 20016
Tel.: 202-463-7378

ST. PIERRE AND MIQUELON

I. GENERAL INFORMATION

St. Pierre and Miquelon is an Overseas Department of France, covered by the Hague Convention Abolishing the Requirement for Legalization for Foreign Public Documents.

Documents originating in the United States (or other parties to the Convention) should be sent to the appropriate authority in each member state in order to obtain the Apostille.

For general information on the Hague Convention and the Apostille, see Appendix A.

For information on obtaining the Apostille for documents originating in the United States, see the individual state.

For information on French Consulates, see France.

REPUBLIC OF THE SUDAN

National Holiday: Independence Day, January 1

I. GENERAL INFORMATION

The Embassy and Consulate General in New York have legalization functions. For information on the National U.S.-Arab Chamber of Commerce, see Appendix C.

II. REQUIREMENTS FOR LEGALIZATION

Prior Authentications Required

1. Notarization
2. Authentication of Notary Signature (In most states this may be done directly by the State Secretary of State; if not, the County Clerk authenticates the signature.)
3. State Secretary of State Certification (In states where the Notary Signature may be authenticated directly by the State Secretary of State, steps 2 and 3 are combined.)
4. U.S. Secretary of State Certification
5. National U.S.- Arab Chamber of Commerce Authentication

Materials to be Submitted with Request

1. Original document to be legalized
2. Photocopy of the document
3. Prepaid, self-addressed return envelope

Direct Registration of Notary Public: Not available

Direct Signing of Document Before Consular Official: Not available

Turn Around Time: If the document is personally delivered, it will be ready the following day after 1:00 PM. The New York Consulate will legalize a document immediately if an official is available.

Fee: $200.00 per document

Payment Method: Cash, money order, company check payable to the Embassy of Sudan

III. EMBASSY AND CONSULATE GENERAL

Address, Phone, Hours	*Jurisdiction*
Embassy of the Republic of the Sudan Consular Section 2210 Massachusetts Avenue, NW Washington, DC 20008 Tel.: 202-338-8565 Fax: 202-667-4206 10:00 AM - 1:00 PM	Entire United States
Consulate General 655 Third Avenue, Fifth Floor New York, NY 10017 Tel.: 212-573-6033 Fax: 212-573-6160 10:00 AM - 5:00 PM	Entire United States

REPUBLIC OF SURINAME

National Holiday: Independence Day, November 25

I. GENERAL INFORMATION

Suriname is a party to the Hague Convention Abolishing the Requirement for Legalization for Foreign Public Documents.

A document should be sent to the appropriate authority in the state or territory in which the document is notarized in order to obtain the Apostille. For information on obtaining the Apostille for documents originating in the United States, see the procedures specified for each of the individual states under United States jurisdiction in Chapter 2. For the enumeration of Federal authorities competent to provide the Apostille, see Appendix D.

For the text of the Hague Convention, the Apostille, and a list of the parties to the Convention, see Appendix A.

For information purposes, the Embassy and Consulate General of Suriname are listed below.

II. EMBASSY AND CONSULATE GENERAL

Address, Phone, Hours	*Jurisdiction*
Embassy of the Republic of Suriname 4301 Connecticut Avenue, NW Washington, DC 20008 Tel.: 202-244-7488 Fax: 202-244-5878 9:00 AM - 5:00 PM	Entire United States
Consulate General 7235 NW 19th Street, Suite A Miami, FL 33126 Tel.: 305-593-2163 Fax: 305-599-1034 8:00 AM - 5:00 PM	Entire United States

KINGDOM OF SWAZILAND

National Holidays: April 19, September 6

I. GENERAL INFORMATION

The Kingdom of Swaziland is a party to the Hague Convention Abolishing the Requirement for Legalization for Foreign Public Documents.

A document should be sent to the appropriate authority in the state or territory in which the document is notarized in order to obtain the Apostille. For information on obtaining the Apostille for documents originating in the United States, see the procedures specified for each of the individual states under United States jurisdiction in Chapter 2. For the enumeration of Federal authorities competent to provide the Apostille, see Appendix D.

For the text of the Hague Convention, the Apostille, and a list of the parties to the Convention, see Appendix A.

For information purposes, the Embassy of Swaziland is listed below.

II. EMBASSY

Embassy of the Kingdom of Swaziland
Suite 3M
3400 International Drive, NW
Washington, DC 20008
Tel.: 202-362-6683
Fax: 202-244-8059
9:00 AM - 4:30 PM

KINGDOM OF SWEDEN

National Holiday: Swedish National Day, June 6

I. GENERAL INFORMATION

The Embassy and Consulate General have legalization functions. Sweden may open a Consulate General in Los Angeles.

II. REQUIREMENTS FOR LEGALIZATION

Prior Authentications Required

1. Notarization
2. Authentication of Notary Signature (In most states this may be done directly by the State Secretary of State; if not, the County Clerk authenticates the signature.)
3. State Secretary of State Certification (In states where the Notary Signature may be authenticated directly by the State Secretary of State, steps 2 and 3 are combined.)
4. U.S. Secretary of State Certification

Materials to be Submitted with Request

1. Original document to be legalized
2. Prepaid, self-addressed return envelope

Direct Registration of Notary Public: Not available

Direct Signing of Document Before Consular Official: Not available

Turn Around Time: If the document is personally delivered, there will be a delay of approximately two days before legalization.

Fee: $21.00 per document or signature

Payment Method: Cash, money order, certified check, check payable to the Embassy or Consulate General of Sweden

III. EMBASSY AND CONSULATE GENERAL

Address, Phone, Hours	*Jurisdiction*
Embassy of the Kingdom of Sweden 1501 M Street, NW, Suite 900 Washington, DC 20005-1702 Tel.: 202-467-2600 Fax: 202-467-2699 9:00 AM - 4:00 PM	Maryland Virginia Washington, DC
Consulate General One Dag Hammerskjold Plaza, 45th Floor New York, NY 10017-2201 Tel.: 212-583-2550 Fax: 212-755-2732 9:00 AM - 12:30 PM 1:30 PM - 4:00 PM	Entire United States

SWISS CONFEDERATION

National Holiday: Anniversary of the Founding of the Swiss Confederation, August 1

I. GENERAL INFORMATION

Switzerland is a party to the Hague Convention Abolishing the Requirement for Legalization for Foreign Public Documents.

A document should be sent to the appropriate authority in the state or territory in which the document is notarized in order to obtain the Apostille. For information on obtaining the Apostille for documents originating in the United States, see the procedures specified for each of the individual states under United States jurisdiction in Chapter 2. For the enumeration of Federal authorities competent to provide the Apostille, see Appendix D.

For the text of the Hague Convention, the Apostille, and a list of the parties to the Convention, see Appendix A.

For information purposes, the Embassy, Permanent Observer Mission and Consulates General of Switzerland are listed below.

Swiss consular officials also legalize documents for Liechtenstein and represent Cuba in diplomatic matters. Cuban legalizations are processed through a separate agency located in the Embassy's Cuban Interest Section. For Cuban legalizations, see the Cuban entry in this section.

Payment Method: The Embassy accepts checks made out to the Embassy of Switzerland. For the Consulates, verify whether checks will be accepted and, if so, the name of the payee.

II. EMBASSY, PERMANENT OBSERVER MISSION AND CONSULATES GENERAL

Address, Phone, Hours	*Jurisdiction*
Embassy of the Swiss Confederation 2900 Cathedral Avenue, NW Washington, DC 20008-3499 Tel.: 202-745-7900 Fax: 202-387-2564 9:00 AM - 12:00 PM	Delaware Kentucky Maryland Virginia Washington, DC West Virginia US possessions without Swiss representation
Permanent Observer Mission to the United Nations 757 Third Avenue, 21st Floor New York, NY 10017-7092 Tel.: 212-421-1480 Fax: 212-751-2104	UN matters only
Consulate General 1275 Peachtree Street, NE, Suite 425 Atlanta, GA 30309-3555 Tel.: 404-870-2000 Fax: 404-870-2011	Alabama Florida Georgia Mississippi North Carolina South Carolina Tennessee
Consulate General Olympia Center, Suite 2301 737 North Michigan Avenue Chicago, IL 60611 Tel.: 312-915-0061 Fax: 312-915-0388	Illinois Indiana Iowa Michigan Minnesota Missouri Nebraska North Dakota Ohio South Dakota Wisconsin Wyoming

Address, Phone, Hours	*Jurisdiction*
Consulate General First Interstate Bank Plaza, Suite 5670 1000 Louisiana Houston, TX 77002-5013 Tel.: 713-650-0000 Fax: 713-650-1321	Arkansas Colorado Kansas Louisiana New Mexico Oklahoma Texas British Cayman Islands
Consulate General 11766 Wilshire Boulevard, Suite 1400 Los Angeles, CA 90025 Tel.: 310-575-1145 Fax: 310-575-1982	Arizona California (south) counties with zip codes of 90000 to 93500
Consulate General Rolex Building, 8th Floor 665 Fifth Avenue New York, NY 10022-6981 Tel.: 212-758-2560 Fax. 212-207-8024	Connecticut Maine Massachusetts New Hampshire New Jersey New York Pennsylvania Rhode Island Vermont Puerto Rico US Virgin Islands
Consulate General 456 Montgomery Street, Suite 1500 San Francisco, CA 94104-1233 Tel.: 415-788-2272 Fax: 415-788-1402	Alaska California (north) counties with zip codes over 93501 Hawaii Idaho Montana Nevada Oregon Utah Washington

SYRIAN ARAB REPUBLIC

National Holiday: National Day, April 17

I. GENERAL INFORMATION

The Embassy and Consulate General have legalization functions.

II. REQUIREMENTS FOR LEGALIZATION

Prior Authentications Required
1. Notarization
2. Authentication of Notary Signature (In most states this may be done directly by the State Secretary of State; if not, the County Clerk authenticates the signature.)
3. State Secretary of State Certification (In states where the Notary Signature may be authenticated directly by the State Secretary of State, steps 2 and 3 are combined.)
4. U.S. Secretary of State Certification

Materials to be Submitted with Request
1. Original document to be legalized
2. Photocopy of the document
3. Prepaid, self-addressed return envelope

Direct Registration of Notary Public: Not available

Direct Signing of Document Before Consular Official: Not available

Turn Around Time: If the document is personally delivered, it may be legalized the same day, depending on the document.

Fee: $10.00 per document or signature

Payment Method: Money order, cashier's check, company check payable to the Embassy or Consulate General of Syria

III. EMBASSY AND CONSULATE GENERAL

Address, Phone, Hours	*Jurisdiction*
Embassy of the Syrian Arab Republic 2215 Wyoming Avenue, NW Washington, DC 20008 Tel.: 202-232-6313 Fax: 202-265-4585 10:00 AM - 2:00 PM	Entire United States
Consulate General 5433 Westheimer Street, Suite 1020 Houston, TX 77056 Tel.: 713-622-8860 10:00 AM - 4:00 PM	Entire United States
Cuban Interest Section 2630 and 2639 16th Street, NW Washington, DC 20008 Tel.: 202-797-8518	

TANZANIA

National Holidays: New Year's Day, January 1; Zanzibar Revolution Day, January 12; Eid El Fitr*, February 9 and 10; Good Friday, March 28; Easter Monday, March 31; Idd El Hajj*, April 17; Union Day (National Day), April 26; Workers' Day, May 1; Saba Saba (International Trade Fair Day), July 7; Maulid*, July 17; Farmers' Day (Nane Nane), August 8; Independence Day, December 9; Christmas, December 25; Boxing Day, December 26**

* Indicates Moslem holiday confirmation of which depends on sighting of moon

** If holiday falls on Saturday or Sunday, the office will be closed on Monday

I. GENERAL INFORMATION

Tanzania has an Embassy in the United States but no Consulates. Documents from anywhere in the United States may be sent to the Embassy for legalization.

II. REQUIREMENTS FOR LEGALIZATION

Prior Authentications Required

1. Notarization
2. Authentication of Notary Signature (In most states this may be done directly by the State Secretary of State; if not, the County Clerk authenticates the signature.)
3. State Secretary of State Certification (In states where the Notary Signature may be authenticated directly by the State Secretary of State, steps 2 and 3 are combined.)
4. U.S. Secretary of State Certification

Materials to be Submitted with Request

1. Original document to be legalized
2. Photocopy of the document
3. Prepaid, self-addressed return envelope

Direct Registration of Notary Public: Not available

Direct Signing of Document Before Consular Official: Not available

Turn Around Time: If the document is personally delivered, there will be a delay of one day before legalization.

Fee: $10.00 per document or signature

Payment Method: Cash, money order, certified check, company check payable to the Embassy

III. EMBASSY

Address, Phone, Hours	*Jurisdiction*
Embassy of Tanzania 2139 R Street, NW Washington, DC 20008 Tel.: 202-939-6125 Fax: 202-797-7408 9:00 AM - 5:00 PM	Entire United States

KINGDOM OF THAILAND

National Holiday: Birthday of His Majesty the King, December 5

I. GENERAL INFORMATION

The Embassy and Consulates General have legalization functions. Each will legalize documents originating in its jurisdiction.

II. REQUIREMENTS FOR LEGALIZATION

Prior Authentications Required
1. Notarization
2. Authentication of Notary Signature (In most states this may be done directly by the State Secretary of State; if not, the County Clerk authenticates the signature.)
3. State Secretary of State Certification (In states where the Notary Signature may be authenticated directly by the State Secretary of State, steps 2 and 3 are combined.)
4. U.S. Secretary of State Certification

Materials to be Submitted with Request
1. Original document to be legalized
2. Copy of document (all pages)
3. Prepaid, self-addressed return envelope

Direct Registration of Notary Public: Not available

Direct Signing of Document Before Consular Official: Not available

Turn Around Time: If the document is personally delivered, there will be a delay of one to two days before legalization. Allow a week if submitting documents by mail.

Fee: $5.00 per document or signature

Payment Method: Cash, money order payable to the Royal Thai Embassy

III. EMBASSY AND CONSULATES GENERAL

Address, Phone, Hours	*Jurisdiction*
Royal Thai Embassy Consular Section 1024 Wisconsin Avenue, NW Washington, DC 20007 Tel.: 202-944-3600, ext. 766 Fax: 202-944-3611 9:30 AM - 12:30 PM 2:00 PM - 4:00 PM	Entire United States
Consulate General 35 East Wacker Drive Chicago, IL 60601 Tel.: 312-236-2447	Illinois Indiana Iowa Kentucky Michigan Mississippi
Consulate General 801 North La Brea Avenue Los Angeles, CA 90038 Tel.: 213-937-1984/5	California
Consulate General 351 East 52nd Street New York, NY 10022 Tel.: 212-754-1770 9:00 AM - 12:30 PM 1:30 PM - 4:30 PM	Connecticut Maine Massachusetts New Hampshire New Jersey New York Ohio Pennsylvania Rhode Island Vermont

REPUBLIC OF TOGO

National Holiday: Independence Day, April 27

I. GENERAL INFORMATION

Both the Embassy and the Honorary Consulate in Miami have legalization functions. The requirements listed below are for the Embassy. Requirements at the Honorary Consulate may differ.

II. REQUIREMENTS FOR LEGALIZATION

Prior Authentications Required

1. Notarization
2. Authentication of Notary Signature (In most states this may be done directly by the State Secretary of State; if not, the County Clerk authenticates the signature.)
3. State Secretary of State Certification (In states where the Notary Signature may be authenticated directly by the State Secretary of State, steps 2 and 3 are combined.)
4. U.S. Secretary of State Certification

Materials to be Submitted with Request

1. Original document to be legalized
2. Prepaid, self-addressed return envelope

Direct Registration of Notary Public: Not available

Direct Signing of Document Before Consular Official: Not available

Turn Around Time: If the document is personally delivered, it must be left for two days for legalization.

Fee: $6.00 per document or signature

Payment Method: Money order payable to the Embassy or Honorary Consulate of Togo

III. EMBASSY AND HONORARY CONSULATE

Address, Phone, Hours	*Jurisdiction*
Embassy of the Republic of Togo 2208 Massachusetts Avenue, NW Washington, DC 20008 Tel.: 202-234-4212 Fax: 202-232-3190 9:00 AM - 4:00 PM	Entire United States
Honorary Consul Michael S. Hacker, Esq. First Union Financial Center, Suite 3800 200 South Biscayne Boulevard Miami, FL 33131-2310 Tel.: 305-371-4286 Fax: 305-371-4288	Entire United States

KINGDOM OF TONGA

National Holiday: Emancipation Day, June 4

I. GENERAL INFORMATION

Tonga is a party to the Hague Convention Abolishing the Requirement for Legalization for Foreign Public Documents.

A document should be sent to the appropriate authority in the state or territory in which the document is notarized in order to obtain the Apostille. For information on obtaining the Apostille for documents originating in the United States, see the procedures specified for each of the individual states under United States jurisdiction in Chapter 2. For the enumeration of Federal authorities competent to provide the Apostille, see Appendix D.

For the text of the Hague Convention, the Apostille, and a list of the parties to the Convention, see Appendix A.

TUNISIA

National Holiday: March 20, March 21, April 9, May 1, July 25, August 13, November 7, three religious holidays

I. GENERAL INFORMATION

Requirements may vary, depending on the document.

II. REQUIREMENTS FOR LEGALIZATION

Prior Authentications Required

1. Notarization
2. Authentication of Notary Signature (In most states this may be done directly by the State Secretary of State; if not, the County Clerk authenticates the signature.)
3. State Secretary of State Certification (In states where the Notary Signature may be authenticated directly by the State Secretary of State, steps 2 and 3 are combined.)
4. U.S. Secretary of State Certification

Materials to be Submitted with Request

1. Original document to be legalized
2. Prepaid, self-addressed return envelope

Direct Registration of Notary Public: Not available

Direct Signing of Document Before Consular Official: Not available

Turn Around Time: If the document is personally delivered, there will be a delay of 24 hours before legalization.

Fee: $3.40 per document or signature

Payment Method: Cash, money order, certified check, company check payable to the Embassy of Tunisia

III. EMBASSY

Address, Phone, Hours	*Jurisdiction*
Embassy of Tunisia Consular Section 1515 Massachusetts Avenue, NW Washington, DC 20005 Tel.: 202-862-1850 Fax: 202-862-1858 9:00 AM - 1:00 PM 2:00 PM - 5:00 PM	Entire United States

REPUBLIC OF TURKEY

National Holiday: Anniversary of the Declaration of the Republic, October 29

I. GENERAL INFORMATION

The Embassy and Consulates General have legalization functions. Each will legalize documents originating in its jurisdiction.

II. REQUIREMENTS FOR LEGALIZATION

Prior Authentications Required
1. Notarization
2. Authentication of Notary Signature (In most states this may be done directly by the State Secretary of State; if not, the County Clerk authenticates the signature.)

Materials to be Submitted with Request
1. Original document to be legalized
2. Photocopy of the document
3. Prepaid, self-addressed return envelope

Direct Registration of Notary Public: Not available

Direct Signing of Document Before Consular Official: Not available

Turn Around Time: If the document is personally delivered, legalization will be handled immediately if possible. Otherwise, documents will be legalized within 24 hours of receipt.

Fee: $19.00

Payment Method: Cash, company check, money order payable to the Embassy of Turkey

III. EMBASSY AND CONSULATES GENERAL

Address, Phone, Hours	*Jurisdiction*
Embassy of the Republic of Turkey 1714 Massachusetts Avenue, NW Washington, DC 20036 Tel.: 202-659-0742 Fax: 202-659-0744	Maryland Washington, DC Virginia West Virginia Bahamas
Consulate General 1990 Post Oak Boulevard, Suite 1300 Houston, TX 77056 Tel.: 713-622-5849 Fax: 713-622-6639	Alabama Arkansas Louisiana Mississippi New Mexico Oklahoma Tennessee Texas
Consulate General 4801 Wilshire Boulevard, Suite 310 Los Angeles, CA 90010 Tel.: 213-937-0118 Fax: 213-932-0061	Alaska Arizona California Colorado Hawaii Idaho Montana Nevada Oregon Utah Washington Wyoming U.S. Pacific Islands
Consulate General 821 United Nations Plaza, 5th Floor New York, NY 10017 Tel.: 212-949-0160 Fax: 212-983-1293	Connecticut Delaware Florida Georgia Kentucky Maine Massachusetts New Hampshire New Jersey

Address, Phone, Hours	*Jurisdiction*
	New York North Carolina Pennsylvania Rhode Island South Carolina Vermont Puerto Rico
Consulate General 360 N. Michigan Avenue, Suite 1405 Chicago, IL 60601 Tel.: 312-263-0644 Fax: 312-263-1449	Illinois Indiana Iowa Kansas Michigan Minnesota Missouri Nebraska North Dakota Ohio South Dakota Wisconsin

TURKS AND CAICOS ISLANDS

I. GENERAL INFORMATION

The Turks and Caicos Islands are a dependency of the United Kingdom, covered by the Hague Convention Abolishing the Requirement for Legalization for Foreign Public Documents.

A document should be sent to the appropriate authority in the state or territory in which the document is notarized in order to obtain the Apostille. For information on obtaining the Apostille for documents originating in the United States, see the procedures specified for each of the individual states under United States jurisdiction in Chapter 2. For the enumeration of Federal authorities competent to provide the Apostille, see Appendix D.

For the text of the Hague Convention, the Apostille, and a list of the parties to the Convention, see Appendix A.

For information on United Kingdom Consulates, see the United Kingdom.

REPUBLIC OF UGANDA

I. REQUIREMENTS FOR LEGALIZATION

Prior Authentications Required
1. Notarization
2. Authentication of Notary Signature (In most states this may be done directly by the State Secretary of State; if not, the County Clerk authenticates the signature.)
3. State Secretary of State Certification (In states where the Notary Signature may be authenticated directly by the State Secretary of State, steps 2 and 3 are combined.)
4. U.S. Secretary of State Certification

Materials to be Submitted with Request
1. Original document to be legalized
2. Photocopy of the document
3. Prepaid, self-addressed return envelope

Direct Registration of Notary Public: Not available

Direct Signing of Document Before Consular Official: Not available

Turn Around Time: If the document is personally delivered, there will be a delay of 24 hours for legalization.

Fee: $30.00 per document or signature

Payment Method: Money order or company check, payable to the Embassy of the Republic of Uganda

II. EMBASSY

Embassy of the Republic of Uganda — Entire United States
5911 16th Street, NW
Washington, DC 20011
Tel.: 202-726-7100
Fax: 202-726-1727
9:00 AM - 5:00 PM

UKRAINE

National Holiday: August 24

I. GENERAL INFORMATION

The Embassy and Consulates General have legalization functions. Each will legalize documents originating in its jurisdiction.

II. REQUIREMENTS FOR LEGALIZATION

Prior Authentications Required
1. Notarization
2. Authentication of Notary Signature (In most states this may be done directly by the State Secretary of State; if not, the County Clerk authenticates the signature.)
3. State Secretary of State Certification (In states where the Notary Signature may be authenticated directly by the State Secretary of State, steps 2 and 3 are combined.)
4. U.S. Secretary of State Certification

Materials to be Submitted with Request
1. Original document to be legalized
2. Prepaid, self-addressed return envelope

Direct Registration of Notary Public: Not available

Direct Signing of Document Before Consular Official: The procedure of certifying the signature of a private person is available at the Embassy. The signer must present identification such as a driver's license or passport.

Time Delay: If the document is presented by hand for legalization, there will be a delay of three days before legalization.

Fee: $20.00 per document or signature (processed within nine days); $40.00 for expedited service (processed within three days); $120.00 per copy for power of attorney concerning real estate in Ukraine

Payment Method: Money order, company check payable to the Embassy or Consul General of Ukraine

III. EMBASSY AND CONSULATES GENERAL

Embassy of Ukraine 3350 M Street, NW Washington, DC 20007 Tel.: 202-333-0606 Fax: 202-333-0817 9:15 AM - 11:30 PM	Alabama Alaska Arizona Arkansas California Colorado Delaware Florida Georgia Hawaii Idaho Kentucky Louisiana Maryland Mississippi Missouri Montana Nevada New Mexico North Carolina Ohio Oklahoma Oregon Puerto Rico South Carolina Tennessee Texas Utah Virginia Washington Washington, DC West Virginia Wyoming
Consulate General 10 East Huron Street Chicago, IL 60611 Tel.: 312-642-4385/8	Illinois Indiana Iowa Kansas Michigan Minnesota

Address, Phone, Hours	*Jurisdiction*
	Nebraska North Dakota South Dakota Wisconsin
Consulate General 240 East 49th Street New York, NY 10017 Tel.: 212-371-5690	Connecticut Maine Massachusetts New Hampshire New Jersey New York Pennsylvania Rhode Island Vermont

UNITED ARAB EMIRATES

National Holiday: National Day, December 2

I. GENERAL INFORMATION

The United Arab Emirates have an Embassy in the United States but no Consulates. Documents from anywhere in the United States may be sent to the Embassy for legalization. Only documents legalized by the Embassy of the United Arab Emirates will be accepted in the United Arab Emirates.

II. REQUIREMENTS FOR LEGALIZATION

Prior Authentications Required

1. Notarization
2. Authentication of Notary Signature (In most states this may be done directly by the State Secretary of State; if not, the County Clerk authenticates the signature.)
3. State Secretary of State Certification (In states where the Notary Signature may be authenticated directly by the State Secretary of State, steps 2 and 3 are combined.)
4. U.S. Secretary of State Certification

Commercial/Shipping Documents

1. All such documents should be certified by one of the following before being presented to the Embassy: National U.S.-Arab Chamber of Commerce in Washington, DC; U.S.-Arab Chamber of Commerce in Chicago; North East Chamber of Commerce in New York; U.S.-Arab Chamber of Commerce in San Francisco
2. The final destination/ultimate consignee must be indicated on all documents and the certificate of origin must contain the following statements:
   a. We hereby certify that the vessel or airline will not call nor does it intend to call at any Israeli port prior to destination.*
   b. We hereby certify that the goods stated herein originated and were wholly produced and/or manufactured by (Name of Manufacturer).

* The requirements of the Export Administration Act (50 U.S.C. 2401 et seq.) should be considered before making this certification.

Materials to be Submitted with Request

1. Original document to be legalized
2. Prepaid, self-addressed return envelope

Direct Registration of Notary Public: Not available

Direct Signing of Document Before Consular Official: Not available

Turn Around Time: If the document is personally delivered, there will be a delay of three to four working days before legalization.

Fee

For general powers of attorney and court documents: $30.00
For other legal documents: $15.00
For corporate power of attorney, commercial agreement, contract, sales agreement, articles of incorporation registration, certificates/stock distribution: $300.00
For commercial invoices, depending on value: $30.00 - $600.00

Payment Method: Cash, money order, certified check payable to the Embassy of the United Arab Emirates

III. EMBASSY

Embassy of the United Arab Emirates — Entire United States
Consular Section
Suite 600
3000 K Street, NW
Washington, DC 20007
Tel.: 202-338-6500
Fax: 202-337-7029
9:00 AM - 1:00 PM

UNITED KINGDOM OF GREAT BRITAIN AND NORTHERN IRELAND

National Holiday: Birthday of the Queen, June 11

I. GENERAL INFORMATION

The United Kingdom is a party to the Hague Convention Abolishing the Requirement for Legalization for Foreign Public Documents.

A document should be sent to the appropriate authority in the state or territory in which the document is notarized in order to obtain the Apostille. For information on obtaining the Apostille for documents originating in the United States, see the procedures specified for each of the individual states under United States jurisdiction in Chapter 2. For the enumeration of Federal authorities competent to provide the Apostille, see Appendix D.

For the text of the Hague Convention, the Apostille, and a list of the parties to the Convention, see Appendix A.

For information purposes, the Embassy, Consulates General, Consulates and Honorary Consulates are listed below.

British consular offices can legalize documents for British dependencies.

II. EMBASSY, CONSULATES GENERAL, CONSULATES AND HONORARY CONSULATES

Address, Phone, Hours	*Jurisdiction*
Embassy of the United Kingdom of Great Britain and Northern Ireland Consular Section 19 Observatory Circle, NW Washington, DC 20008-3611 Tel.: 202-588-7800 Fax: 202-588-7850 8:30 AM - 12:30 PM	Delaware Kentucky Maryland Virginia Washington, DC West Virginia

Note: The Embassy handles only consular matters for the residents of Kentucky and West Virginia.

Address, Phone, Hours	*Jurisdiction*
Consulate General Marquis One Tower, Suite 2700 245 Peachtree Center Avenue Atlanta, GA 30303 Tel.: 404-524-5856 Fax: 404-524-3153	Alabama Florida Georgia Mississippi North Carolina South Carolina Tennessee

Note: Residents of the above states should refer to the New York Consulate for visa applications. Residents of Florida should contact the Orlando Consulate for consular matters, and communicate directly with the Atlanta Consulate General for emergency/after hours problems.

Consulate General Federal Reserve Plaza 600 Atlantic Avenue, 25th Floor Boston, MA 02210 Tel.: 617-248-9555 Fax: 617-248-9578	Maine Massachusetts New Hampshire Rhode Island Vermont

Note: The Boston Consulate General is available for consular matters only.

Consulate General The Wrigley Building, Suite 1300 400 N. Michigan Avenue Chicago, IL 60611 Tel.: 312-346-1810 Fax: 312-464-0661/7	Illinois Indiana Iowa Kansas Kentucky Michigan Minnesota Missouri Nebraska North Dakota Ohio South Dakota West Virginia Wisconsin

Note: Residents of Kentucky and West Virginia should refer to the Washington DC Consular Section for consular matters; residents of

Michigan and Ohio should refer to the Cleveland Consulate for consular matters.

Address, Phone, Hours	*Jurisdiction*
Consulate 55 Public Square, Suite 1650 Cleveland, OH 44113-1963 Tel.: 216-621-7675 Fax: 216-621-2615	Michigan (Consular matters) Ohio (Consular matters)
Consulate General 2911 Turtle Creek Boulevard, Suite 940 Dallas, TX 75219 Tel.: 214-521-4090 Fax: 214-521-4807	Arizona Colorado Louisiana New Mexico Oklahoma Texas

Note: The Dallas Consulate General offers limited services dealing with trade matters.

Consulate General 1000 Louisiana, Suite 1900 Houston, TX 77002 Tel.: 713-659-6270 Fax: 713-659-7094	Arkansas Colorado Louisiana New Mexico Oklahoma Texas
Consulate General 11766 Wilshire Boulevard, Suite 400 Los Angeles, CA 90025 Tel.: 310-477-3322, ext. 249 Fax: 310-575-1450	Arizona California Hawaii Nevada: Clark County Utah Guam Trust Territories of the Pacific: Wake, Johnson, Mariana Islands

Note: For consular matters, residents of Alaska, Northern California, Idaho, Montana, Oregon and Wyoming should refer to the San Francisco Consulate. The Los Angeles Consulate General issues visas for all western states and provides full consular services for states listed within its jurisdiction.

Address, Phone, Hours	*Jurisdiction*
Consulate Brickell Bay Office Tower 1001 South Bayshore Drive, Suite 2110 Miami, FL 33131 Tel.: 305-374-1522 Fax: 305-374-8196	Florida

Note: The Miami Consulate deals with trade matters only.

Consulate General 845 Third Avenue New York, NY 10022 Tel.: 212-745-0200 Fax: 212-754-3062	Connecticut Maine Massachusetts New Hampshire New Jersey New York Pennsylvania Puerto Rico Rhode Island Vermont Virgin Islands

Note: The New York Consulate processes visa applications for Alabama, Florida, Georgia, Mississippi, North Carolina, South Carolina and Tennessee. Residents of Maine, Massachusetts, New Hampshire, Rhode Island, and Vermont should refer to the Boston Consulate for consular matters.

Vice Consulate 200 South Orange Avenue, Suite 2110 Orlando, FL 32801 Tel.: 407-426-7855 Fax: 407-426-9343	Florida

Note: For consular matters outside of regular hours, residents of Florida should refer to Atlanta Consulate.

Address, Phone, Hours	*Jurisdiction*
Consulate General 1 Sansome Street, Suite 850 San Francisco, CA 94104 Tel.: 415-981-3034 Fax: 415-434-2018	Alaska California (northern) Idaho Montana Nevada (except for Clark County) Wyoming

Note: San Francisco has jurisdiction for consular and commercial matters only.

Consulate 820 First Interstate Center 999 Third Avenue Seattle, WA 98104 Tel.: 206-622-9255 Fax: 206-622-4728	Oregon Washington
Honorary Consulate Mr. Charles (Peter) Mather III Mather & Company 226 Walnut Street Philadelphia, PA 19106 Tel.: 215-925-0118 Fax: 215-351-9012	Under authority of New York Consulate General
Honorary Consulate Dr. Dan Court American Airlines Building, Suite 1100 1509 Lopez Landron Santurce, PR 00911 Tel.: 787-721-5193 Fax: 787-723-6965	Under authority of New York Consulate General

URUGUAY

National Holiday: Independence Day, August 25

I. GENERAL INFORMATION

The Embassy, Consulates General and Honorary Consulates have legalization functions. Each will legalize documents originating in its jurisdiction. The requirements set forth below are for the Embassy and the New York Consulate General.

II. REQUIREMENTS FOR LEGALIZATION

Prior Authentications Required
The Embassy requires steps 1 through 4.
The New York Consulate requires steps 1 and 2.

1. Notarization
2. Authentication of Notary Signature (In most states this may be done directly by the State Secretary of State; if not, the County Clerk authenticates the signature.)
3. State Secretary of State Certification (In states where the Notary Signature may be authenticated directly by the State Secretary of State, steps 2 and 3 are combined.)
4. U.S. Secretary of State Certification

Materials to be Submitted with Request
1. Original document to be legalized
2. Prepaid, self-addressed return envelope

Direct Registration of Notary Public: Not available

Direct Signing of Document Before Consular Official: The procedure of certifying the signature of a private person is available at all Consulates. The signer must bring two witnesses. Processing time is three working days.

Turn Around Time: If the document is personally delivered, there will be a delay of two working days before legalization at the Embassy and the New York Consulate General.

Fee: Fees vary according to the document presented for legalization. Contact the nearest Consulate to verify current fees.

Payment Method: Cash, money order, certified check, company check, personal check at the Embassy in Washington DC payable to the Embassy of Uruguay; cash or money order at the New York Consulate General payable to the Consulate of Uruguay

III. EMBASSY, CONSULATES GENERAL AND HONORARY CONSULATES

Address, Phone, Hours	*Jurisdiction*
Embassy of Uruguay Consular Section Third Floor 2715 M Street, NW Washington, DC 20007 Tel.: 202-331-4219 Fax: 202-331-8142 9:30 AM - 4:00 PM	Indiana Kentucky Maryland Ohio Virginia Washington, DC West Virginia
Consulate General 1077 Ponce de Leon Boulevard Coral Gables, FL 33134 Tel.: 305-443-9764 Fax: 305-443-7802	Alabama Florida Georgia North Carolina South Carolina Tennessee
Honorary Consulate Medical Building 67 Union Street Natick, MA 01760 Tel.: 617-650-7936	Boston
Honorary Consulate 2 Canal Street, Suite 2002 New Orleans, LA 70130 Tel.: 504-525-8354	Arkansas Louisiana Mississippi Oklahoma Texas

Address, Phone, Hours	*Jurisdiction*
Consulate General 747 Third Avenue, 21st Floor New York, NY 10017 Tel.: 212-753-8581	Connecticut Delaware Illinois Iowa Maine Massachusetts Michigan Minnesota Missouri New Hampshire New Jersey New York Pennsylvania Rhode Island Vermont
Honorary Consulate Himalaya, 254 Monterrey Urb. Puerto Rico, 00926 Tel.: 809-764-7941 Fax: 809-282-8033	Puerto Rico
Consulate General 429 Santa Monica Boulevard, Suite 400 Santa Monica, CA 90401 Tel.: 310-394-5777	Alaska Arizona California Colorado Hawaii Idaho Kansas Missouri Montana Nebraska New Mexico Nevada North Dakota South Dakota Utah Wisconsin Wyoming

Address, Phone, Hours	*Jurisdiction*
Honorary Consulate Lane, Powell, Spears, Lubersky 420 Fifth Avenue, Suite 4100 Seattle, WA 99101 Tel.: 804-625-3658	Oregon Washington

REPUBLIC OF UZBEKISTAN

National Holiday: Independence Day, September 1

I. REQUIREMENTS FOR LEGALIZATION

Prior Authentications Required
1. Notarization
2. State Secretary of State Certification
3. U.S. Secretary of State Certification

Materials to be Submitted with Request
1. Original document to be legalized
2. Photocopy of the document
3. Prepaid, self-addressed return envelope

Direct Registration of Notary Public: Not available

Direct Signing of Document Before Consular Official: The procedure of certifying the signature of a private person is available. An appointment should be made and the signer must present his/her passport as identification.

Turn Around Time: If the document is personally delivered, it must be left for three days for legalization. If the document is mailed, allow five to seven days for legalization.

Fee: $25.00 per document or signature

Payment Method: Money order, certified check payable to the Embassy of Uzbekistan

II. EMBASSY

Embassy of the Republic of Uzbekistan
1746 Massachusetts Avenue, NW
Washington, DC 20036
Tel.: 202-530-7291
Fax: 202-530-7294
10:00 AM - 1:00 PM

REPUBLIC OF VENEZUELA

National Holiday: Independence Day, July 5

I. GENERAL INFORMATION

The Consulates General have legalization functions. Each will legalize documents originating in its jurisdiction. The Embassy does not legalize documents. The requirements given below are for the Chicago and New York Consulates General.

II. REQUIREMENTS FOR LEGALIZATION

Prior Authentications Required

1. Notarization
2. Authentication of Notary Signature (In most states this may be done directly by the State Secretary of State; if not, the County Clerk authenticates the signature.)
3. State Secretary of State Certification required from states not in Embassy's jurisdiction (In states where the Notary Signature may be authenticated directly by the State Secretary of State, steps 2 and 3 are combined.)

Materials to be Submitted with Request

1. Original document to be legalized
2. Prepaid, self-addressed return envelope

Direct Registration of Notary Public: Not available

Direct Signing of Document Before Consular Official: Not available

Turn Around Time: If the document is personally delivered, there will be a delay of 48 hours before legalization.

Fee: $50.00 - $70.00, depending on the document

Payment Method: Money order or company check

III. EMBASSY AND CONSULATES GENERAL

Address, Phone, Hours	*Jurisdiction*
Embassy of the Republic of Venezuela Consular Section 1099 30th Street, NW Washington, DC 20007 Tel.: 202-342-2214 Fax: 202-342-6820 9:00 AM - 1:00 PM	Kentucky Maryland Ohio Virginia Washington, DC West Virginia
Consulate General 545 Boylston Street, 6th Floor Boston, MA 02603 Tel.: 617-266-9355/68 Fax: 617-266-2350	Maine Massachusetts New Hampshire
Consulate General 20 N. Wacker Drive, Suite 1925 Chicago, IL 60606 Tel.: 312-236-9655/9 Fax: 312-580-1010	Illinois Indiana Iowa Michigan Minnesota Nebraska North Dakota South Dakota Wisconsin
Consulate General 2700 Post Oak Boulevard, Suite 1500 Houston, TX 77056 Tel.: 713-961-5141/2/66 Fax: 713-961-1485	Kansas New Mexico Oklahoma Texas
Consulate General 1101 Brickell Avenue, Suite 901 Miami, FL 33131 Tel.: 305-577-0302 Fax: 305-372-5167	Florida Georgia North Carolina South Carolina

Address, Phone, Hours	*Jurisdiction*
Consulate General 1908 World Trade Center 2 Canal Street New Orleans, LA 70130 Tel.: 504-522-3284/6700 Fax: 504-522-7092	Alabama Arkansas Louisiana Mississippi Missouri Tennessee
Consulate General 7 East 51st Street New York, NY 10022 Tel.: 212-826-1660 Fax: 212-644-7471	Connecticut Delaware New Jersey New York Pennsylvania Rhode Island Vermont
Consulate General 455 Market Street, Suite 220 San Francisco, CA 94105 Tel.: 415-512-8340/1/2/7 Fax: 415-512-7693	Alaska Arizona California Colorado Hawaii Idaho Montana Nevada Oregon Utah Washington Wyoming
Consulate General Edificio Mercantil Plaza Piso 6, Oficina 601 Ave. Ponce de Leon Hato Rey, PR 00908 Tel.: 809-766-4250/1 Fax: 809-766-4255	Puerto Rico Virgin Islands

SOCIALIST REPUBLIC OF VIETNAM

National Holiday: September 2

I. GENERAL INFORMATION

The Embassy does not have legalization functions. To legalize documents, it is necessary to contact the appropriate department in Vietnam. For information contact the Embassy (listed below) by telephone or visit the Embassy website at www.Vietnam Embassy - USA.org.

II. EMBASSY

Embassy of the Socialist Republic of Vietnam
Suite 501
1233 20th Street, NW
Washington, DC 20036
Tel.: 202-861-2291
Fax: 202-861-0917
9:30 AM - 12:00 PM

WALLIS AND FUTUNA ISLANDS

I. GENERAL INFORMATION

Wallis and Futuna Islands is an Overseas Territory of France, covered by the Hague Convention Abolishing the Requirement for Legalization for Foreign Public Documents.

A document should be sent to the appropriate authority in the state or territory in which the document is notarized in order to obtain the Apostille. For information on obtaining the Apostille for documents originating in the United States, see the procedures specified for each of the individual states under United States jurisdiction in Chapter 2. For the enumeration of Federal authorities competent to provide the Apostille, see Appendix D.

For the text of the Hague Convention, the Apostille, and a list of the parties to the Convention, see Appendix A.

For information on French Consulates, see France.

WESTERN SAMOA

I. GENERAL INFORMATION

Legalizations for Western Samoa are handled by New Zealand. For New Zealand Consulates, see the Dominion of New Zealand. For information purposes, the Embassy of Western Samoa is listed below.

II. EMBASSY

Embassy of Western Samoa
Suite 800
820 Second Avenue
New York, NY 10017
Tel.: 212-599-6196

THE REPUBLIC OF YEMEN

National Holiday: May 22; local holidays are also observed.

I. REQUIREMENTS FOR LEGALIZATION

Prior Authentications Required
1. Notarization
2. Authentication of Notary Signature (In most states this may be done directly by the State Secretary of State; if not, the County Clerk authenticates the signature.)
3. State Secretary of State Certification (In states where the Notary Signature may be authenticated directly by the State Secretary of State, steps 2 and 3 are combined.)
4. U.S. Secretary of State Certification

Requirements for Commercial Invoices and Certificates of Origin
1. The commercial invoices and certificates of origin must be certified by the National U.S.-Arab Chamber of Commerce and then presented to the Embassy of Yemen for legalization. Please see Appendix C, the National U.S.-Arab Chamber of Commerce, for information on document preparation and other details.

Materials to be Submitted with Request
1. Original document to be legalized
2. Photocopy of the document
3. Prepaid, self-addressed return envelope if the document is mailed to the Embassy

Direct Registration of Notary Public: Not available

Direct Signing of Document Before Consular Official: Not available

Turn Around Time: If the document is personally delivered, it must be left for two days for legalization. If the document is mailed, the average turn around time is two days.

Fee:
$100.00 per document or signature
$30.00 per sheet for commercial invoices and certificates of origin

Payment Method: Money order, certified check, company check payable to the Yemen Consulate

II. EMBASSY

Yemen Embassy Consulate Section, Suite 705 2600 Virginia Avenue, NW Washington, DC 20037 Tel.: 202-965-4760 Fax: 202-337-2717 9:00 AM - 1:00 PM	Entire United States

YUGOSLAVIA

National Holiday: October 24

I. GENERAL INFORMATION

Yugoslavia is a party to the Hague Convention Abolishing the Requirement for Legalization for Foreign Public Documents.

A document should be sent to the appropriate authority in the state or territory in which the document is notarized in order to obtain the Apostille. For information on obtaining the Apostille for documents originating in the United States, see the procedures specified for each of the individual states under United States jurisdiction in Chapter 2. For the enumeration of Federal authorities competent to provide the Apostille, see Appendix D.

For the text of the Hague Convention, the Apostille, and a list of the parties to the Convention, see Appendix A.

For instances in which legalization by a Yugoslav official is still necessary, the requirements for legalization are given below.

II. REQUIREMENTS FOR LEGALIZATION

Materials to be Submitted with Request

1. Original document to be legalized
2. Photocopy of the document
3. Prepaid, self-addressed return envelope

Fee: $45 for a single signature, $27 for a second signature

III. EMBASSY

Embassy of Yugoslavia 2410 California Street, NW Washington, DC 20008 Tel.: 202-462-6566 Fax: 202-797-9663 9:00 AM - 4:00 PM	Entire United States

REPUBLIC OF ZAMBIA

National Holiday: October 24

I. GENERAL INFORMATION

Zambia has an Embassy in the United States but no Consulates. Documents from anywhere in the United States may be sent to the Embassy for legalization.

II. REQUIREMENTS FOR LEGALIZATION

Prior Authentications Required

1. Notarization
2. Authentication of Notary Signature (In most states this may be done directly by the State Secretary of State; if not, the County Clerk authenticates the signature.)
3. State Secretary of State Certification (In states where the Notary Signature may be authenticated directly by the State Secretary of State, steps 2 and 3 are combined.)
4. U.S. Secretary of State Certification

Materials to be Submitted with Request

1. Original document to be legalized
2. Prepaid, self-addressed return envelope

Direct Registration of Notary Public: Not available

Direct Signing of Document Before Consular Official: Not available

Turn Around Time: If the document is personally delivered, it will generally be legalized immediately if the workload permits.

Fee: None

III. EMBASSY

Address, Phone, Hours	*Jurisdiction*
Embassy of the Republic of Zambia 2419 Massachusetts Avenue, NW Washington, DC 20008 Tel.: 202-265-9717 Fax: 202-332-0826 9:00 AM - 5:00 PM (April - October) 9:00 AM - 4:00 PM (November - March)	Entire United States

REPUBLIC OF ZIMBABWE

National Holiday: April 18

I. GENERAL INFORMATION

The Embassy will legalize documents for the United States of America and other countries in which Zimbawe has no representation provided such documents are channeled through their Embassy.

II. REQUIREMENTS FOR LEGALIZATION

Prior Authentications Required
1. Notarization
2. Authentication of Notary Signature (In most states this may be done directly by the State Secretary of State; if not, the County Clerk authenticates the signature.)
3. State Secretary of State Certification (In states where the Notary Signature may be authenticated directly by the State Secretary of State, steps 2 and 3 are combined.)
4. U.S. Secretary of State Certification

Materials to be Submitted with Request
1. Original document to be legalized
2. Prepaid, self-addressed return envelope

Direct Registration of Notary Public: Not available

Direct Signing of Document Before Consular Official: Not available

Turn Around Time: If the document is personally delivered, the document will be legalized immediately if the work load is not too great.

Fee: $10.00 per document or signature

Payment Method: Cash, money order, certified check, company check

III. EMBASSY

Address, Phone, Hours	*Jurisdiction*
Embassy of the Republic of Zimbabwe 1608 New Hampshire Avenue, NW Washington, DC 20009 Tel.: 202-332-7100 Fax: 202-483-9326 9:00 AM - 1:00 PM 2:00 AM - 4:00 PM	Entire United States Countries in which Zimbawe has no representation

CHAPTER 2

LEGALIZATION WITHIN THE UNITED STATES

ALABAMA

I. GENERAL INFORMATION

Authentication of Notary Public Signature
The Notary Public Signature may be authenticated only by the county Probate Judge, except in Jefferson County, where the Circuit Clerk also authenticates notarial signatures. After authentication, the document is ready for submission to the State Secretary of State for certification, if that is required prior to legalization.

If an Apostille is desired, however, intervening authentication by the Probate Judge is not necessary (see below).

Certification of Probate Judge Authentication
This is done by the Alabama Secretary of State's Office. After authentication, the document is ready for submission to the U.S. Secretary of State for certification.

Apostille
The Apostille, for countries which are party to the Hague Convention, may be obtained by submitting the notarized document directly to the Secretary of State's Office, expressly requesting the Apostille, and identifying the country involved. (To obtain an Apostille, prior authentication by the Probate Judge is not necessary.)

Materials to be Submitted with Request
1. Original document to be legalized
2. Prepaid, self-addressed return envelope is required only for return mail service other than First Class.

Fees
Authentication of Probate Judge Signature: $5.00
Apostille: $5.00

Payment Method: Cash, certified check, company check, personal check, money order

II. SECRETARY OF STATE

Office of the Secretary of State 334-242-7476
Room S-105, State Capitol
600 Dexter Avenue
Montgomery, AL 36130
Attention: Authentication Division

III. PROBATE JUDGES

Address to Probate Judge, _______________ County

County	*Address*	*Telephone*
Autauga	134 North Court Street Room 104 Prattville, AL 36067	334-361-3725
Baldwin	PO Box 459 Courthouse Square Bay Minette, AL 36507	334-937-0260
Barbour	PO Box 758 EuFaula, AL 36072	334-775-8371
Bibb	103 Davidson Drive Centreville, AL 35042	205-926-3108
Blount	220 Second Avenue E. Room 106 Oneonta, AL 35121	205-625-4191
Bullock	PO Box 472 Union Springs, AL 36089	334-738-2250
Butler	PO Box 756 Greenville, AL 36037	334-382-3612
Calhoun	1702 Noble Street Suite 103 Anniston, AL 36201	205-236-8231

County	*Address*	*Telephone*
Chambers	Courthouse 2 Lafayette Street Lafayette, AL 36862	334-864-4380
Cherokee	100 Main Street Centre, AL 35960	205-927-3363
Chilton	PO Box 270 Clanton, AL 35046	205-755-1555
Choctaw	117 S. Mulberry Street Butler, AL 36904	205-459-2417
Clarke	PO Box 10 Grove Hill, AL 36451	334-275-3251
Clay	PO Box 1120 Ashland, AL 36251	205-354-2197
Cleburne	120 Vickery Street Room 201 Heflin, AL 36264	205-463-2951
Coffee	230 Court Street Elba, AL 36323	334-897-2211
Colbert	PO Box 47 Tuscumbia, AL 35674	205-386-8542
Conecuh	PO Box 149 Evergreen, AL 36401	334-578-1221
Coosa	PO Box 218 Rockford, AL 35136	205-377-4919
Covington	PO Drawer 789 Andalusia, AL 36420	334-222-3189
Crenshaw	PO Box 328 Luverne, AL 36049	334-335-6568

County	*Address*	*Telephone*
Cullman	500 Second Avenue, SW Cullman, AL 35055	205-739-3530
Dale	1702 Highway 123 E. Suite G Ozark, AL 36360	334-774-6025
Dallas	PO Box 997 Selma, AL 36702-0997	334-874-2500
DeKalb	111 Grand Avenue SW Suite 200 Fort Payne, AL 35967	205-845-8510
Elmore	PO Box 280 Wetumpka, AL 36092	334-567-1138
Escambia	PO Box 557 Brewton, AL 36427	334-867-0297
Etowah	800 Forrest Avenue Gadsden, AL 35901	205-549-5334
Fayette	PO Box 509 Fayette, AL 35555	205-932-4519
Franklin	PO Box 70 Russellville, AL 35653	205-332-8801
Geneva	PO Box 430 Geneva, AL 36340	334-684-2276
Greene	PO Box 790 Eutaw, AL 35462	205-372-3340
Hale	PO Box 396 Greensboro, AL 36744	334-624-8740
Henry	101 Court Abbeville, AL 36310	334-585-3257

County	*Address*	*Telephone*
Houston	PO Box 6406 Dothan, AL 36302	334-677-4740
Jackson	Courthouse Scottsboro, AL 35768	205-574-9290
Jefferson	716 North 21st Street Room 117 Birmingham, AL 35263	205-325-5428
Jefferson (Bessemer Div.)	1801 Third Avenue North Bessemer, AL 35020	205-481-4100
Lamar	PO Box 338 Vernon, AL 35592	205-695-7333
Lauderdale	PO Box 1059 Florence, AL 35631	205-760-5750
Lawrence	14330 Court Street Suite 102 Moulton, AL 35650	205-974-2439
Lee	PO Box 666 Opelika, AL 36803-0666	334-745-9761
Limestone	County Courthouse 310 W. Washington Street Athens, AL 35611	205-233-6427
Lowndes	PO Box 5 Hayneville, AL 36040	334-548-2365
Macon	PO Box 659 Tuskegee, AL 36083	334-724-4371
Madison	100 Northside Square Room 700 Huntsville, AL 35801	205-532-3330

County	*Address*	*Telephone*
Marengo	PO Box 480668 Linden, AL 36748	205-295-5226
Marion	PO Box 1687 Hamilton, AL 35570	205-921-2471
Marshall	424 Blount Avenue Guntersville, AL 35976	205-571-7764
Mobile	PO Box 7 Mobile, AL 36601	334-690-8540
Monroe	PO Box 665 Monroeville, AL 36461	334-743-4107
Montgomery	PO Box 223 Montgomery, AL 36101-0223	334-832-1244
Morgan	PO Box 848 Decatur, AL 35602	205-351-4678
Perry	PO Box 478 Marion, AL 36756	334-683-2210
Pickens	PO Box 370 Carrollton, AL 35447	205-367-2010
Pike	PO Drawer 1147 Troy, AL 36081-1147	334-566-6474
Randolph	PO Box 249 Wedowee, AL 36278	205-357-4933
Russell	PO Box 700 Phenix City, AL 36868	334-298-7979
Saint Clair	PO Box 397 Ashville, AL 35953	205-594-2120

County	*Address*	*Telephone*
Shelby	County Courthouse PO Box 467 Columbiana, AL 35051	205-669-3712
Sumter	PO Box 1040 Livingston, AL 35470	205-652-7281
Talladega	PO Box 755 Talladega, AL 35161	205-362-4175
Tallapoosa	125 N. Broadnax Street Room 131 Dadeville, AL 36853	205-825-4266
Tuscaloosa	PO Box 20113 Tuscaloosa, AL 35401	205-349-3870
Walker	PO Box 502 Jasper, AL 35502-1447	205-384-7281
Washington	PO Box 549 1 Court Street Chatom, AL 36518	334-847-2201
Wilcox	PO Box 668 Camden, AL 36726	334-682-4881
Winston	PO Box 27 Courthouse Square Double Springs, AL 35553	205-489-5219

ALASKA

I. GENERAL INFORMATION

Authentication of Notary Public Signature
Authentication is done only by the Lt. Governor's Office. After such authentication, the document is ready for submission to the U.S. Secretary of State for certification, if that is required prior to legalization.

Apostille
For countries which are party to the Hague Convention, the Apostille may be obtained by submitting the notarized document directly to the Lieutenant Governor's Office, expressly requesting the Apostille, and identifying the country involved.

Materials to be Submitted with Request
1. Original notarized document to be authenticated
2. Prepaid, self-addressed return envelope is required for return mail service other than first class mail

Fees
Authentication of Notary Public Signature: $2.00
Apostille: $2.00

Payment Method: Money order, certified check, company check, personal check

II. LIEUTENANT GOVERNOR'S OFFICE

Lieutenant Governor — 907-465-3509
PO Box 110015
Juneau, Alaska 99811

AMERICAN SAMOA

I. GENERAL INFORMATION

For information on legalization, please communicate with the Office of the Governor.

II. OFFICE OF THE GOVERNOR

Office of the Governor
American Samoa Government
Pago Pago, American Samoa 96799
Tel.: 684-633-4116
Attention: Marilyn Tilo

ARIZONA

I. GENERAL INFORMATION

Authentication of Notary Public Signature
Authentication can be done either by the appropriate Clerk of the Superior Court or by the Secretary of State's Office. After authentication by the Secretary of State, the document is ready for submission to the U.S. Secretary of State for certification, if that is required prior to legalization.

Apostille
For countries which are party to the Hague Convention, the Apostille may be obtained by submitting the notarized document directly to the Secretary of State's Office, expressly requesting the Apostille, and identifying the country involved. (Prior authentication by the Clerk of the Superior Court is not necessary.)

Materials to be Submitted with Request
1. Original notarized document to be authenticated.
2. Prepaid, self-addressed return envelope is not required but is appreciated

Fee: $3.00 for Apostilles and certifications

Payment Method: Money order, company check, personal check

II. SECRETARY OF STATE

Secretary of State — 520-542-4086
Att: Notary Department
1700 W. Washington
Phoenix, AZ 85007

III. CLERKS OF THE SUPERIOR COURT

County	*Address*	*Telephone*
Apache	PO Box 365 St. Johns, AZ 85936	520-337-4364 extension 261

County	*Address*	*Telephone*
Cochise	PO Box CK Bisbee, AZ 85603	520-432-9360
Coconino	Courthouse Flagstaff, AZ 86001	520-779-6535 extension 728
Gila	1400 East Ash Street Globe, AZ 85501	520-425-3231 extension 246
Graham	Courthouse 800 Main Street Safford, AZ 85546	520-428-3100
Greenlee	PO Box 1027 Clifton, AZ 85533	520-865-4242
La Paz	PO Box 730 Parker, AZ 85334	520-669-6131
Maricopa	PO Box 52826 Phoenix, AZ 85072-2826	520-506-7400
Mohave	401 E. Spring Street Kingman, AZ 86401	520-753-0713 extension 4321
Navajo	PO Box 668 Holbrook AZ 86025	520-524-6161 extension 283
Pima	110 West Congress Tucson, AZ 85701	520-740-3282
Pinal	PO Box 889 Florence, AZ 85232	520-868-6296
Santa Cruz	PO Box 1265 Nogales, AZ 85621	520-761-7808
Yavapai	Courthouse Prescott, AZ 86301	520-771-3312

County	*Address*	*Telephone*
Yuma	168 South Second Street Yuma, AZ 85364	520-329-2162

ARKANSAS

I. GENERAL INFORMATION

Authentication of Notary Public Signature
Authentication can be done only by the Secretary of State's Office. After authentication, the document is ready for submission to the U.S. Secretary of State for certification, if that is required prior to legalization.

Apostille
For countries which are party to the Hague Convention, the Apostille may be obtained by submitting the notarized document directly to the Secretary of State's Office, expressly requesting the Apostille, and identifying the country involved.

Materials to be Submitted with Request
1. Original notarized document to be authenticated
2. Stamped, self-addressed return envelope is required only for return mail service other than first class. (Authenticated documents require a larger than ordinary envelope.)

Fees
Authentication of Notary Public Signature: $5.00 (certification)
Apostille: $10.00

Payment Method: Cash, money order, certified check, personal check, company check for correct amount

II. SECRETARY OF STATE

Secretary of State, Notary Division 501-682-3409
State Capitol 888-233-0325
Little Rock, AR 72201-1094

CALIFORNIA

I. GENERAL INFORMATION

Authentication of Notary Public Signature
Authentication can be done by the appropriate County Clerk or by the Secretary of State as required by the individual country. After authentication by the Secretary of State, the document is ready for submission to the U.S. Secretary of State for certification, if that is required prior to legalization.

Apostille
For countries which are party to the Hague Convention, the Apostille may be obtained by submitting the notarized document directly to the Secretary of State's Office, expressly requesting the Apostille, and identifying the country involved. (Prior authentication by the County Clerk is not required by the Secretary of State, but some countries do require County Clerk certification.)

Materials to be Submitted with Request
1. Original notarized document to be authenticated
2. Prepaid, self-addressed return envelope

Fees
Authentication of Notary Public Signature: $20.00
Apostille: $20.00

Payment Method: Money order, certified check, company check, personal check payable to Secretary of State

II. SECRETARY OF STATE

Secretary of State
Notary Public Section
1500 11th Street, 2nd Floor
Sacramento, CA 95814

916-652-3595

Mailing Address
Secretary of State
Notary Public Division
PO Box 942877
Sacramento, CA 94277-0001

COLORADO

I. GENERAL INFORMATION

Authentication of Notary Public Signature
In most cases, the Notary Public Signature may be authenticated only by the Secretary of State's Office. After authentication, the document is ready for submission to the U.S. Secretary of State for certification.

Apostille
For countries which are party to the Hague Convention, the Apostille may be obtained by submitting the notarized document directly to the Secretary of State's Office, expressly requesting the Apostille, and identifying the country involved.

Materials to be Submitted with Request
1. Original notarized document to be authenticated
2. Prepaid, self-addressed return envelope is not required but is appreciated

Fee: Authentication: $2.00
Apostille: $2.00
Expedited Service (while client waits): Add $15.00 for each document (Total: $17.00 each)

Payment Method: Cash, certified check, personal check, company check payable to "Secretary [or Department] of State"

II. SECRETARY OF STATE

Secretary of State — 303-894-2680
Notary Division
1560 Broadway, Suite 200
Denver, CO 80202

CONNECTICUT

I. GENERAL INFORMATION

Authentication of Notary Public Signature
Authentication can be done by the Secretary of State's Office. After authentication by the Secretary of State, the document is ready for submission to the U.S. Secretary of State for certification, if that is required prior to legalization.

Apostille
For countries which are party to the Hague Convention, the Apostille may be obtained by submitting the notarized document directly to the Secretary of State's Office, expressly requesting the Apostille, and identifying the country involved. (Prior authentication by the Town Clerk is not necessary.)

Materials to be Submitted with Request
1. Cover letter with name, address, and daytime telephone number of person submitting the request and the country of destination
2. Original notarized document to be authenticated
3. Prepaid, self-addressed return envelope is not required but will speed up the process; a prepaid courier airbill may be used.

Fees
Authentication of Notary Public Signature: $20.00
Certification of Town Clerk Authentication: $20.00
Apostille: $20.00
Expedited service: $25.00 per item ordered

Payment Method: Money order, certified check, personal check, or company check payable to the Secretary of State, Master and VISA cards

II. SECRETARY OF STATE

Secretary of State 860-566-4135
Attention: Authentication Unit
30 Trinity Street
Hartford, CT 06106

DELAWARE

I. GENERAL INFORMATION

Authentication of Notary Public Signature
Authentication can be done by the appropriate County Clerk or by the Secretary of State's Office. After authentication by the Secretary of State, the document is ready for submission to the U.S. Secretary of State for certification, if that is required prior to legalization.

Apostille
For countries which are party to the Hague Convention, the Apostille may be obtained by submitting the notarized document directly to the Secretary of State's Office, expressly requesting the Apostille, and identifying the country involved. (Prior authentication by the County Clerk is not necessary.)

Materials to be Submitted with Request
1. Original notarized document to be authenticated or a legible facsimile
2. Prepaid, self-addressed return envelope is required only for return mail other than first class

Fees
Authentication of Notary Public Signature: $2.00
Apostille: $10.00

Payment Method: Cash, money order, certified check, company check, personal check payable to Secretary of State, Delaware

II. SECRETARY OF STATE

Department of State 302-739-3077
Division of Corporations
PO Box 898, Townsend Building
Federal and Duke of York Streets
Dover, DE 19903

FLORIDA

I. GENERAL INFORMATION

Authentication of Notary Public Signature
Authentication can, in most cases, be done only by the Secretary of State's Office. After authentication by the Secretary of State, the document is ready for submission to the U.S. Secretary of State for certification, if that is required prior to legalization.

Apostille
For countries which are party to the Hague Convention, the Apostille may be obtained by submitting the notarized document directly to the Secretary of State's Office, expressly requesting the Apostille, and identifying the country involved.

Materials to be Submitted with Request
1. Original notarized document to be authenticated
2. Prepaid, self-addressed return envelope is required only for return mail service other than first class.

Fees
Authentication of Notary Public Signature: $10.00
Apostille: $10.00

Payment Method: Money order, certified check, company check, personal check payable to the Secretary of State

II. SECRETARY OF STATE

Department of State 904-488-7521
Bureau of Notaries
Capitol Building, Room 1801
Tallahassee, FL 32399

GEORGIA

I. GENERAL INFORMATION

Note: Recent Georgia legislation has transferred notarial authentication power to the Georgia Superior Court Clerks' Cooperative Authority. **The U.S. Secretary of State, however, as of this writing (October 31, 1997) has not approved the Clerks' Cooperative Authority issuance.** Consequently, if an Apostille is required, the applicant is urged first to telephone the Office of the Georgia Secretary of State at 404-656-8288 to learn which Georgia office has the power to grant the Apostille. The procedures in effect until October 31, 1997 are summarized below.

Authentication of Notary Public Signature

Authentication is accomplished by submitting a notarized document to the Clerk of the Superior Court who appointed the notary. Upon completion of the Clerk's certification, the document is forwarded to the Election Division (404-656-2854) for the Great Seal. The document may then be submitted to the U.S. Secretary of State for further certification.

Apostille

Until further notice, for countries which are party to the Hague Convention, the Apostille may be obtained by first obtaining notarial authentication from the appointing Clerk of Superior Court and then submitting the document to the Secretary of State's Office, expressly requesting the Apostille, and identifying the country involved.

Materials to be Submitted with Request

1 Original notarized document to be authenticated (Only original document is necessary and only original document can be certified.)
2. Prepaid, self-addressed return envelope not required but appreciated

Fees

Authentication of Notary Public Signature: $2.00
Certification of County Clerk Authentication: $10.00
Apostille: $3.00

Payment Method: Cash, certified check, personal check, company check

II. SECRETARY OF STATE

Secretary of State 404-656-2885
Notary Division, West Tower, Suite 820
2 Martin Luther King Jr. Drive, SE
Atlanta, GA 30334

GUAM

I. GENERAL INFORMATION

For information on legalization, please communicate with the Attorney General of Guam.

The Clerk and Deputy Clerks of the United States District Court of Guam also have the authority to issue the Apostille.

Fee
Certificate of Authority: $25.00
Apostille: $25.00

II. ATTORNEY GENERAL

Attorney General Calvin E. Holloway, Sr. Tel.: 011-671-475-3324
Office of the Attorney General Fax: 011-671-472-2493
Suite 2-200E, Judicial Center Building
120 W. O'Brien Drive
Agana, Guam 96910

Note that Guam is 15 hours ahead of Eastern Standard Time.

HAWAII

I. GENERAL INFORMATION

Authentication of Notary Public Signature
Authentication can be done by the Clerk of the Circuit Court. After authentication by the Clerk of the Circuit Court, the document is ready for submission to the Lt. Governor's Office for certification if that is required prior to legalization.

Apostille
For countries which are party to the Hague Convention, the Apostille may be obtained by submitting the notarized document directly to the Secretary of State's Office, expressly requesting the Apostille, and identifying the country involved.

Materials to be Submitted with Request
1. Original notarized document to be authenticated
2. Prepaid, self-addressed return envelope is required only for return service other than first class mail

Fees
Certification of County Clerk Authentication: $1.00 (subject to change)
Apostille: $1.00 (subject to change)

Payment Method: Cash, money order, certified check, company check, personal check

II. LT. GOVERNOR

Office of the Lt. Governor 808-586-0255
PO Box 3226
Honolulu, HI 96801

III. CLERKS OF THE CIRCUIT COURT

County	*Address*	*Telephone*
Honolulu	Circuit Court of First Circuit Legal Document Section Ka-ahumanu Hale 777 Punchbowl Street Honolulu, HI 96813	808-539-4301
Maui	Circuit Court of Second Circuit Legal Document Section Hoapili Hale 2145 Main Street Wailuku, Maui, HI 96793	808-244-2979
Hawaii	Circuit Court of Third Circuit Court Document Section Hilo State building 75 Aupuni Street Hilo, HI 96720	808-961-7400
Kauai	Circuit Court of Fifth Court Legal Document Section 3059 Umi Street Lihue, Kauai, HI 96766	808-246-3300

IDAHO

I. GENERAL INFORMATION

Authentication of Notary Public Signature
The Notary Public Signature may be authenticated only by the Secretary of State's Office. After authentication, the document is ready for submission to the U.S. Secretary of State for certification, if that is required prior to legalization.

Apostille
For countries which are party to the Hague Convention, the Apostille may be obtained by submitting the notarized document directly to the Secretary of State's Office, expressly requesting the Apostille, and identifying the country involved.

Materials to be Submitted with Request
1. Original notarized document to be authenticated
2. Prepaid, self-addressed return envelope will be used if submitted

Fees
Authentication of Notary Public signature: $10.00
Apostille: $10.00

Payment Method: Cash, money order, certified check, company check, personal check

II. SECRETARY OF STATE

Secretary of State — 208-334-2300
Notary Public Department
Box 83720
700 West Jefferson
Boise, ID 83720-0080

ILLINOIS

I. GENERAL INFORMATION

Authentication of Notary Public Signature
Authentication can be done either by the appropriate County Clerk or directly by the Secretary of State's Office as required by individual country. After authentication by the Secretary of State, the document is ready for submission to the U.S. Secretary of State for certification, if that is required prior to legalization.

Apostille
For countries which are party to the Hague Convention, the Apostille may be obtained by submitting the notarized document directly to the Secretary of State's Office, expressly requesting the Apostille, and identifying the country involved.

INDIANA

I. GENERAL INFORMATION

Authentication of Notary Public Signature
Authentication can be done either by the appropriate County Clerk or directly by the Secretary of State's Office. After authentication by the Secretary of State, the document is ready for submission to the U.S. Secretary of State for certification, if this is required prior to legalization.

Apostille
For countries which are party to the Hague Convention, the Apostille may be obtained by submitting the notarized document directly to the Secretary of State's Office, expressly requesting the Apostille, and identifying the country involved. (Prior authentication by the County Clerk is not necessary.)

Note
The Secretary of State's Office specifically requires that the following information be clearly presented on the document submitted to the Authentication Deputy:

1. Date of execution of the document by the Notary or Clerk
2. In the case of the attesting Notary, signature, typed or printed name, county of residence, expiration date of commission and Notarial Seal.

Marriage licenses must be authenticated by the appropriate County Clerk before being sent to the Secretary of State's Office. The Secretary of State's Office can authenticate only birth certificates issued by the State of Indiana. These can be ordered from the Department of Health Vital Statistics Division at 317-233-2700.

Materials to be Submitted with Request
1. Original notarized document to be authenticated
2. Prepaid, self-addressed return envelope is preferred but not required

Fees
Authentication of Notary Public signature: $0.50.
Certification of County Clerk authentication: $0.50
Apostille: $0.50

Payment Method: Cash, money order, certified check, company check, personal check

II. SECRETARY OF STATE

Authentications Deputy 317-232-6531
Secretary of State
State House, Room 201
Indianapolis, IN 46204

IOWA

I. GENERAL INFORMATION

Authentication of Notary Public Signature
Authentication can be done only by the Secretary of State's Office. After authentication by the Secretary of State, the document is ready for submission to the U.S. Secretary of State for certification, if that is required prior to legalization.

Apostille
For countries which are party to the Hague Convention, the Apostille may be obtained by submitting the name of the notary and the date on which the document was notarized. The Secretary of State's Office requests that the document not be sent through the mail to avoid its being lost.

Materials to be Submitted with Request
1. Copy of notarized document OR
   Letter stating name of notary, date on which document was notarized, and name of country to which document is being sent
2. Prepaid, self-addressed return envelope is not required but is appreciated

Fees
Authentication of Notary Public Signature: $5.00 per certificate
Apostille: $5.00 per certificate

Payment Method: Money order, certified check, company check, personal check, MasterCard, Visa; make checks payable to the Secretary of State

Facsimile and Telephone Requests
1. Provide name of notary, date on which document was notarized, and name of country to which document is being sent
2. Pay by Visa or MasterCard

II. SECRETARY OF STATE

Secretary of State 515-281-5204
Hoover Building, Second Floor
Des Moines, IA 50319

KANSAS

I. GENERAL INFORMATION

Authentication of Notary Public Signature
The Notary Public Signature may be authenticated only by the Secretary of State's Office. After authentication, the document is ready for submission to the U.S. Secretary of State for certification, if that is required prior to legalization.

Apostille
For countries which are party to the Hague Convention, the Apostille may be obtained by submitting the notarized document directly to the Secretary of State's Office, expressly requesting the Apostille, and identifying the country involved.

Materials to be Submitted with Request
1. Original notarized document to be authenticated
2. Prepaid, self-addressed return envelope is not required but is appreciated

Fees
Authentication of Notary Public Signature: $1.00
Apostille: $5.00

Payment Method: Cash, money order, certified check, personal check, company check

II. SECRETARY OF STATE

Secretary of State 913-296-2236
Attn.: Notary Clerk
Capitol, Second Floor
300 SW 10th Avenue
Topeka, KS 66612-1594

KENTUCKY

I. GENERAL INFORMATION

Authentication of Notary Public Signature
The Notary Public Signature is authenticated by the County Clerk. The County Clerk's authentication is then certified by the Secretary of State's Office. The document is then ready for submission to the U.S. Secretary of State for certification, if that is required prior to legalization.

Apostille
For countries which are party to the Hague Convention, the Apostille may be obtained by submitting the notarized document, which has been certified by the County Clerk, directly to the Secretary of State's Office, expressly requesting the Apostille, and identifying the country involved. Prior authentication by the County Clerk is mandatory.

Materials to be Submitted with Request
1. Original notarized document to be authenticated
2. Prepaid, self-addressed return envelope is required for return mail service other than first class

Fees
Certification of County Clerk authentication: $5.00
Apostille: $5.00

Payment Method: Cash, money order, certified check, company check, personal check

II. SECRETARY OF STATE

Secretary of State's Office — 502-564-7330
Corporate Department — Extension 456
700 Capitol Building, Room 154
Frankfort, KY 40601
Attention: Pat McLean

LOUISIANA

I. GENERAL INFORMATION

Authentication of Notary Public Signature
Authentication can be done by the appropriate Parish Clerk of the Court or the Secretary of State's Office. After authentication by the Secretary of State, the document is ready for submission to the U.S. Secretary of State for certification, if that is required prior to legalization.

Apostille
For countries which are party to the Hague Convention, the Apostille may be obtained by submitting the notarized document directly to the Secretary of State's Office, expressly requesting the Apostille, and identifying the country involved.

Materials to be Submitted with Request
1. Original notarized document to be authenticated
2. Prepaid, self-addressed return envelope is not required but is appreciated; the customer is responsible for air mail delivery and express mail fees if desired

Fees
Authentication of Notary Public signature: $10.00
Certification of County Clerk authentication: $10.00
Apostille: $10.00

Payment Method: Cash, money order, certified check, personal check, company check

II. SECRETARY OF STATE

Secretary of State 504-342-4980
PO Box 94125
Baton Rouge, LA 70804-9125
Attn.: Commissions Section

MAINE

I. GENERAL INFORMATION

Authentication of Notary Public Signature
Authentication can be done only by the Secretary of State's Office. After authentication by the Secretary of State, the document is ready for submission to the U.S. Secretary of State for certification, if that is required prior to legalization.

Apostille
For countries which are party to the Hague Convention, the Apostille may be obtained by submitting the notarized document directly to the Secretary of State's Office, expressly requesting the Apostille, and identifying the country involved.

Materials to be Submitted with Request
1. Original notarized document to be authenticated
2. Prepaid, self-addressed return envelope is required only for return service other than first class mail

Fees
Authentication of Notary Public Signature: $10.00
Apostille: $10.00

Payment Method: Cash, money order, certified check, company check, personal check made out to Secretary of State

II. SECRETARY OF STATE

Department of Secretary of State 207-287-4181
Authentication Division
101 State House Station
Augusta, ME 04333

MARYLAND

I. GENERAL INFORMATION

Authentication of Notary Public Signature
Authentication can be done only by the appropriate County Clerk of the Circuit Court. After authentication by the County Clerk, the document is ready for submission to the Secretary of State for certification, if that is required prior to legalization.

Certification of County Clerk Authentication
Certification is done by the Secretary of State's Office. After authentication by the Secretary of State's Office, the document is ready for submission to the U.S. Secretary of State, if that is required prior to legalization.

Apostille
For countries which are party to the Hague Convention, the Apostille may be obtained by submitting the notarized document to the appropriate Clerk of the Circuit Court for authentication or by obtaining the seal and signature of the issuing agency. Then the document must be submitted to the Secretary of State's Office, expressly requesting the Apostille, and identifying the country involved.

Materials to be Submitted with Request
1. Original notarized document to be authenticated
2. Prepaid, self-addressed return envelope is required

Fees
Certification of County Clerk Authentication: $5.00
Apostille: $5.00

Payment Method: Cash, money order, certified check, company check, personal check payable to the Secretary of State

II. SECRETARY OF STATE

Certification Desk 410-974-5521
Office of the Secretary of State
State House
Annapolis, MD 21401

Walk-in service 410-974-5221
Jeffrey Building, First Floor
16 Francis Street
Annapolis, MD 21401
8:00 AM - 4:30 PM, Monday - Friday

III. CLERKS OF THE CIRCUIT COURT

Address: License Department, Clerk of the Circuit Court
_______ County Courthouse (except for Baltimore County)

County	*Address*	*Telephone*
Allegany	Cumberland, MD 21502	301-777-5922
Anne Arundel	Annapolis, MD 21401	410-222-1434
Baltimore City	412 Court House East Baltimore, MD 21202	410-333-3760
Baltimore County	Courts Building 401 Bosley Avenue Towson, MD 21204	410-887-2609
Calvert	Prince Frederick, MD 20678	410-535-1660
Caroline	PO Box 458 Denton, MD 21629	410-479-1811
Carroll	55 N. Court Street Westminster, MD 21157	410-857-2985
Cecil	County Office Building Elkton, MD 21921	410-996-5375
Charles	PO Box 970 La Plata, MD 20646	301-932-3242
Dorchester	PO Box 150 Cambridge, MD 21613	410-228-0480

County	*Address*	*Telephone*
Frederick	100 W. Patrick Street Frederick, MD 21702	301-694-1960
Garrett	Oakland, MD 21550	301-334-1937
Harford	Bel Air, MD 21014	410-638-3245
Howard	Ellicott City, MD 21043	410-313-2111
Kent	Chestertown, MD 21620	410-778-7460
Montgomery	Judicial Center Rockville, MD 20850	301-217-6752
Prince George's	Upper Marlboro, MD 20772	301-952-3330
Queen Anne's	Centreville, MD 21617	410-758-1773
St. Mary's	PO Box 676 Leonardtown, MD 20640	301-475-4567
Somerset	Princess Anne, MD 21853	410-651-1555
Talbot	Easton, MD 21601	410-822-2611
Washington	Courthouse Annex Hagerstown, MD 21740	301-791-3085
Wicomico	Salisbury, MD 21801	410-543-6551
Worcester	Room 2218 Snow Hill, MD 21863	410-632-1221

MASSACHUSETTS

I. GENERAL INFORMATION

Authentication of Notary Public Signature
In most cases, the Notary Public Signature may be authenticated only by the Secretary of State's Office. Recording of notary commissions with a county official is not required, although some notaries may be registered with Superior Court Clerks. After authentication by the Secretary of State's Office, the document is ready for submission to the U.S. Secretary of State for certification, if that is required prior to legalization.

Apostille
For countries which are party to the Hague Convention, the Apostille may be obtained by submitting the notarized document directly to the Secretary of State's Office, expressly requesting the Apostille, and identifying the country involved.

Materials to be Submitted with Request
1. Original notarized document to be authenticated
2. Prepaid, self-addressed return envelope is not required but is appreciated

Fees
Authentication of Notary Public Signature: $3.00
Apostille: $3.00

Payment Method: Cash, money order, certified check, personal check, company check. Checks should be made payable to the Commonwealth of Massachusetts.

II. SECRETARY OF STATE

Secretary of the Commonwealth 617-727-2836
Commissions Section, Room 1719
McCormack Building
One Ashburton Place
Boston, MA 02108

MICHIGAN

I. GENERAL INFORMATION

Authentication of Notary Public Signature
Authentication can be done by the appropriate County Clerk or by the Secretary of State's Office. After authentication by the Secretary of State, the document is ready for submission to the U.S. Secretary of State for certification, if that is required prior to legalization. The request for authentication must state the country of destination. The Michigan Secretary of State, moreover, can issue Certificates of Authority only for a Michigan Notary Public Certificate on a document, a County Clerk Certificate on a document, State Registrar Certification on documents issued by the Michigan Department of Community Health, and Director, Corporations, Securities and Development Bureau on documents issued by the Michigan Department of Consumer and Industry Services. The Michigan Secretary of State cannot certify city officials; original birth, death, marriage or divorce records; or documents from a city clerk, court clerk, or other state.

Apostille
For countries which are party to the Hague Convention, the Apostille may be obtained by submitting the notarized document directly to the Secretary of State's Office, expressly requesting the Apostille, and identifying the country involved. (Prior authentication by the County Clerk is not necessary.)

Materials to be Submitted with Request
1. Original notarized document to be authenticated, with original signatures
2. Prepaid, self-addressed return envelope is required

Fees
Authentication of Notary Public Signature: $1.00
Certification of County Clerk Authentication: $1.00
Certification of State Registrar or Corporations, Securities and Development Bureau Director: $1.00
Apostille: $1.00

Payment Method: Money order, certified check, company check, personal check payable to State of Michigan

Additional Information

Use zip code 48915 if sending document(s) by courier service such as Federal Express. The office of the Secretary of State does not accept or return documents by DHL unless prior arrangements are made: call the office to make these arrangements. Do not use the U.S. Post Office for express or priority mail, since it will not be delivered more quickly than regular mail.

If you have five or more documents, call the office to prearrange certification.

II. SECRETARY OF STATE

Secretary of State 517-373-2531
Office of the Great Seal
Michigan Historical Center, First Floor
717 West Allegan Street
Lansing, MI 48918-1750

MINNESOTA

I. GENERAL INFORMATION

Authentication of Notary Public Signature
Authentication can be done by the Clerk of Court of the appropriate county or by the Secretary of State's Office. After authentication by the Secretary of State's Office, the document is ready for submission to the U.S. Secretary of State for certification, if that is required prior to legalization.

Apostille
For countries which are party to the Hague Convention, the Apostille may be obtained by submitting the notarized document directly to the Secretary of State's Office, expressly requesting the Apostille, and identifying the country involved. (Prior authentication by the Clerk of the Court is not necessary.)

Materials to be Submitted with Request
1. Original notarized document to be authenticated
2. Prepaid, self-addressed return envelope is required only for return service other than first class mail

Fees
Authentication of Notary Public Signature: $5.00
Certification of County Clerk Authentication: $5.00
Apostille: $5.00

Payment Method: Cash, money order, certified check, company check, personal check payable to Secretary of State

II. SECRETARY OF STATE

Secretary of State 612-297-9102
State Office Building, Room 180
100 Constitution Avenue
St. Paul, MN 55155

MISSISSIPPI

I. GENERAL INFORMATION

Authentication of Notary Public Signature
Authentication is done by the Secretary of State's Office. After authentication, the document is ready for submission to the U.S. Secretary of State for certification, if that is required prior to legalization.

Apostille
For countries which are party to the Hague Convention, the Apostille may be obtained by submitting the notarized document directly to the Secretary of State's Office, expressly requesting the Apostille, and identifying the country involved.

Materials to be Submitted with Request
1. Original notarized document to be authenticated
2. Prepaid, self-addressed return envelope is not required but is requested

Fees
Authentication of Notary Public Signature: $2.00
Certification of County Clerk Authentication: $2.00
Apostille: $2.00

Payment Method: Cash, money order, certified check, company check, personal check payable to Secretary of State.

II. SECRETARY OF STATE

Secretary of State 601-359-1615
Notary Department
PO Box 136
Jackson, MS 39025

MISSOURI

I. GENERAL INFORMATION

Authentication of Notary Public Signature
Only some counties record notary commissions, but in all cases the authentication of a notary's signature must be done by the Secretary of State's Office. After authentication by the Secretary of State, the document is ready for submission to the U.S. Secretary of State for certification, if that is required prior to legalization.

Apostille
For countries which are party to the Hague Convention, the Apostille may be obtained by submitting the notarized document directly to the Secretary of State's Office, expressly requesting the Apostille, and identifying the country involved.

Materials to be Submitted with Request
1. Original notarized document to be authenticated
2. Prepaid, self-addressed return envelope is not required but is requested

Fees
Authentication of Notary Public Signature: $10.00
Apostille: $10.00

Payment Method: Cash, money order, certified check, company check, personal check payable to State Director of Revenue

II. SECRETARY OF STATE

Secretary of State's Office 573-751-4756
Attn.: Commission Division
PO Box 784
Jefferson City, MO 65102

MONTANA

I. GENERAL INFORMATION

Authentication of Notary Public Signature
Authentication can be done only by the Secretary of State's Office. After authentication by the Secretary of State, the document is ready for submission to the U.S. Secretary of State for certification, if that is required prior to legalization.

Apostille
For countries which are party to the Hague Convention, the Apostille may be obtained by submitting the notarized document directly to the Secretary of State's Office, expressly requesting the Apostille, and identifying the country involved.

Materials to be Submitted with Request
1. Original <u>notarized</u> document to be authenticated
2. Prepaid, self-addressed return envelope is requested for all services
3. Fee payable to the Secretary of State
4. Letter identifying the country involved and, preferably, giving a day time telephone number in case of problem(s)

Fees (per document)
Authentication of Notary Public Signature: $2.00
Certificate of Notarial Standing: $2.00
Certificate of County Clerk & Recorder Authentication: $2.00
Certificate of Clerk or District Court Authentication: $2.00
Apostille: $2.00

Payment Method: Cash, money order, cashier's check, company check, personal check payable to Secretary of State (cash is not recommended when material is sent by mail or courier).

Additional Information: Documents sent by priority courier service may not be sent to the post office box given below but must be sent to the State Capital, Room 225.

II. SECRETARY OF STATE

Office of the Secretary of State 406-444-5379
Notary Department
State Capitol
PO Box 202801
Helena, MT 59620

NEBRASKA

I. GENERAL INFORMATION

Authentication of Notary Public Signature
Authentication is done by the Secretary of State. After authentication by the Secretary of State, the document is ready for submission to the U.S. Secretary of State for certification, if that is required prior to legalization.

Apostille
For countries which are party to the Hague Convention, the Apostille may be obtained by submitting the notarized document directly to the Secretary of State's Office, expressly requesting the Apostille, and identifying the country involved.

Materials to be Submitted with Request
1. Original notarized document to be authenticated
2. Prepaid, self-addressed return envelope is required only for return service other than first class mail

Fees
Authentication of Notary Public Signature or Certificate of Notarial Standing: $10.00
Apostille: $10.00

Payment Method: Cash, money order, certified check, company check, personal check payable to Secretary of State

II. SECRETARY OF STATE

Secretary of State 402-471-2558
Notary Division, Room 1305
State Capitol Building
PO Box 95104
Lincoln, NE 68509

NEVADA

I. GENERAL INFORMATION

Authentication of Notary Public Signature
Authentication is done directly by the Secretary of State. After authentication by the Secretary of State, the document is ready for submission to the U.S. Secretary of State for certification, if that is required prior to legalization.

Apostille
For countries which are party to the Hague Convention, the Apostille may be obtained by submitting the notarized document directly to the Secretary of State's Office, expressly requesting the Apostille, and identifying the country involved. (Prior authentication by the County Clerk is not necessary.)

Materials to be Submitted with Request
1. Original notarized document to be authenticated
2. Prepaid, self-addressed return envelope

Average Turn Around Time: 10 working days

Fees
Authentication of Notary Public Signature: $20.00
Apostille: $20.00

Payment Method: Money order, certified check, company check, personal check

II. SECRETARY OF STATE

Secretary of State
Capitol Complex
Carson City, NV 89710

702-687-5203

NEW HAMPSHIRE

I. GENERAL INFORMATION

Authentication of Notary Public Signature
Authentication can be done by the appropriate Town or City Clerk or by the Secretary of State's Office. Note, however, that the Secretary of State will not certify Town or City Clerk authentications. After authentication by the Secretary of State, the document is ready for submission to the U.S. Secretary of State for certification, if that is required prior to legalization.

Apostille
For countries which are party to the Hague Convention, the Apostille may be obtained by submitting the notarized document directly to the Secretary of State's Office, expressly requesting the Apostille, and identifying the country involved.

Materials to be Submitted with Request
1. Original notarized document to be authenticated
2. Prepaid, self-addressed return envelope at least 7½ by 10½ in size is required only for return service other than first class mail

Fees
Authentication of Notary public Signature: $5.00
Apostille: $5.00

Payment Method: Cash, money order, certified check, company check, personal check payable to Secretary of State or State of New Hampshire

II. SECRETARY OF STATE

Office of the Secretary of State — 603-271-3242
State House, Room 204
Concord, NH 03301

NEW JERSEY

I. GENERAL INFORMATION

Authentication of Notary Public Signature
Authentication can be done only by the appropriate County Clerk. After authentication, the document is ready for submission to the U.S. Secretary of State for certification, if that is required prior to legalization.

Certification of County Clerk Authentication
Authentication is done by the Secretary of State's Office. After authentication, the document is ready for submission to the U.S. Secretary of State for certification, if that is required prior to legalization.

Apostille
For countries which are party to the Hague Convention, the Apostille may be obtained by submitting the notarized document directly to the Secretary of State's Office, expressly requesting the Apostille, and identifying the country involved. Whether or not prior authentication by the County Clerk is required is determined by the country involved.

Materials to be Submitted with Request
1. Original notarized document to be authenticated
2. Prepaid, self-addressed return envelope is required only if using a courier service such as Federal Express or DHL

Fees
Authentication of Notary Public Signature: $3.00 (County Clerk fee)
Certification of County Clerk Authentication: $25.00
Apostille: $25.00
Expedited service $35.00

Payment Method: Money order, certified check, company check, personal check

II. SECRETARY OF STATE

Secretary of State 609-530-6421
Notary Section
PO Box 452
Trenton, NJ 08625

III. COUNTY CLERKS

County	*Address*	*Telephone/Fax*
Atlantic	5901 Main Street Mays Landing, NJ 08830-1797	609-641-7861 609-625-4738
Bergen	Bergen County Justice Ctr. 10 Main Street, Room 117 Hackensack, NJ 07601-7698	201-646-2000 201-646-0267
Burlington	Court Complex PO Box 6000 49 Rancocas Road Mount Holly, NJ 08060-1397	609-265-5189 609-265-0696
Camden	101 South 5th Street Hall of Justice, Suite 150 Camden, NJ 08103-4002	609-225-7214 609-225-7100
Cape May	7 North Main Street Cape May Courthouse, NJ 08210-5000	609-465-1013 609-465-8625
Cumberland	PO Box 716 60 West Broad Street Bridgeton, NJ 08302-2665	609-451-8000 Ext 211 609-455-1410
Essex	465 King Blvd., Room 247 Newark, NJ 07102-1795	201-621-4921 201-621-5178
Gloucester	Court House, 1st Floor Box 129 Woodbury, NJ 08096-3327	609-853-3241 609-853-3327
Hudson	584 Newark Avenue Jersey City, NJ 07306-2018	201-795-6112 201-795-2581
Hunterdon	71 Main Street Hall of Records Flemington, NJ 08822-1495	908-788-1214 908-782-4068

County	*Address*	*Telephone*
Mercer	Court House PO Box 8068 Trenton, NJ 08650-8068	609-989-6477 609-989-1111
Middlesex	PO Box 1110 New Brunswick, NJ 08903-1110	908-745-4202/3827 908-745-2170
Monmouth	300 Halls Mill Road Freehold, NJ 07728-1254	908-431-7794 908-409-4887
Morris	PO Box 315 Morristown, NJ 07963-0315	201-285-6066 201-285-5233
Ocean	PO Box 2191 Court House, Room 105 Toms River, NJ 08754-2191	908-929-2018 908-349-4336
Passaic	401 Grand Street Paterson, NJ 07505	201-225-3632 201-754-1920
Salem	92 Market Street PO Box 18 Salem, NJ 08079-1913	609-935-7510 Ext. 212/206 609-935-8882
Somerset	PO Box 3000 20 Grove Street Somerville, NJ 08876-1262	908-231-7013 908-253-8853
Sussex	4 Park Place Newton, NJ 07860-1795	201-579-0900 201-383-7493
Union	Court House, Room 105 Elizabeth, NJ 07207-6099	908-527-4998/9 908-558-2589
Warren	Court House Belvidere, NJ 07823-1500	908-475-6214 908-475-2370

NEW MEXICO

I. GENERAL INFORMATION

Authentication of Notary Public Signature
Authentication can be done only by the Secretary of State's Office. After authentication by the Secretary of State, the document is ready for submission to the U.S. Secretary of State for certification, if that is required prior to legalization.

Note: a certificate verifying notarial standing in the absence of a notarized document can be provided on request.

Apostille
For countries which are party to the Hague Convention, the Apostille may be obtained by submitting the notarized document directly to the Secretary of State's Office, expressly requesting the Apostille, and identifying the country involved.

Materials to be Submitted with Request
1. Original notarized document to be authenticated
2. Photocopy with legible signature of Notary Public, seal or stamp
2. Prepaid, self-addressed return envelope is required only for return service other than first class

Fees
Authentication of Notary Appointment: $3.00 each
Apostille: $3.00 each

Payment Method: Cash, money order, certified check, company check, personal check payable to Secretary of State or New Mexico Secretary of State

II. SECRETARY OF STATE

Secretary of State
Room 420
State Capitol
Santa Fe, NM 87503

505-827-3600
800-477-3632

NEW YORK

I. GENERAL INFORMATION

Authentication of Notary Public Signature
Authentication must be done by the appropriate County Clerk. After authentication by the County Clerk, the document is ready for submission to the State Secretary of State for certification, if that is required prior to legalization or for the Apostille.

Certification of County Clerk Authentication
Authentication is done by the New York Secretary of State's Office. The country for which legalization is required must be identified. After authentication, the document is ready for submission to the U.S. Secretary of State for certification, if that is required prior to legalization.

Apostille
For countries which are party to the Hague Convention, the Apostille may be obtained by submitting the notarized document to the County Clerk and then to the Secretary of State's Office, expressly requesting authentication and identifying the specific country involved.

Materials to be Submitted with Request
1. Original notarized document to be authenticated
2. Prepaid, self-addressed return envelope is required for return service and first class mail

Fees
Certification of County Clerk Authentication: $10.00
Apostille: $10.00

Payment Method: Money order, certified check, personal check or business check in an amount not to exceed $500.00 payable to Department of State; checks for over $500.00 must be certified.

II. SECRETARY OF STATE

Documents may be mailed to either office.

Secretary of State
Miscellaneous Records
Certification Unit
162 Washington Avenue
Albany, NY 12231
Tel.: 518-474-4770

Department of State
Counsel's Office, 6th Floor
270 Broadway
New York, NY 10007
Tel.: 212-417-5684

III. COUNTY CLERKS

County	*Address*	*Telephone*
Albany	Albany, NY 12207	518-487-5000
Allegany	Belmont, NY 14813	716-268-9270
Bronx	North Bronx, NY 10451	718-590-3644
Broome	Binghamton, NY 13901	607-778-2451
Cattaraugus	Little Valley, NY 14755	716-938-9111
Cayuga	Auburn, NY 12031	315-253-1271
Chautauqua	Mayville, NY 14757	716-753-4331
Chemung	Elmira, NY 14901	607-737-2920
Chenango	Norwich, NY 13815	607-337-1450
Clinton	Plattsburgh, NY 12901	518-565-4700
Columbia	Hudson, NY 12534	518-828-3339
Cortland	Cortland, NY 13045	607-753-5021
Delaware	Delhi, NY 13753	607-746-2123

County	*Address*	*Telephone*
Dutchess	Poughkeepsie, NY 12601	914-431-1856
Erie	Buffalo, NY 14202	716-858-6718
Essex	Elizabethtown, NY 12932	518-873-6301 Extension 265
Franklin	Malone, NY 12953	518-483-6767
Fulton	Johnstown, NY 12095	518-762-0555
Genesee	Batvia, NY 14416	716-344-2550
Greene	Catskill, NY 12414	518-943-2050
Hamilton	Lake Pleasant, NY 12108	518-548-7111
Herkimer	Herkimer, NY 13350	315-867-1002
Jefferson	Watertown, NY 13601	315-785-3801
Kings	Brooklyn, NY 11201	718-643-8011
Lewis	Lowville, NY 13367	315-376-2414
Livingston	Geneseo, NY 14450	716-243-7000
Madison	Wampsville, NY 13161	315-366-2261
Monroe	Rochester, NY 14614	716-428-5151
Montgomery	Fonda, NY 12068	518-853-3431
Nassau	Mineola, NY 11501	516-571-1445
New York	Manhattan, NY 10007	212-374-8589
Niagara	Lockport, NY 14094	716-439-7022
Oneida	Utica, NY 13501	315-798-5773

County	*Address*	*Telephone*
Onondaga	Syracuse, NY 13202	315-435-2226
Ontario	Canandaigua, NY 14424	716-396-4200
Orange	Goshen, NY 10924	914-294-5151
Orleans	Albion, NY 14411	716-589-5334
Oswego	Oswego, NY 13126	315-349-8385
Otsego	Cooperstown, NY 13326	607-547-4200
Putnam	Carmel, NY 10512	914-225-3641
Queens	Jamaica, NY 11424	718-520-3702
Rensselaer	Troy, NY 12180	518-270-4080
Richmond	Staten Island, NY 10301	718-390-5386
Rockland	New City, NY 10956	914-638-5069
St. Lawrence	Canton, NY 13617	315-379-2237
Saratoga	Ballston Spa, NY 12020	518-885-2213
Schenectady	Schenectady, NY 12305	518-388-4225
Schoharie	Schoharie, NY 12157	518-295-8316
Schuyler	Watkins Glen, NY 14891	607-535-2132
Seneca	Waterloo, NY 13165	315-539-5655
Steuben	Bath, NY 14810	607-776-9631
Suffolk	Riverhead, NY 11901	516-852-2000/99

County	*Address*	*Telephone*
Sullivan	Monticello, NY 12701	914-794-3000 Extension 5012
Tioga	Oswego, NY 13827	607-687-3133
Tompkins	Ithaca, NY 14850	607-274-5431
Ulster	Kingston, NY 12401	914-331-9300 Extension 488
Warren	Lake George, NY 12845	518-761-6429
Washington	Fort Edward, NY 12828	518-747-3374
Wayne	Lyons, NY 14489	315-946-5972
Westchester	White Plains, NY 10601	914-285-3070
Wyoming	Warsaw, NY 14569	716-786-8810
Yates	Penn Yan, NY 14527	315-536-5120

NORTH CAROLINA

I. GENERAL INFORMATION

Authentication of Notary Public Signature
Authentication can be done only by the appropriate Register of Deeds Office. (If the Notary's signature is not required to be certified but just the authority of the Notary, contact the Notary Public Division.) After authentication, the document is submitted to the Secretary of State's Office. After authentication by the Secretary of State, the document is ready for submission to the U.S. Secretary of State for certification, if that is required prior to legalization. The country of intended use must be stated for each submitted document.

Apostille
For countries which are party to the Hague Convention, the Apostille may be obtained by submitting the notarized document to the appropriate Register of Deeds for authentication and then to the Secretary of State's Office, expressly requesting the Apostille, and identifying the country involved.

Materials to be Submitted with Request
1. Original notarized document to be authenticated
2. Prepaid, self-addressed return envelope is required for return service other than first class mail; Federal Express/Airbourne/UPS/Airbill numbers are required

Fees
Certification of Register of Deeds Authentication: $6.25
Apostille: $6.25

Payment Method: Cash, money order, certified check, company check, personal check payable to Secretary of State

II. SECRETARY OF STATE

Secretary of State's Office 919-733-4104
Authentication Division
300 N. Salisbury Street, Room 302
Legislative Office Building
Raleigh, NC 27603-5909
8:00 AM - 4:30 PM

III. REGISTERS OF DEEDS

County	*Address*	*Telephone*
Alamance	118 W. Harden Street Graham, NC 27253	910-570-6565
Alexander	201 First Street, SW, Ste. 3 Taylorsville, NC 28681	704-632-3152
Alleghany	PO Box 186 Sparta, NC 28675	910-372-4342
Anson	PO Box 352 Wadesboro, NC 28170	704-694-3212
Ashe	PO Box 367 Jefferson, NC 28640	910-246-9338
Avery	Courthouse, PO Box 87 Newland, NC 28657	704-733-8260
Beaufort	PO Box 514 Washington, NC 27889	919-946-2323
Bertie	PO Box 340 Windsor, NC 27983	919-794-5309
Bladen	Courthouse, PO Box 247 Elizabethtown, NC 28337	910-862-6710
Brunswick	PO Box 87 Bolivia, NC 28422	910-253-4371
Buncombe	60 Court Plaza Asheville, NC 28801-3563	704-255-5541
Burke	PO Box 936 Morgantown, NC 28655	704-438-5450

County	*Address*	*Telephone*
Cabarrus	PO Box 707 Concord, NC 28056	704-788-8112
Caldwell	905 West Avenue, NW Lenoir, NC 28645	704-757-1310
Camden	PO Box 190 Camden, NC 27921	919-335-4077
Carteret	PO Box 630 Beaufort, NC 28516	919-728-8474
Caswell	PO Box 98 Yanceyville, NC 27379	910-694-4193
Catawba	PO Box 65 Newton, NC 28658	704-465-1573
Chatham	PO Box 756 Pittsboro, NC 27312	919-542-8235
Cherokee	Courthouse Murphy, NC 28906	704-837-2613
Chowan	PO Box 487, Courthouse Edenton, NC 27932	919-482-2619
Clay	PO Box 118 Hayesville, NC 28904	704-389-6301
Cleveland	PO Box 1210 Shelby, NC 28150	704-484-4834
Columbus	PO Box 1086, Courthouse Whiteville, NC 28472	910-640-6625
Craven	PO Box 1528 New Bern, NC 28563	919-636-6617

County	*Address*	*Telephone*
Cumberland	PO Box 2039 Fayetteville, NC 28302	910-678-7775
Currituck	PO Box 71 Currituck, NC 27929	919-232-3297
Dare	PO Box 70 Manteo, NC 27954	919-473-3438
Davidson	PO Box 464 Lexington, NC 27293	704-242-2003
Davie	123 S. Main Street Mocksville, NC 27028	704-634-2513
Duplin	PO Box 448 Kenansville, NC 28349	910-296-2108
Durham	PO Box 1107 Durham, NC 27702	919-560-0480
Edgecombe	PO Box 386 Tarboro, NC 27886	919-641-7928
Forsyth	PO Box 20639 Winston-Salem, NC 27101-0639	910-727-2903
Franklin	PO Box 545 Louisburg, NC 27549	919-496-3500
Gaston	PO Box 1578 Gastonia, NC 28053	704-866-3180
Gates	PO Box 471 Gatesville, NC 27938	919-357-0850
Graham	PO Box 406 Robbinsville, NC 28771	704-479-7971

County	*Address*	*Telephone*
Granville	PO Box 427 Oxford, NC 27565	919-693-6314
Greene	PO Box 86 Snow Hill, NC 28580	919-747-3620
Guilford	PO Box 3427 Greensboro, NC 27402	910-373-7556
Halifax	PO Box 67 Halifax, NC 27839	919-583-2101
Harnett	PO Box 279 Lillington, NC 227546	910-893-7542
Haywood	Courthouse Waynesville, NC 28786	704-452-6635
Henderson	113 North Main Street Hendersonville, NC 28739	704-697-4901
Hertford	PO Box 36 Winton, NC 27986	919-358-7850
Hoke	304 North Main Street Raeford, NC 28376	910-875-2035
Hyde	PO Box 294 Swan Quarter, NC 27885	919-926-3011
Iredell	PO Box 904 Statesville, NC 28677	704-872-7468
Jackson	Courthouse Sylva, 28779	704-586-4055
Johnston	PO Box 118 Smithfield, NC 27577	919-989-5160

County	*Address*	*Telephone*
Jones	PO Box 189 Trenton, NC 28585	919-448-2551
Lee	PO Box 2040 Sanford, NC 27331-2040	919-774-4821
Lenoir	PO Box 3239 Kinston, NC 28502	919-523-2390
Lincoln	PO Box 218 Lincolnton, NC 28092	704-736-8534
Macon	5 West Main Franklin, NC 28734	704-524-6421
Madison	PO Box 66 Marshall, NC 28753	704-649-3131
Martin	PO Drawer 348 Williamston, NC 27892	919-792-1683
McDowell	1 South Main Street Marion, NC 28752	704-652-4727
Mecklenburg	County Office Building Room 101 720 East Fourth Street Charlotte, NC 28202	704-336-2443
Mitchell	PO Box 82 Bakersville, NC 28705	704-688-2139
Montgomery	PO Box 695 Troy, NC 27371	910-576-4271
Moore	PO Box 1210 Carthage, NC 28327	910-947-6370
Nash	PO Box 974 Nashville, NC 27856	919-459-9825

County	*Address*	*Telephone*
New Hanover	314 Princess Street, 216 Wilmington, NC 28401	910-341-4530
Northampton	PO Box 128 Jackson, NC 27845	919-534-2511
Onslow	109 Old Bridge Street Jacksonville, NC 28540	910-347-3451
Orange	208 South Cameron Hillsborough, NC 27278	919-732-8181
Pamlico	PO Box 433 Bayboro, NC 28515	919-745-4421
Pasquotank	PO Box 154 Elizabeth City, NC 27907	919-335-4367
Pender	PO Box 43 Burgaw, NC 28425	910-259-1225
Perquimans	Courthouse, Box 74 Hertford, NC 27944	919-426-5660
Person	Courthouse Square Roxboro, NC 27573	910-597-7221
Pitt	PO Box 35 Greenville, NC 27835	919-830-4128
Polk	PO Box 308 Columbus, NC 28722	704-894-8450
Randolph	PO Box 4066 Asheboro, NC 27204	910-318-6960
Richmond	PO Box 1563 Rockingham, NC 28379	910-997-8250

County	*Address*	*Telephone*
Robeson	Courthouse, Box 22 Lumberton, NC 28358	910-671-3040
Rockingham	PO Box 56 Wentworth, NC 27375	910-342-8820
Rowan	PO Box 2568 Salisbury, NC 28145	704-638-3102
Rutherford	PO Box 551 Rutherford, NC 28139	704-287-6156
Sampson	PO Box 256 Clinton, NC 28328	910-592-8026
Scotland	Box 769 Laurinburg, NC 28353	910-277-2575
Stanley	PO Box 97 Albemarle, NC 28002	704-983-7235
Stokes	PO Box 67 Danbury, NC 27016	910-593-2811
Surry	PO Box 303 Dobson, NC 27017	910-386-9235
Swain	PO Box 417 Bryson City, NC 28713	704-488-9273
Transylvania	Courthouse 12 E. Main Street Brevard, NC 28712	704-884-3162
Tyrrell	PO Box 449 Columbia, NC 27925	919-796-2901
Union	PO Box 248 Monroe, NC 28111	704-283-3797

County	*Address*	*Telephone*
Vance	122 Young Street, Ste. F Henderson, NC 27536	919-438-4155
Wake	PO Box 1897 Raleigh, NC 27602	919-856-5460
Warren	PO Box 506 Warrenton, NC 27589	919-257-3265
Washington	PO Box 1007 Plymouth, NC 27962	919-793-2325
Watauga	Courthouse, Box 9 Boone, NC 28607	704-265-8052
Wayne	PO Box 267 Goldsboro, NC 27530	919-731-1449
Wilkes	County Courthouse Main Street Wilkesboro, NC 28697	919-651-7351
Wilson	115 East Nash Street Wilson, NC 27893	919-399-2935
Yadkin	PO Box 211 Yadkinville, NC 27055	910-679-4225
Yancey	Courthouse, Room 4 Burnsville, NC 28714	704-682-2174

NORTH DAKOTA

I. GENERAL INFORMATION

Authentication of Notary Public Signature
Authentication can be done only by the Secretary of State's Office. After authentication by the Secretary of State, the document is ready for submission to the U.S. Secretary of State for certification, if that is required prior to legalization.

Apostille
For countries which are party to the Hague Convention, the Apostille may be obtained by submitting the notarized document directly to the Secretary of State's Office, expressly requesting the Apostille, and identifying the country involved.

Materials to be Submitted with Request
1. Original notarized document to be authenticated
2. Prepaid, self-addressed return envelope is required only for return service other than first class mail.

Fees
Authentication of Notary Public Signature: $10.00
Apostille: $10.00

Payment Method: Cash, money order, certified check, company check, personal check payable to Secretary of State, credit card (Visa, MasterCard, Discover)

II. SECRETARY OF STATE

Secretary of State
State Capitol
600 East Boulevard Avenue
Bismarck, ND 58505-0500

701-328-2900

OHIO

I. GENERAL INFORMATION

Authentication of Notary Public Signature
Authentication can be done only by the appropriate county Clerk of Court of Common Pleas, unless the Notary is an Ohio attorney, in which case the authentication can be done by the Secretary of State's Office.

Certification of Clerk of Common Pleas Authentication
Certification is done by the Secretary of State's Office. After authentication, the document is ready for submission to the U.S. Secretary of State for certification, if that is required prior to legalization. Certified copies (having an original seal and signature) of birth and death certificates, as well as signatures of judges on certified copies of documents filed with the courts, also can be authenticated. Signatures of Deputy Clerks and copies of signatures, however, can not be certified.

Apostille
For countries which are party to the Hague Convention, the Apostille may be obtained by first submitting the notarized document to the appropriate Clerk of Court of Common Pleas for authentication. The notarized document is then submitted to the Secretary of State's Office, expressly requesting the Apostille, and identifying the country involved. (If the document has been notarized by a Notary who is an Ohio attorney, the document may be sent directly to the Secretary of State's Office for the Apostille.)

Materials to be Submitted with Request
1. Original notarized document to be authenticated
2. Prepaid, self-addressed return envelope is required only for return service other than first class mail

Fees
Certification of Clerk of Court of Common Pleas Authentication: $5.00
Apostille: $5.00

Payment Method: Money order or check payable to the Ohio Secretary of State or State of Ohio.

II. SECRETARY OF STATE

Secretary of State 614-466-2585
Elections Department
30 East Broad Street, 14th Floor
Columbus, Ohio 43266-0418

III. CLERKS OF COURTS OF COMMON PLEAS

County	*Address*
Adams	Courthouse West Union, OH 45693
Allen	Courthouse Lima, OH 45802
Ashland	Courthouse Ashland, OH 44805
Ashtabula	Courthouse Jefferson, OH 44047
Athens	Courthouse Athens, OH 45701
Auglaize	Courthouse Wapakoneta, OH 45895
Belmont	Courthouse St. Clairsville, OH 43950
Brown	Courthouse Georgetown, OH 45121
Butler	Courthouse Hamilton, OH 45012
Carroll	Courthouse Carrollton, OH 44615

County	*Address*
Champaign	Courthouse Urbana, OH 43078
Clark	Courthouse Springfield, OH 45502
Clermont	Courthouse Batavia, OH 45103
Clinton	Courthouse Wilmington, OH 45177
Columbiana	Courthouse Lisbon, OH 44432
Coshocton	Courthouse Coshocton, OH 43812
Crawford	Courthouse Bucyrus, OH 44820
Cuyahoga	Courthouse Cleveland, OH 44113
Darke	Courthouse Greenville, OH 45331
Defiance	Courthouse Defiance, OH 43512
Delaware	Courthouse Delaware, OH 43015
Erie	Courthouse Sandusky, OH 44870
Fairfield	Courthouse Lancaster, OH 43130

County	*Address*
Fayette	Courthouse Washington Courthouse, OH 43160
Franklin	Courthouse Columbua, OH 43215
Fulton	Courthouse Wauseon, OH 43567
Gallia	Courthouse Gallipolis, OH 45631
Geauga	Courthouse Chardon, OH 44024
Greene	Courthouse Xenia, OH 45385
Guernsey	Courthouse Cambridge, OH 43725
Hamilton	Courthouse Cincinnati, OH 45202
Hancock	Courthouse Findlay, OH 45840
Hardin	Courthouse Kenton, OH 43326
Harrison	Courthouse Cadiz, OH 43907
Henry	Courthouse Napleon, OH 43545
Highland	Courthouse Hillsboro, OH 45133

County	*Address*
Hocking	Courthouse Logan, OH 43138
Holmes	Courthouse Millersburg, OH 44654
Huron	Courthouse Norwalk, OH 44857
Jackson	Courthouse Jackson, OH 45640
Jefferson	Courthouse Steubenville, OH 43952
Knox	Courthouse Mount Vernon, OH 43050
Lake	Courthouse Painesville, OH 44077
Lawrence	Courthouse Ironton, OH 45638
Licking	Courthouse Newark, OH 43055
Logan	Courthouse Bellefontaine, OH 43311
Lorain	Courthouse Elyria, OH 44035
Lucas	Courthouse Toledo, OH 43624
Madison	Courthouse London, OH 43140

County	*Address*
Mahoning	Courthouse Youngstown, OH 44503
Marion	Courthouse Marion, OH 43302
Medina	Courthouse Medina, OH 44256
Meigs	Courthouse Pomeroy, OH 45769
Mercer	Courthouse Celina, OH 45822
Miami	Courthouse Troy, OH 45373
Monroe	Courthouse Woodsfield, OH 43793
Montgomery	Courthouse Dayton, OH 45402
Morgan	Courthouse McConnelsville, OH 43576
Morrow	Courthouse Mount Gilead, OH 43338
Muskingum	Courthouse Zanesville, OH 43701
Noble	Courthouse Caldwell, OH 43724
Ottawa	Courthouse Port Clinton, OH 43452

County	*Address*
Paulding	Courthouse Paulding, OH 45879
Perry	Courthouse New Lexington, OH 43764
Pickaway	Courthouse Circleville, OH 43113
Pike	Courthouse Waverly, OH 45690
Portage	Courthouse Ravenna, OH 44266
Preble	Courthouse Eaton, OH 45320
Putnam	Courthouse Ottawa, OH 45875
Richland	Courthouse Mansfield, OH 44902
Ross	Courthouse Chillicothe, OH 45601
Sandusky	Courthouse Fremont, OH 43420
Scioto	Courthouse Portsmouth, OH 45662
Seneca	Courthouse Tiffin, OH 44883
Shelby	Courthouse Sidney, OH 45365

County	*Address*
Stark	Courthouse Canton, OH 44702
Summit	Courthouse Akron, OH 44308
Trumbull	Courthouse Warren, OH 44482
Tuscarawas	Courthouse New Philadelphia, OH 44663
Union	Courthouse Marysville, OH 43040
Van Wert	Courthouse Van Wert, OH 45891
Vinton	Courthouse McArthur, OH 45651
Warren	Courthouse Lebanon, OH 45036
Washington	Courthouse Marietta, OH 45750
Wayne	Courthouse Wooster, OH 44691
Williams	Courthouse Bryan, OH 43506
Wood	Courthouse Bowling Green, OH 43402
Wyandot	Courthouse Upper Sandusky, OH 43351

OKLAHOMA

I. GENERAL INFORMATION

Authentication of Notary Public Signature
Authentication can be done by the Court Clerk in the appropriate county. After authentication, the document is ready for submission to the U.S. Secretary of State for certification, if that is required prior to legalization. If an Apostille is desired, however, intervening authentication by the Court Clerk is not necessary (see below).

Certification of Court Clerk Authentication
Authentication is done by the Secretary of State's Office. After authentication, the document is ready for submission to the U.S. Secretary of State for certification, if that is required prior to legalization.

Apostille
For countries which are party to the Hague Convention, the Apostille may be obtained by submitting the notarized document directly to the Secretary of State's Office, expressly requesting the Apostille, and identifying the country involved.

Materials to be Submitted with Request
1. Original notarized document to be authenticated
2. Prepaid, self-addressed return envelope

Fees (Secretary of State)
Certification of Court Clerk Authentication: $20.00
Apostille: $25.00

Fee (County Clerk)
Authentication of Notary Public Signature: $3.00

Payment Method: Cash, money order, certified check, company check, personal check payable to Secretary of State

II. SECRETARY OF STATE

Secretary of State 405-521-4211/2
101 State Capitol Building
2300 N. Lincoln Boulevard
Oklahoma City, OK 73105-4847

III. COUNTY COURT CLERKS

Address correspondence to _____ County Court Clerk.

County	*Address*	*Telephone*
Adair	Adair County PO Box 426 Stilwell, OK 74960-0426	918-696-7633
Alfalfa	Alfafa County 300 S. Grand Cherokee, OK 73728	405-596-3523
Atoka	Atoka County 201 E. Court Street Atoka, OK 74525	405-889-3565
Beaver	Beaver County PO Box 327 Beaver, OK 73932	405-625-3191
Beckham	Beckham County PO Box 520 Sayre, OK 73662	405-928-3330
Blaine	Blaine County 212 N. Wiegel Street Watonga, OK 73772	405-623-5970
Bryan	Bryan County Fourth and Evergreen Durant, OK 74701	405-924-1446
Caddo	Caddo County PO Box 10 Anadarko, OK 73005	405-247-3393
Canadian	Canadian County PO Box 730 El Reno, OK 73036	405-262-1070 ext. 275

County	*Address*	*Telephone*
Carter	Carter County PO Box 1236 Ardmore, OK 73401	405-223-5253
Cherokee	Cherokee County 213 W. Delaware, Room 300 Tahlequah, OK 74464	405-456-0691
Choctaw	Choctaw County 300 E. Jefferson Hugo, OK 74743	405-326-7554
Cimarron	Cimarron County PO Box 788 Boise City, OK 73933	405-544-2221
Cleveland	Cleveland County 200 S. Peters Norman, OK 73069	405-321-6402
Coal	Coal County 3 North Main Coalgate, OK 74538	405-927-2281
Comanche	Comanche County 300 S.W. 5th Lawton, OK 73501	405-355-4017
Cotton	Cotton County 301 N. Broadway Walters, OK 73572-1271	405-875-3029
Craig	Craig County 301 W. Canadian Vinita, OK 74301	918-256-2445
Creek	Creek County PO Box 1410 Sapupla, OK 74067	918-227-2525

County	*Address*	*Telephone*
Custer	Custer County Third and B Street Arapaho, OK 73620	405-323-3233
Delaware	Delaware County PO Box 407 Jay, OK 74346	918-253-4420
Dewey	Dewey County PO Box 278 Taloga, OK 73667-0278	405-328-5521
Ellis	Ellis County PO Box 217 Arnett, OK 73832	405-885-7255
Garfield	Garfield County 114 W. Broadway Enid, OK 73701	405-237-0232
Garvin	Garvin County Grant and Willow Street Pauls Valley, OK 73075	405-238-5596
Grady	Grady County Fourth and Choctaw Chickasha, OK 73018	405-224-7446
Grant	Grant County 112 Guthrie Medford, OK 73759	405-395-2828
Greer	Greer County PO Box 216 Mangum, OK 73554-0216	405-782-3665
Harmon	Harmon County 114 Hollis Street Hollis, OK 73550	405-688-3617

County	*Address*	*Telephone*
Harper	Harper County 311 S.E. First Street Buffalo, OK 73834	405-735-2010
Haskell	Haskell County 202 E. Main Stigler, OK 74462	918-967-3323
Hughes	Hughes County 200 N. Broadway Holdenville, OK 74848	405-379-3384
Jackson	Jackson County 101 N. Main, Room 303 Altus, OK 73521	405-482-0448
Jefferson	Jefferson County 220 W. Main Waurika, OK 73537	405-228-2961
Johnston	Johnston County 400 W. 8th Street Tishomingo, OK 73460	405-371-3281
Kay	Kay County PO Box 428 Newkirk, OK 73750	405-362-3350
Kingfisher	Kingfisher County Main Street and Broadway Kingfisher, OK 73750	405-375-3813
Kiowa	Kiowa County 316 S. Main Hobart, OK 73651	405-726-5125
Latimer	Latimer County 109 N. Central Wilberton, OK 74576	918-465-2011

County	*Address*	*Telephone*
LeFlore	LeFlore County 110 Front Street Poteau, OK 74953	918-647-3181
Lincoln	Lincoln County PO Box 307 Chandler, OK 74834	405-258-1309
Logan	Logan County 301 E. Harrison Guthrie, OK 73044	405-282-0123
Love	Love County 405 W. Main Street Marietta, OK 73448	405-276-2235
McClain	McClain County Second and Washington Purcell, OK 73080	405-527-3221
McCurtain	McCurtain County 109 N. Central Idabel, OK 74745	405-286-3693
McIntosh	McIntosh County 110 N. First Eufaula, OK 74432	918-689-2282
Major	Major County E. Broadway and Ninth Fairview, OK 73737	405-277-4690
Marshall	Marshall County PO Box 58 Madill, OK 73446	405-795-3278
Mayes	Mayes County PO Box 867 Pryor, OK 74361	918-825-2185

County	*Address*	*Telephone*
Murray	Murray County 10th and Wyandotte Sulphur, OK 73086	405-622-3223
Muskogee	Muskogee County Court and State Street Muskogee, OK 74401	918-682-8731
Noble	Noble County PO Box 793 Perry, OK 73077	405-336-5187
Nowata	Nowata County 229 North Maplen Nowata, OK 74048	918-273-0127
Okfuskee	Osfuskee County Third and Atlanta Street Okemah, OK 74859	918-623-0525
Oklahoma	Oklahoma County 320 Robert S. Kerr, Rm. 413 Oklahoma City, OK 73102	405-278-1705
Okmulgee	Okmulgee County 315 West 7th Street Okmulgee, OK 74447	918-756-3042
Osage	Osage County 600 Grandview Pawhuska, OK 74056	918-287-4104
Ottawa	Ottawa County 102 East Central Miami, OK 74354	918-542-2801
Pawnee	Pawnee County 500 Harrison, # 300 Pawnee, OK 74058	918-762-2547

County	*Address*	*Telephone*
Payne	Payne County 606 South Husband Stillwater, OK 74074	405-372-4774
Pittsburg	Pittsburg County Second and Carl Albert Pkwy. McAlester, OK 74501	918-423-4859
Pontotoc	Pontotoc County Thirteenth and Broadway Ada, OK 74820	405-332-5763
Pottawatomie	Pottawatomie County 325 N. Broadway Shawnee, OK 74801	405-273-3624
Pushmataha	Pushmataha County 203 S.W. Third Antlers, OK 74523	405-298-2274
Roger Mills	Roger Mills County L.L. Males Blvd. & Broadway Cheyenne, OK 73628	405-497-3361
Roger	Rogers County 219 S. Missouri Claremore, OK 74017	918-341-5711
Seminole	Seminole County PO Box 130 Wewoka, OK 74884	405-257-6236
Sequoyah	Sequoyah County 120 E. Chickasaw Sallisaw, OK 74955	918-775-4411
Stephens	Stephens County 12th and Willow Duncan, OK 73533	405-255-8460

County	*Address*	*Telephone*
Texas	Texas County PO Box 1081 Guymon, OK 73942	405-338-3003
Tillman	Tillman County PO Box 116 Frederick, OK 73542	405-323-3023
Tulsa	Tulsa County 500 South Denver Tulsa, OK 74102	918-596-5420
Wagoner	Wagoner County PO Box 249 Wagoner, OK 74477	918-485-4508
Washington	Washington County 420 S. Johnstone Street Bartlesville, OK 74003	918-337-2870
Washita	Washita County PO Box 397 Cordell, OK 73632	405-832-3836
Woods	Woods County PO Box 924 Alva, OK 73717	405-327-3119
Woodward	Woodward County 1600 Main Street Woodward, OK 73801	405-256-3413

OREGON

I. GENERAL INFORMATION

Authentication of Notary Public Signature
Authentication can be done by the Secretary of State. After authentication by the Secretary of State, the document is ready for submission to the U.S. Secretary of State for certification, if that is required prior to legalization.

Apostille
For countries which are party to the Hague Convention, the Apostille may be obtained by submitting the notarized document directly to the Secretary of State's Office, expressly requesting the Apostille, and identifying the country involved. (Prior authentication by the County Clerk is not necessary.)

Materials to be Submitted with Request
1. Original notarized document to be authenticated
2. Prepaid, self-addressed return envelope is not required for first class mail return service but is appreciated

Fees
Authentication of Notary Public Signature: $10.00
Apostille: $10.00

Payment Method: Money order, certified check, company check, personal check payable to State of Oregon, Visa or MasterCard

II. SECRETARY OF STATE

Secretary of State — 503-986-2200
Corporation Division - Notary Section
Suite 151
255 Capitol Street, NE
Salem, OR 97310-1327

PENNSYLVANIA

I. GENERAL INFORMATION

Authentication of Notary Public Signature
Authentication can be done by the appropriate County Clerk or directly by the Secretary of State's Office. After authentication by the Secretary of State, the document is ready for submission to the U.S. Secretary of State for certification, if that is required prior to legalization.

Apostille
For countries which are party to the Hague Convention, the Apostille may be obtained by submitting the notarized document directly to the Secretary of State's Office, expressly requesting the Apostille, and identifying the country involved. (Prior authentication by the County Clerk is not necessary.)

Materials to be Submitted with Request
1. Original notarized document to be authenticated
2. Cover letter stating name of country in which document(s) will be used
2. Prepaid, self-addressed return envelope is required; pre-paid air bill for return by a courier service

Fees
Authentication of Notary Public Signature: $15.00
Apostille: $15.00

Payment Method: Cash (only at counter, for orders under $25.00), money order, certified check, company check, personal check issued by a United States bank and payable to the Commonwealth of Pennsylvania

Turn Around Time: Allow 10 to 15 working days for processing. Requests are completed in the order they are received. Expedited service is not available.

II. SECRETARY OF STATE

Department of State 717-787-5280
Bureau of Commissions, Elections and
Legislation
Certification Division
Room 304, North Office Building
Harrisburg, PA 17120

PUERTO RICO

I. GENERAL INFORMATION

Apostille
The Apostille may be obtained from the Division of Certifications.

Fee
Apostille: $3.00

II. DIVISION OF CERTIFICATIONS

Division of Certifications
Department of State of Puerto Rico
PO Box 9023271
San Juan, PR 00902-3271
Tel.: 787-723-6785

RHODE ISLAND

I. GENERAL INFORMATION

Authentication of Notary Public Signature
Authentication can be done only by the Secretary of State's Office. After authentication by the Secretary of State, the document is ready for submission to the U.S. Secretary of State for certification, if that is required prior to legalization.

Apostille
For countries which are party to the Hague Convention, the Apostille may be obtained by submitting the notarized document directly to the Secretary of State's Office, expressly requesting the Apostille, and identifying the country involved.

Materials to be Submitted with Request
1. Original notarized document to be authenticated
2. Prepaid, self-addressed return envelope is required only for return service other than first class mail.

Fees
Authentication of Notary Public Signature: $5.00
Apostille: $5.00

Payment Method: Cash, money order, certified check, company check, personal check payable to Secretary of State

Additional Information: For over-the-counter service, call the office in 48 hours in advance with the notary name, country, and number of documents.

II. SECRETARY OF STATE

Office of the Secretary of State 401-277-1487
Notary Division
100 North Main Street
Providence, RI 02903

SOUTH CAROLINA

I. GENERAL INFORMATION

Authentication of Notary Public Signature
Authentication can be done by either the Clerk of Court or the Register of Mesne Conveyance of the appropriate county or by the Secretary of State's Office. After authentication by the Secretary of State, the document is ready for submission to the U.S. Secretary of State for certification, if that is required prior to legalization.

Apostille
For countries which are party to the Hague Convention, the Apostille may be obtained by submitting the notarized document directly to the Secretary of State's Office, expressly requesting the Apostille, and identifying the country involved. (Prior authentication by the County Clerk is not necessary.)

Materials to be Submitted with Request
1. Original notarized document to be authenticated
2. Prepaid, self-addressed return envelope

Fees
Authentication of Notary Public Signature: $2.00
Apostille: $2.00
(Per certification)

Payment Method: Cash, money order, certified check, company check, personal check payable to Secretary of State

II. SECRETARY OF STATE

Secretary of State 803-734-2119
PO Box 11350
Columbia, SC 29211

SOUTH DAKOTA

I. GENERAL INFORMATION

Authentication of Notary Public Signature
Authentication can be done only by the Secretary of State's Office. After authentication by the Secretary of State, the document is ready for submission to the U.S. Secretary of State for certification, if that is required prior to legalization.

Apostille
For countries which are party to the Hague Convention, the Apostille may be obtained by submitting the notarized document directly to the Secretary of State's Office, expressly requesting the Apostille, and identifying the country involved.

Materials to be Submitted with Request
1. Original notarized document to be authenticated
2. Prepaid, self-addressed return envelope is requested but not required unless other than first class mail

Fees
Authentication of Notary Public Signature: $2.00
Apostille: $2.00 per certification

Payment Method: Cash, money order, certified check, company check, personal check payable to Secretary of State, Visa, MasterCard

II. SECRETARY OF STATE

Secretary of State
State Capitol Building
500 East Capitol, Suite 204
Pierre, SD 57501-5077

605-773-5666
(direct line)

TENNESSEE

I. GENERAL INFORMATION

Note
With effect from July 1, 1993, every elected Notary Public serves as a Notary Public at Large for the State of Tennessee. The Tennessee Department of State authenticates the State Registrar's signature on originals or certified copies of vital records through direct submission to the Secretary of State's Office. Signatures of former County Clerks and State Registrars can also be authenticated for their term of office.

Authentication of Notary Public Signature
Authentication of documents notarized by a Notary Public at Large for the State of Tennessee can not be done by the Secretary of State's Office. For notarial powers that expire after July 1, 1997, signatures of Notaries at Large all must be authenticated through the respective counties of election for those powers that expire after July 1, 1997. After authentication by the Secretary of State, the document is ready for submission to the U.S. Secretary of State for certification, if that is required prior to legalization.

Authentication of documents notarized by a County Notary Public must be done by the appropriate County Clerk. Certification of the County Clerk's authentication is done by the Secretary of State's Office.

Apostille
For countries which are party to the Hague Convention, the Apostille may be obtained by submitting the notarized document directly to the Secretary of State's Office, expressly requesting the Apostille, and identifying the country involved. The document must be notarized by a Notary Public; however, the notarized document must first be authenticated by the appropriate County Clerk and then submitted to the Secretary of State's Office expressly requesting an Apostille and identifying the country involved. The State Registrar's signature may be provided by the Secretary of State.

Materials to be Submitted with Request
1. Original notarized document to be authenticated
2. Prepaid, self-addressed return envelope is required only for return service other than first class mail

Fees

Authentication of Notary Public Signature: $2.00 (if applicable) per document

Authentication of County Clerk Signature: $2.00 per document

Apostille: $2.00 per document

Payment Method: Cash, money order, certified check, company check, personal check payable to Secretary of State or State of Tennessee

II. SECRETARY OF STATE

Secretary of State 615-741-3699
James K. Polk Building, Suite 1800
Nashville, TN 37243-0306

TEXAS

I. GENERAL INFORMATION

Authentication of Notary Public Signature and Apostille
Both certifications can be done only by the Secretary of State's Office. A letter stating the name of the Notary Public, the expiration date of notarial power, and the date the document was authorized is required. In the case of the Apostille, the country in which the document is to be used should also be indicated. An appropriate certificate establishing notarial standing will issue from the Secretary of State's Office. The notarized document should not be sent.

Materials to be Submitted with Request
1. Prepaid, self-addressed return envelope is required only for return service other than first class mail

Fees
Certification of Notarial Authority: $10.00
Apostille: $10.00

Payment Method: Money order, certified check, company check, personal check

II. SECRETARY OF STATE

Secretary of State
Notary Public Section
1019 Brazos
Austin, TX 78701

512-463-5705

UTAH

I. GENERAL INFORMATION

Authentication of Notary Public Signature
Authentication is done by the Notary Division of the Department of Commerce for documents for use in the United States, or by the Lieutenant Governor's Office for documents required by a foreign government. After authentication by the Lieutenant Governor's Office, the document is ready for submission to the U.S. Secretary of State for certification, if that is required prior to legalization.

Apostille
For countries which are party to the Hague Convention, the Apostille may be obtained by submitting the notarized document directly to the Lieutenant Governor's Office, expressly requesting the Apostille, and identifying the country involved. (Prior authentication by the County Clerk is not necessary.)

Materials to be Submitted with Request
1. Original notarized document to be authenticated
2. Prepaid, self-addressed return envelope is required only for return service other than first class mail

Fees
Lieutenant Governor's Office fee for Apostille: $5.00
Department of Commerce and Lieutenant Governor's Office fee for authentication of Notary Public signature: $10.00

Payment Method: Cash, money order, certified check, company check, personal check payable to the State of Utah

II. DEPARTMENT OF COMMERCE
LIEUTENANT GOVERNOR'S OFFICE

Within the United States

Department of Commerce 801-530-6078
PO Box 146705
Salt Lake City, UT 84114-6705

For Apostille and Notary Authentication for Foreign Governments

Lieutenant Governor's Office 801-538-1040
Attention: Marilyn Hollingworth
203 State Capitol
Salt Lake City, UT 84114

VERMONT

I. GENERAL INFORMATION

Authentication of Notary Public Signature
Authentication can be done by the County Clerk or by the Secretary of State's Office. After authentication by the Secretary of State, the document is ready for submission to the U.S. Secretary of State for certification, if that is required prior to legalization.

Apostille
For countries which are party to the Hague Convention, the Apostille may be obtained by submitting the notarized document directly to the Secretary of State's Office, expressly requesting the Apostille, and identifying the country involved. (Prior authentication by the County Clerk is not necessary.)

Materials to be Submitted with Request
1. Original notarized document to be authenticated
2. Prepaid, self-addressed return envelope is required only for return service other than first class mail. On request, documents will be returned through certified mail. An additional $2.00 fee is required for this service.

Fees
Authentication of Notary Public Signature: $2.00
Certification of County Clerk Authentication: $2.00
Apostille: $2.00

Payment Method: Cash, money order, certified check, company check, personal check payable to State of Vermont

II. SECRETARY OF STATE

Secretary of State 802-828-2363
109 State Street
Montpelier, VT 05609-1103

VIRGIN ISLANDS

I. GENERAL INFORMATION

Apostille
The Apostille may be obtained from the Lieutenant Governor's office. The Clerk and Deputy Clerks of the United States District Court of the Virgin Islands also have the authority to issue Apostilles.

Fees
Apostille: $5.00
Certification: $5.00

Payment Method: Check payable to the Government of the Virgin Islands

II. LIEUTENANT GOVERNOR

Lieutenant Governor K. Mapp 809-774-2991
Kongens Gade #18
St. Thomas, Virgin Islands 00802
Fax: 809-774-6953

VIRGINIA

I. GENERAL INFORMATION

Note
An original document with an ink signature requires the following information for notarization: city and county of Commonwealth of Virginia, Notary statement, date of signature, legible Notary signature, date of expiration of commission, and legible Notary seal.

Authentication of Notary Public Signature
Authentication can be done by the appropriate County Clerk or directly by the Secretary of Commonwealth's Office. After authentication by the Secretary of Commonwealth, the document is ready for submission to the U.S. Secretary of State for certification, if that is required by the Embassy under consideration.

Vital Records
Documents from the Virginia Department of Health, Bureau of Vital Records (birth and death certificates and marriage and divorce documents) must be requested to have an ink signature and date on the document signed by the Registrar or Deputy Registrar of Vital Records. A Notary cannot sign state documents.

Court documents must be requested to have the Clerk of the Court sign and date them. A Notary cannot sign a court document.

Apostille
For countries which are party to the Hague Convention, the Apostille may be obtained by submitting the notarized document directly to the Secretary of Commonwealth's Office, with a cover letter of request expressly requesting the Apostille, and identifying the country involved. (Prior authentication by the County Clerk is not necessary.)

Materials to be Submitted with Request
1. Original notarized document or signed state or court document to be authenticated
2. Cover letter of request providing name, address and telephone number and name of country to which the document will be sent
3. Prepaid, self-addressed return envelope is required; courier service (FedEx, UPS) with a tracking system is recommended
4. Check with the proper fee

Turn Around Time: It is necessary to make an appointment to personally deliver documents for authentication. Call 804-786-2441 for an appointment.

Fees
Authentication of Notary Public Signature: $10.00
Certification of County Clerk Authentication: $10.00
Apostille: $10.00

Payment Method: Cash, money order, certified check, company check, personal check payable to the Secretary of the Commonwealth; overnight mail service prepaid by check or money order

II. SECRETARY OF THE COMMONWEALTH

Secretary of the Commonwealth 804-786-2441
PO Box 2454
Richmond, VA 23218
Attn: Authentication

For overnight mail service:
Secretary of the Commonwealth
Attn. Authentication
Capitol Square
Old Finance Building
Richmond, VA 23219

WASHINGTON

I. GENERAL INFORMATION

Authentication of Notary Public Signature
Authentication of Notary Public signature can be done by the Department of Licensing. Authentication of documents signed by a Notary, certified by county or state officials, and/or certified by authorized officials representing the Washington Education System can be done by the Secretary of State's Office. After such authentication, the document is ready for submission to the U.S. Secretary of State for certification, if that is required prior to legalization.

Apostille
For countries which are party to the Hague Convention, the Apostille may be obtained by submitting the notarized document directly to the Secretary of State's Office, expressly requesting the Apostille, and identifying the country involved.

Materials to be Submitted with Request
1. Original notarized document to be authenticated or certified copy with an original certification
2. Prepaid, self-addressed return envelope is required
3. Telephone number

Time Delay: If the document is presented by hand for legalization, it will be legalized the same day. Note that there is a maximum of five documents for same-day service. If more than five documents are to be legalized, an appointment must be made to pick up the legalized documents.

Additional Information
Some countries require different forms of authentication. To insure that the proper form is used, indicate the country for which the document is intended.
If you have further questions, contact the Authentication Clerk at 360-902-4161.

Fees
Authentication of Notary Public Signature: $15.00 per document
Apostille: $15.00

Payment Method: Cash, money order, certified check, company check, personal check; checks and money orders payable to Secretary of State

II. SECRETARY OF STATE

Secretary of State 360-902-4161
Legislative Building, 2nd Floor
PO Box 40220
Olympia, WA 98504-0220
Attention: Authentication Clerk
10:00 AM - 3:00 PM

III. DEPARTMENT OF LICENSING

Department of Licensing 360-753-3836
Notaries Division
405 Black Lake Boulevard, Building 2
Olympia, WA 98502

WASHINGTON, DC

I. GENERAL INFORMATION

Authentication of Notary Public Signature
Authentication is done by the Office of the Secretary of State of the District of Columbia, Notarial Section. After authentication by the Office of the Secretary of the District of Columbia, the document is ready for submission to the U.S. Secretary of State for certification, if that is required prior to legalization.

Apostille
For countries which are party to the Hague Convention, the Apostille may be obtained by submitting the notarized document directly to the Office of the Secretary of the District of Columbia, Notarial Section, expressly requesting the Apostille, and identifying the country involved.

Materials to be Submitted with Request
1. Original notarized document to be authenticated
2. Prepaid, self-addressed return envelope is required

Fees
Authentication of Notary Public Signature for Domestic Use: $10.00
Authentication of Notary Public Signature for Foreign Use: $10.00
Apostille: $10.00

Payment Method: Cash, money order, certified check, company check, personal check (all checks must be in exact amount)

II. SECRETARY OF STATE

District of Columbia Government 202-727-3117
Office of the Secretary of the District of Columbia
Office of Notary and Authentication
Suite 230
717 14th Street, NW
Washington, DC 20005
9:00 AM - 1:00 PM

WEST VIRGINIA

I. GENERAL INFORMATION

Authentication of Notary Public Signature
If the document is notarized by a Statewide Notary Public, authentication can be done directly by the Secretary of State's Office. After authentication by the Secretary of State, the document is ready for submission to the U.S. Secretary of State for certification, if that is required prior to legalization.

Certification of County Clerk Authentication
Certification is done by the Secretary of State's Office for documents notarized and authenticated by a County Clerk. After such authentication, the document is ready for submission to the U.S. Secretary of State for certification, if that is required prior to legalization.

Apostille
For countries which are party to the Hague Convention, the Apostille may be obtained by submitting the notarized document directly to the Secretary of State's Office, expressly requesting the Apostille, and identifying the country involved.

Materials to be Submitted with Request
1. Original notarized document to be authenticated
2. Prepaid, self-addressed return envelope is required only for return service other than first class mail

Fees
Authentication of Notary Public Signature: $10.00
Certification of County Clerk Authentication: $10.00
Apostille: $10.00

Payment Method: Cash, money order, certified check, company check, personal check payable to Secretary of State

II. SECRETARY OF STATE

Secretary of State 304-558-6000
1900 Kanawha Boulevard
Building 1, Suite 157K
Charleston, WV 25305

III. COUNTY CLERKS

County	*Address*	*Telephone*
Barbour	Philipp, WV 26416	304-457-2232
Berkeley	Martinsburg, WV 25401	304-267-3000
Boone	Madison, WV 25130	304-369-3925
Braxton	Sutton, WV 26601	304-765-2833
Brooke	Wellsburg, WV 26070	304-737-3661
Cabell	Huntington, WV 25701	304-526-8625
Calhoun	Grantsville, WV 26147	304-354-6725
Clay	Clay, WV 25043	304-587-4259
Doddridge	West Union, WV 26456	304-873-2631
Fayette	Fayetteville, WV 25840	304-574-1200
Gilmer	Glenville, WV 26351	304-462-7641
Grant	Petersburg, WV 26847	304-257-4550
Greenbrier	Lewisburg, WV 24901	304-645-2373
Hampshire	Romney, WV 36757	304-822-5112
Hancock	New Cumberland, WV 20047	304-564-3311
Hardy	Moorefield, WV 26836	304-538-2929
Harrison	Clarksburg, WV 26301	304-624-8611
Jackson	Ripley, WV 25721	304-372-2011

County	*Address*	*Telephone*
Jefferson	Charles Town, WV 25414	304-725-9761 Extension 215
Kanawha	Charleston, WV 25301	304-357-0110
Lewis	Weston, WV 26452	304-269-3371
Lincoln	Hamlin, WV 25523	304-824-7500 Extension 201
Logan	Logan, WV 25601	304-752-2000
Marion	Fairmont, WV 26554	304-367-5440
Marshall	Moundsville, WV 26041	304-845-1220
Mason	Pt. Pleasant, WV 25550	304-675-1997
McDowell	Welch, WV 24801	304-436-8344
Mercer	Princeton, WV 24740	304-425-9546
Mineral	Keyser, WV 26726	304-788-3924
Mingo	Williamson, WV 25661	304-235-1638
Monongalia	Morgantown, WV 26505	304-291-7230
Monroe	Union, WV 24983	304-772-3096
Morgan	Berkeley Springs, WV 25411	304-258-2774
Nicholas	Summersville, WV 26651	304-872-3630
Ohio	Wheeling, WV 26003	304-234-3656
Pendleton	Franklin, WV 26807	304-358-2505
Pleasants	St. Marys, WV 26170	304-684-3542

County	*Address*	*Telephone*
Pocahontas	Marlinton, WV 24954	304-799-4549
Preston	Kingwood, WV 26537	304-329-0070
Putnam	Winfield, WV 25213	304-755-2824
Raleigh	Beckley, WV 25801	304-255-9123
Randolph	Elkins, WV 26241	304-636-0543
Ritchie	Harrisville, WV 26362	304-643-2164
Roane	Spencer, WV 25276	304-927-2860
Summers	Hinton, WV 25951	304-466-3770
Taylor	Grafton, WV 25951	304-265-1401
Tucker	Parsons, WV 26287	304-478-2414
Tyler	Middlebourne, WV 26149	304-758-2102
Upshur	Buckhannon, WV 26201	304-472-1068
Wayne	Wayne, WV 25570	304-272-5101
Webster	Webster Springs, WV 26288	304-847-2508
Wetzel	New Martinsville, WV 26155	304-455-1390
Wirt	Elizabeth, WV 26143	304-275-4271
Wood	Parkersburg, WV 26101	304-424-1850
Wyoming	Pineville, WV 24874	304-732-8000

WISCONSIN

I. GENERAL INFORMATION

Note
For authentication of vital records, i.e., birth, marriage, and death certificates, please call in advance for special instructions. Also call in advance for court documents such as divorce decrees, adoption orders and probate records.

Authentication of Notary Public Signature
In most cases, authentication can be done only by the Secretary of State's Office. County recording of notary commissions is optional. Submit the document directly to the Secretary of State's Office and identify the country involved. After authentication by the Secretary of State, the document is ready for submission to the U.S. Secretary of State for certification, if that is required prior to legalization.

Apostille
For countries which are party to the Hague Convention, the Apostille may be obtained by submitting the notarized document directly to the Secretary of State's Office and identifying the country involved.

Materials to be Submitted with Request
1. Original notarized document to be authenticated
2. Prepaid, self-addressed return envelope is required

Fees
Authentication of Notary Public Signature: $5.00
Certification of Clerk of the Circuit Court Authentication: $5.00
Apostille: $5.00

Payment Method: Cash, money order, certified check, company check, personal check payable to Secretary of State

II. SECRETARY OF STATE

Office of the Secretary of State 608-266-5503
Attn.: Notary Records

Street Address
30 West Mifflin Street, 10th Floor
Madison, WI 53702

Mailing Address
PO Box 7848
Madison, WI 53707-7848

WYOMING

I. GENERAL INFORMATION

Authentication of Notary Public Signature
Authentication can be done only by the Secretary of State's Office. After authentication by the Secretary of State, the document is ready for submission to the U.S. Secretary of State for certification, if that is required prior to legalization.

Apostille
For countries which are party to the Hague Convention, the Apostille may be obtained by submitting the notarized document directly to the Secretary of State's Office, expressly requesting the Apostille, and identifying the country involved.

Materials to be Submitted with Request
1. Original notarized document to be authenticated
2. Prepaid, self-addressed return envelope is not required

Fees
Authentication of Notary Public Signature: $3.00
Certification of County Clerk Authentication: $3.00
Apostille: $3.00

Payment Method: Cash, money order, certified check, company check, personal check

II. SECRETARY OF STATE

Secretary of State
Notaries Division
State Capitol
Cheyenne, WY 83002

307-777-5342/33

[illegible]

[illegible]

1. GENERAL INFORMATION

Authentication of Notary Public signatures

[illegible]

[illegible]

[illegible]

[illegible]

[illegible]

[illegible]

2. [illegible]

[illegible]

APPENDICES

APPENDIX A

THE HAGUE CONVENTION TEXT
LIST OF MEMBERS TO THE HAGUE CONVENTION

CONVENTION ABOLISHING THE REQUIREMENT OF LEGALIZATION FOR FOREIGN PUBLIC DOCUMENTS

The States signatory to the present Convention,

Desiring to abolish the requirement of diplomatic or consular legalisation for foreign public documents,

Have resolved to conclude a Convention to this effect and have signed upon the following provisions:

ARTICLE 1

The present Convention shall apply to public documents which have been executed in the territory of one contracting State and which have to be produced in the territory of another contracting State.

For the purposes of the present Convention, the following are deemed to be public documents:

(a) Documents emanating from an authority or an official connected with the courts or tribunals of the State, including those emanating from a public prosecutor, a clerk of a court or a process server ("huissier de justice");
(b) Administrative documents;
(c) Notarial acts;
(d) Official certificates which are placed on documents signed by persons in their private capacity, such as official certificates recording the registration of a document or the fact that it was in existence on a certain date and official and notarial authentication of signatures.

However, the present Convention shall not apply:

(a) To documents executed by diplomatic or consular agents;
(b) To administrative documents dealing directly with commercial or customs operations.

ARTICLE 2

Each contracting State shall exempt from legalisation documents to which the present Convention applies and which have to be produced in its territory. For the purposes of the present Convention, legalisation means only the formality by which the diplomatic or consular agents of the country in which the document has to be produced certify the authenticity of the signature, the capacity in which the person signing the document has acted and, where appropriate, the identity of the seal or stamp which it bears.

ARTICLE 3

The only formality which may be required in order to certify the authenticity of the signature, the capacity in which the person signing the document has acted and, where appropriate, the identity of the seal or stamp which it bears, is the addition of the certificate described in Article 4, issued by the competent authority of the State from which the document emanates.

However, the formality mentioned in the preceding paragraph cannot be required when either the laws, regulations, or practice in force in the State where the document is produced or an agreement between two or more contracting States have abolished or simplified it, or exempt the document itself from legalisation.

ARTICLE 4

The certificate referred to in the first paragraph of Article 3 shall be placed on the document itself or on an "allonge"; it shall be in the form of the model annexed to the present Convention.

It may, however, be drawn up in the official language of the authority which issues it. The standard terms appearing therein may be in a second language also. The title "Apostille (Convention de La Haye du 5 octobre 1961)" shall also be in the French language.

ARTICLE 5

The certificate shall be issued at the request of the person who has signed the document or of any bearer.

When properly filled in, it will certify the authenticity of the signature, the capacity in which the person signing the document has acted and, where appropriate, the identity of the seal or stamp which the document bears.

The signature, seal and stamp on the certificate are exempt from all certification.

ARTICLE 6

Each contracting State shall designate by reference to their official function, the authorities who are competent to issue the certificate referred to in the first paragraph of Article 3.

It shall give notice of such designation to the Ministry of Foreign Affairs of the Netherlands at the time it deposits its instrument of ratification or of accession or its declaration of extension. It shall also give notice of any change in the designated authorities.

ARTICLE 7

Each of the authorities designated in accordance with Article 6 shall keep a register or card index in which it shall record the certificates issued, specifying:

(a) The number and date of the certificate,

(b) The name of the person signing the public document and the capacity in which he has acted, or in the case of unsigned documents, the name of the authority which has affixed the seal or stamp.

At the request of any interested person, the authority which has issued the certificate shall verify whether the particulars in the certificate correspond with those in the register or card index.

ARTICLE 8

When a treaty, convention or agreement between two or more contracting States contains provisions which subject the certification of a signature, seal or stamp to certain formalities, the present Convention will only override such provisions if those formalities are more rigorous than the formality referred to in Articles 3 and 4.

ARTICLE 9

Each contracting State shall take the necessary steps to prevent the performance of legalisations by its diplomatic or consular agents in cases where the present Convention provides for exemption.

ARTICLE 10

The present Convention shall be open for signature by the States represented at the Ninth session of the Hague Conference on Private International Law and Iceland, Ireland, Liechtenstein and Turkey.

It shall be ratified and the instruments of ratification shall be deposited with the Ministry of Foreign Affairs of the Netherlands.

ARTICLE II

The present Convention shall enter into force on the sixtieth day after the deposit of the third instrument of ratification referred to in the second paragraph of Article 10.

The Convention shall enter into force for each signatory State which ratifies subsequently on the sixtieth day after the deposit of its instrument of ratification.

ARTICLE 12

Any State not referred to in Article 10 may accede to the present Convention after it has entered into force in accordance with the first paragraph of Article 11. The instrument of accession shall be deposited with the Ministry of Foreign Affairs of the Netherlands.

Such accession shall have effect only as regards the relations between the acceding State and those contracting States which have not raised an objection to its accession in the six months after the receipt of the notification referred to in sub-paragraph (d) of Article 15. Any such objection shall be notified to the Ministry of Foreign Affairs of the Netherlands.

The Convention shall enter into force as between the acceding State and the States which have raised no objection to its accession on the sixtieth day after the expiry of the period of six months mentioned in the preceding paragraph.

ARTICLE 13

Any State may, at the time of signature, ratification or accession, declare that the present Convention shall extend to all the territories for the international relations of which it is responsible, or to one or more of them. Such a declaration shall take effect on the date of entry into force of the Convention for the State concerned.

At any time thereafter, such extension shall be notified to the Ministry of Foreign Affairs of the Netherlands.

When the declaration of extension is made by a State which has signed and ratified, the Convention shall enter into force for the territories concerned in accordance with Article 11. When the declaration of extension is made by a State which has acceded, the Convention shall enter into force for the territories concerned in accordance with Article 12.

ARTICLE 14

The present Convention shall remain in force for five years from the date of its entry into force in accordance with the first paragraph of Article 11, even for States which have ratified it or acceded to it subsequently.

If there has been no denunciation, the Convention shall be renewed tacitly every five years.

Any denunciation shall be notified to the Ministry of Foreign Affairs of the Netherlands at least six months before the end of the five year period.

ARTICLE 15

The Ministry of Foreign Affairs of the Netherlands shall give notice to the States referred to in Article 10, and to the States which have acceded in accordance with Article 12, of the following:

(a) The notifications referred to in the second paragraph of Article 16;

(b) The signatures and ratifications referred to in Article 10;

(c) The date on which the present Convention enters into force in accordance with the first paragraph of Article 11;

(d) The accessions and objections referred to in Article 12 and the date on which such accessions take effect;

(e) The extensions referred to in Article 13 and the date on which they take effect;

(f) The denunciations referred to in the third paragraph of Article 14.

In witness whereof the undersigned, being duly authorized thereto, have signed the present Convention.

Done at The Hague the 5th October 1961, in French and in English, the French text prevailing in case of divergence between the two texts, in a single copy which shall be deposited in the archives of the Government of the Netherlands, and of which a certified copy shall be sent, through the diplomatic channel, to each of the States represented at the Ninth session of the Hague Conference on Private International Law and also to Iceland, Ireland, Liechtenstein and Turkey.

ANNEX TO THE CONVENTION

Model of Certificate

The certificate will be in the form of a square
with sides at least 9 centimeters long.

APOSTILLE
(Convention de La Haye du 5 octobre 1961)

1. Country: ____________________
This public document
2. has been signed by ___________
3. acting in the capacity of ____________________
4. bears the seal/stamp of ______________________________
____

Certified

5. at _________________ 6. the _____________________
7. by ____
8. N° ____
9. Seal/stamp: 10. Signature:
____________________ ________________________

PARTIES TO THE HAGUE CONVENTION

Andorra
Angola
Anguilla
Antigua and Barbuda
Argentina
Armenia
Aruba
Australia
Austria
Bahamas
Barbados
Belarus
Belgium
Belize
Bermuda
Bosnia & Herzegovina
Botswana
British Antarctic Terr.
British Virgin Islands
Brunei/Darussalam
Cayman Islands
Channel Islands
Comoros Islands
Croatia
Cyprus
Djibouti
Dominica
El Salvador
Falkland Islands
Fiji
Finland
France
French Guiana
French Polynesia
Germany
Gibralter
Greece
Grenada
Guadeloupe
Guernsey
Hong Kong
Hungary
Isle of Man
Israel
Italy
Japan
Jersey
Kiribati
Latvia
Lesotho
Liberia
Liechtenstein
Luxembourg
Macedonia
Malawi
Malta
Marshall Islands
Martinique
Mauritius
Mexico
Montserrat
Mozambique
Netherlands
Netherlands Antilles
New Caledonia
Norway
Panama
Portugal
Reunion
Russian Federation
St. Helena
St. Kitts & Nevis
St. Lucia
St. Pierre & Miquelon
St. Vinc. & the Gren.
San Marino
Seychelles
Slovenia
Solomon Islands
South Africa
S. Georgia & S. Sandwich
Spain.
Suriname
Swaziland
Tonga
Turkey
Turks and Caicos
Tuvalo
United Kingdom
United States
Vanuatu
Wallis and Futuna
Yugoslavia

APPENDIX B

PROTOCOL ON UNIFORMITY OF POWERS OF ATTORNEY WHICH ARE TO BE UTILIZED ABROAD LIST OF MEMBERS TO THE PROTOCOL

PROTOCOL OF UNIFORMITY OF POWERS OF ATTORNEY WHICH ARE TO BE LEGALIZED ABROAD

ARTICLE I

Powers of attorney granted in the countries, comprising the Pan American Union, for utilization abroad, shall conform to the following rules:

1. If the power of attorney is executed by or on behalf of a natural person, the attesting official (notary, registrar, clerk of court, judge or any other official upon whom the law of the respective country confers such functions) shall certify from his own knowledge to the identity of the appearing party and to his legal capacity to execute the instrument.

2. If the power of attorney is executed in the name of a third person, or if it is delegated or if there is a substitution by the agent, the attesting official, in addition to certifying, in regard to the representative who executes the power of attorney, or delegates or makes a substitution, to the requirements mentioned in the foregoing paragraph, shall also certify that such representative has in fact the authority to represent the person in whose name he appears, and that this representation is legal according to such authentic documents as for this purpose are exhibited to said attesting official and which the latter shall mention specifically, giving their dates, and their origin or source.

3. If the power of attorney is executed in the name of a juridical person, in addition to the certification referred to in the foregoing paragraphs, the attesting official shall certify, with respect to the juridical person in whose name the power is executed, to its due organization, its home office, its present legal existence, and that the purposes for which the instrument is granted are within the scope of the objects or activities of the juridical person; which declarations shall be based on the documents which for that purpose are presented to the official, such as the instrument of organization, bylaws, resolutions of the board of directors or other governing bodies, and such other legal documents as shall substantiate the authority conferred. The attesting official shall specifically mention these documents, giving their dates and their origin.

ARTICLE II

The certification made by the attesting official pursuant to the provisions of the foregoing article shall not be impugned except by proof to the contrary produced by the person challenging its accuracy.

For this purpose, it shall not be necessary to allege falsity of the document if the objection is founded only on an erroneous legal construction or interpretation made by the official in his certification.

ARTICLE III

It shall be unnecessary for the grantee of a power of attorney to signify therein his acceptance of the mandate, such acceptance being conclusively presumed by the grantee's acting under the power.

ARTICLE IV

Special powers of attorney to authorize acts of ownership granted in any of the countries of the Pan American Union, for use in another member country, must specify in concrete terms the nature of the powers conferred, to enable the grantee to exercise all the rights necessary for the proper execution of the power with respect to property as well as to the taking of all necessary steps before the tribunals or administrative authorities in defense thereof.

General powers of attorney for the administration of property shall be sufficient, if expressly granted with that general character, to empower the grantee to consummate all manner of administrative acts, including the prosecution and defense of law suits and administrative and judicial proceedings, in connection with the administration of the property.

General powers of attorneys for law suits, collections or administrative or judicial proceedings, when so worded as to indicate that they confer all general powers and all such special powers as, according to the law, ordinarily require a special clause, shall be deemed to be granted without any limitation or restriction whatever.

The provisions of this article shall have the character of a special rule which shall prevail over such general rules to the contrary as the legislation of the respective country may establish.

ARTICLE V

Powers of attorney granted in any of the member countries of the Pan American Union, which are executed in conformity with the rules of this Protocol, shall be given full faith and credit, provided, however, that they are legalized in accordance with the special rules governing legalization.

ARTICLE VI

Powers of attorney granted abroad and in a foreign language may be translated into the language of the country of their destination and the translation incorporated as part of the text of the instrument thereof. In such case, the translation, so authorized by the grantor, shall be deemed accurate in every particular. The translation of the power of attorney may also be made in the country where the power is to be utilized, in accordance with the local usage or pertinent laws of such a country.

ARTICLE VII

Powers granted in a foreign country do not require as a prerequisite their registration or protocolization thereof in designated offices. However, this rule will not prevail when the registration or protocolization of such instruments is required by the law as a special formality in specific cases.

ARTICLE VIII

Any person who may, pursuant to the pertinent legislation, intervene or become a party in a judicial or administrative proceeding for the defense of his interests, may be represented by a volunteer, on condition, however, that such representative shall furnish the necessary legal authority in writing, or that, pending the due substantiation of his authority, such representative shall furnish bond, at the discretion of the competent tribunal or administrative authority, to respond for the costs or damages which his action may occasion.

ARTICLE IX

In the case of powers of attorney, executed in any of the countries of the Pan American Union in accordance with the foregoing provisions, to be utilized in any member country of the Union, notaries duly commissioned as such under the laws of their respective countries shall be deemed to have authority to exercise functions and powers equivalent to those accorded to native notaries by the laws and regulations of (name of country), without prejudice, however, to the necessity of protocolization of the instrument in the cases referred to in Article VII.

ARTICLE X

What has been said in the foregoing articles with respect to notaries shall apply with equal force to the authorities or officials that exercise notarial functions under the laws of their respective countries.

ARTICLE XI

The original of the present Protocol in Spanish, Portuguese, English and French under the present date shall be deposited in the Pan American Union and opened for signature by the states, members of the Pan American Union.

ARTICLE XII

The present Protocol is operative as respects each High Contracting Party on the date of signature by such Party. It shall be open for signature on behalf of any of the states, members of the Pan American Union, and shall remain operative indefinitely, but any Party may terminate its own obligations hereunder three months after it has given to the Pan American Union notice of such intention.

Notwithstanding the stipulations of the foregoing paragraph any state desiring to do so may sign the present Protocol ad referendum, which Protocol in this case, shall not take effect, with respect to such state, until after the deposit of the instrument of ratification, in conformity with its constitutional procedure.

ARTICLE XIII

Any state desiring to approve the present Protocol with modifications may indicate, when signing the Protocol, the form in which the instrument will be given effect within its territory.

IN WITNESS WHEREOF, the undersigned Plenipotentiaries, having deposited their full powers found to be in due and proper form, sign this Protocol on behalf of their respective governments, and affix thereto their seals on the dates appearing opposite their signatures.

RESERVATIONS AND DECLARATIONS MADE AT THE TIME OF SIGNING

BOLIVIA

The Representative of Bolivia signs this Protocol with the following clarification regarding Article I, Section 2:

"For the correct application of Article I, Section 2 of the Protocol on Uniformity of Powers of Attorney in the territory of the Republic of Bolivia, it is necessary that the notary or official charged with the authentication of documents insert in the Powers of Attorney which are issued by delegation or by substitution the integral text of the original Powers of Attorney and of all those documents which prove the legal capacity of the person conferring the power."

COLOMBIA

The Plenipotentiary of Colombia signs the Protocol on Powers of Attorney ad referendum to approval by the National Congress, making the reservation that the Legislation of Colombia, in Article 2590 of the Civil Code, provides that notaries are responsible only for the formal part and not for the substance of the acts and contracts which they authenticate.

MEXICO

The Government of the United Mexican States, in accepting the provisions of Article IV, makes the express declaration that aliens who are required, for the performance of certain acts, to enter into the agreement or waiver referred to in Section I of Article 27 of the Political Constitution of the United Mexican States, must grant a special power of attorney, expressly including as one of its provisions the agreement and waiver above mentioned. Section I of Article 27 of the Constitution reads as follows: Only Mexicans by birth or by naturalization, and Mexican companies, have the right to acquire the ownership of lands, waters, and their appurtenances or to obtain concessions for the exploitation of mines, waters, or mineral fuels in the Mexican Republic. The State may grant the same right to aliens, provided they enter into an agreement before the Secretariat of Foreign Relations to be considered as Mexicans with respect to such property, and not to invoke, therefore, the protection of their governments in any matter relating thereto; under the penalty, in the event they violate the agreement, of forfeiture to the nation of property they have acquired by reason thereof. Under no circumstances may foreigners acquire direct ownership of lands and waters within a zone of one hundred kilometers along the seashore."

VENEZUELA

The Representative of Venezuela signed the Protocol with the following modification of Paragraph I of Article I:

"1. If the power of attorney is executed by or on behalf of a natural person, the attesting official (notary, registrar, clerk of court, judge or any other official upon whom the law of the respective country confers such functions) shall certify from his own knowledge to the identity of the appearing party and to his legal capacity to execute the instrument, according to documents which the latter has produced."

RESERVATIONS AND DECLARATIONS
MADE AT THE TIME OF RATIFYING

COLOMBIA

With the reservation made at the time of signing.

EL SALVADOR

(a) Article IX, as respects its application in El Salvador, shall be considered as reading as follows:

"Article IX. The powers of attorney granted in any of the countries of the Pan American Union in accordance with the foregoing provisions and in conformity with the laws of the country of origin, shall, for their utilization in any other country of the Union, be considered as granted before a competent notary of the country in which they may be used, without prejudice, however, to the necessity of protocolization of the instrument in the cases referred to in Article VII."

(b) The reservation is made to Article VIII that official activity of the attorney, as plaintiff or defendant, cannot be admitted in judicial or administrative matters for which Salvadorean laws require that representation be accredited by a special power of attorney.

MEXICO

With the reservation made at the time of signing.

VENEZUELA

With the reservation made at the time of signing.

Signatories	Date of Signature	Date of Deposit of Instrument of Ratification
Bolivia	September 26, 1940	
Brazil[1]	September 6, 1940	
Colombia	May 25, 1940	June 10, 1940
El Salvador	May 21, 1940	February 6, 1941
Mexico	December 5, 1951	June 26, 1953
Nicaragua	May 27, 1940	
Panama	April 10, 1940	April 15, 1942
United States	October 3, 1941	November 3, 1941
Venezuela	February 20, 1940	

[1] Brazil did not sign ad referendum, and consequently the Protocol entered into force with respect to Brazil on September 26, 1940.

APPENDIX C

NATIONAL U.S.-ARAB CHAMBER OF COMMERCE

NATIONAL U.S.-ARAB CHAMBER OF COMMERCE

I. GENERAL INFORMATION

The National U.S.-Arab Chamber of Commerce has a national office in Washington, DC and offices in Chicago, Houston, Los Angeles, New York, and San Francisco. Documents may be legalized at the national office in Washington, DC, the New York office, and the Houston office. Bahrain, Jordan, Kuwait, Lebanon, Omar, Qatar, Saudi Arabia, Sudan, Syria, Tunisia, the United Arab Emirates, and Yemen require all legal and commercial documents to be certified by the National U.S.-Arab Chamber of Commerce. Of these countries, Kuwait and Oman require only steps 1 and 2 listed under Prior Authentications.

The National U.S.-Arab Chamber of Commerce office in Washington, in addition to providing authentication service, will also forward authenticated documents to any embassy by its messenger. The legalization fee and two stamped envelopes, one addressed to the appropriate embassy and the other addressed to the sender, must be included with the authenticated documents. An additional fee of $10.00 is charged for this service.

II. REQUIREMENTS FOR LEGALIZATION

Prior Authentications Required

1. Notarization
2. Authentication of Notary Signature by the County Clerk of the county in which the document is executed
3. State Secretary of State Certification
4. U.S. Secretary of State Certification

Materials to be Submitted with Request

1. Original document to be legalized
2. Copy of document, identified as Chamber copy
3. Prepaid self-addressed return envelope or prepaid courier waybill for return by overnight courier

Direct Registration of Notary Public: Not available

Direct Signing of Document Before Consular Official: Not available

Turn Around Time: If the document is personally delivered, it can be legalized immediately if the work load permits.

Fee: $15.00 per document or signature

Payment Method: Certified check, company check, money order (checks/money orders should show company name, address and telephone number and be made payable to the National U.S.-Arab Chamber of Commerce)

III. OFFICES

Address, Phone, Hours	*Jurisdiction*
National Office Suite 550 1100 New York Avenue, NW Washington, DC 20005 Tel.: 202-289-5920 Fax: 202-289-5939 9:30 AM - 12:30 PM 1:30 PM - 3:30 PM	Entire United States
Chicago Office[1] 208 West LaSalle Street, Suite 706 Chicago, IL 60604 Tel.: 312-782-0320 Fax: 312-782-7379	
Houston Office 1330 Post Oak Boulevard, Suite 1600 Houston, TX 77056 Tel.: 713-963-4620 Fax: 713-963-4609 9:00 AM - 12:00 PM 1:00 PM - 3:00 PM	Entire United States

[1] The Chicago Office does not certify documents. Submit documents notarized in Illinois to the Washington DC, New York, or Houston office.

Address, Phone, Hours	*Jurisdiction*
Los Angeles Office 8939 S. Sepulveda Boulevard, Suite 430 Los Angeles, CA 90045 Tel.: 310-646-1499 Fax: 310-646-2462 9:00 AM - 1:00 PM	Alaska Arizona California Colorado Hawaii Idaho Montana Nevada New Mexico Oregon Utah Washington Wyoming (Jurisdiction of above shared with San Francisco office)
New York Office 420 Lexington Avenue, Suite 2739 New York, NY 10170 Tel.: 212-986-8024 Fax: 212-986-0216	Northeast and mid Atlantic states
San Francisco Office PO Box 42228 San Francisco, CA 94142-2218 Tel.: 415-389-9200 Fax: 415-389-7111 9:00 AM - 12:00 PM	Alaska Arizona California Colorado Hawaii Idaho Montana Nevada New Mexico Oregon Utah Washington Wyoming (Jurisdiction of above shared with Los Angeles office)

APPENDIX D

UNITED STATES DEPARTMENT OF STATE DOCUMENT CERTIFICATION REQUIREMENTS

FEDERAL AUTHORITIES COMPETENT TO PROVIDE APOSTILLE

UNITED STATES DEPARTMENT OF STATE

I. GENERAL INFORMATION

Fee: $4.00

Time Delay: If the document is presented by hand for legalization, there will be a delay of from three to five days before legalization.

II. DEPARTMENT OF STATE

U.S. Department of State
Office of Authentication
Columbia Plaza (State Annex #1)
518 Twenty-Third Street, NW
Washington, DC 20520
Tel.: 202-663-3868
7:30 AM - 11:00 AM

FEDERAL AUTHORITIES COMPETENT TO PROVIDE APOSTILLE

In brief, the following Federal officials are authorized to provide the Apostille prescribed in the Hague Convention: Authentication Offices and Acting Authentication Offices, U.S. Department of State, Clerks and Deputy Clerks of The Supreme Court of the United States, the Courts of Appeals for the First through the Eleventh Circuits and the District of Columbia Circuit and the Federal Circuit, the United States District Courts, the United States Court of Claims, the United States Court of International Trade, the United States Claims Court, the District Court of Guam, the District Court of the Virgin Islands, and the District Court for the Northern Mariana Islands.

In addition, officials in the various states are authorized to provide the Apostille as noted in Chapter 2.